NARI SHAKTI

NARI SHAKTI

INDIAN WOMEN
TAKE **CENTRE STAGE**

Edited by

Uma Ganesh *and*
Ganesh Natarajan

Pune International Centre

RUPA

Published by
Rupa Publications India Pvt. Ltd 2024
7/16, Ansari Road, Daryaganj
New Delhi 110002

Sales centres:
Bengaluru Chennai
Hyderabad Jaipur Kathmandu
Kolkata Mumbai Prayagraj

P-ISBN: 978-93-6156-756-8
E-ISBN: 978-93-6156-354-6

First impression 2024

10 9 8 7 6 5 4 3 2 1

The moral right of the authors has been asserted.

Printed in India

This book is dedicated to the mothers of India, who balance countless roles with grace, who are the epitome of utter selflessness, boundless compassion and unconditional love, while inspiring us to be the best versions of ourselves!

CONTENTS

FOREWORD

As a woman, I firmly believe that most women face four major hurdles in life. The first is the internal struggle a girl child goes through with the messaging she receives since childhood—be it restrictions to her body language, her thought process, or the expectations to abide by social conventions. Together, these form their personal script. The second is the lack of support and encouragement from her immediate family. The third is the attitude she faces in the professional space. The question that arises, time and again, is whether organizations are ready and willing to accept a woman on the basis of her *merit* and *competence*? And the last hurdle is lack of successful role models for women to emulate.

Therefore, we need to ask ourselves whether the differences between men and women are purely biological in origin or whether women are victims of social conditioning and a patriarchal stranglehold. Renowned American cultural anthropologist Margaret Mead observed that men and women are more alike than different. It is the way one is 'nurtured', and not 'nature', that makes all the difference. Differences and belief systems are institutionalized through messaging, and reinforced in the psyche through generations.

In India, statistics indicate that the top rankers today in schools and colleges are mainly women. Yet, this is not adequately reflected in the number of women holding top positions or even the sheer number of women employed in the organized workforce at all levels. Is this because women have been conditioned to sabotage their own ambition, profession and intelligence by glorifying, among others, the roles of a wife and a mother? In short, women have not been taken seriously. What is worse is some women with excellent education have not taken *themselves* seriously due to their personal scripts.

Even in the twenty-first century, many business families in educated urban settings find it difficult to encourage or allow their daughters to join the family business or develop an alternate professional identity.

The conversation about women entering the professional space is still far ahead of India's social reality. At the ground level, we as a country fare poorly on most social indicators when it comes to our women. Even in 2024, female foeticide is prevalent all over India, not only among the poor as is widely believed, but also among well-to-do and educated families. If a girl child is not accepted at birth, how can we expect families to invest in her during the rest of her life?

Acquiring education is the next struggle for the girl child. In several parts of urban and rural India, the thought that the girl child is a liability, or *paraya dhan* (to be handed over to her in-laws, her rightful family), stops their family from investing in their future. If by some stroke of luck a girl child is given a good education, the constant messaging is that a job is a stop-gap arrangement till she finds a suitable husband. After marriage, in most cases, a woman working is acceptable only if the husband's income is insufficient. Contrast this with the messaging most men receive since childhood. Their entire upbringing is strongly focused on career building. So, while a woman is groomed to fulfil the needs of those around her, a man is taught to realize his aspirations and goals.

'Behind every successful man, there is a woman,' goes the popular saying. However, often a husband is not taught to respect, encourage and nurture his wife's career; in fact, in many cases, a wife is successful *in spite* of her husband.

Over the years, more and more women have joined the workforce because they want to stand on their own feet and not depend on their families or partners. Unfortunately, most stagnate at junior to middle-level positions; the glass ceiling for top positions is still tough for women to break. Add to that the post-Covid-19 decline in the number of women in the workforce which, hopefully, is a temporary phenomenon.

On a lighter note, as Canadian feminist Charlotte Whitton had put it: 'Whatever women do, they must do twice as well as men to be thought half as good.' Luckily, this is not difficult.

On the matter of women's employment, India ranks 10th among 130 countries, a pressing concern that needs to be urgently addressed.

In *Nari Shakti*, Uma Ganesh and Ganesh Natarajan, two very accomplished editors, have brought together several distinguished authors to discuss, among other themes, the place of women in society, the opportunities they have and the challenges they face as corporate executives and entrepreneurs, to draw meaningful inferences from the diverse paths women have taken to claim their rightful place in society.

I would like to thank Pune International Centre (PIC) for asking me to write the foreword for this book, and I extend my heartiest congratulations to the authors and editors. This is the third book from PIC in three years, and I wish them well in their laudable thought-leadership efforts.

Anu Aga
Former Chairperson, Thermax Limited,
and a strong supporter of social causes in India

INTRODUCTION
Born Unfree

Uma Ganesh and Ganesh Natarajan

Coinciding with the celebrations of the International Women's Year, 133 governments came together to participate in the first-ever world conference on women in Mexico City, Mexico, in 1975. It concluded with a definitive 'World Plan of Action of the Implementation of the Objectives of the International Women's Year', providing a comprehensive set of guidelines for the advancement of women through the next ten years.

The guidelines were basic interventions and acted as a starting point for the cause of women's development. However, the question of development had to start from the basic premise of allocation and access to resources required for any form of social, economic and political development.

Five years later, in 1980, 12 more member nations joined their predecessors and together, they participated in the 'World Conference of the UN Decade of Women' in Copenhagen, Denmark. A Programme of Action was drawn up by the collective decision of 145 participating nations. It determined that the control of property and resources is central to women's empowerment and cultivating a bargaining power for them. The action plan called for stronger national measures to ensure women's ownership and control of property, as well as improvements in protecting women's rights to inheritance, child custody and nationality[1].

---

[1]UN Women, 'World Conferences on Women', https://tinyurl.com/2s38rxnv. Accessed on 27 August 2024.

The attainment of legal measures to protect and encourage ownership rights of women was a major victory for the women's movement. However, it was still not enough. The next tryst was to determine the methods of achieving gender equality. Hence, after a gap of another five years, the number grew, and almost 157 member nations participated in the 'World Conference to Review and Appraise the Achievements of the UN Decade for Women', held in Nairobi, Kenya. It was in this conference that the concept of women's empowerment was emphasized upon as a methodology to promote gender equality. Defined as the redistribution of social power and resource control in favour of women, the process was idealized to aim for women taking control over their lives: setting their own agendas, gaining skills, solving problems and developing self-reliance.

The data presented in the conference revealed that the improvements in the past years had benefitted only a limited number of women. Thus, the Nairobi Conference was mandated to seek new ways of overcoming obstacles for achieving the objectives of the declared Decade: Equality, Development and Peace. Therefore, to streamline the process and ideas, three categories were established to measure the progress achieved, namely constitutional and legal measures, equality in social participation, and equality in political participation and decision-making.

The Nairobi chapter marked an important turn in the history of women's movements and studies. It recognized that gender equality was not an isolated issue, but encompassed all areas of human activity. It stated, as a matter of fact, the necessity for women to participate in all spheres, not only in those relating to gender. The strategy stated that:

> Despite the considerable progress achieved and the increasing participation of women in society, the Decade has only partially attained its goals and objectives. Although the

earlier years of the Decade were characterized by relatively favorable economic conditions in both the developed and developing countries, deteriorating economic conditions have slowed efforts directed towards promoting the equal participation of women in society and have given rise to new problems. With regard to development, there are indications that in some cases, although the participation of women is increasing, their benefits are not increasing proportionately.[2]

The global society adopted some of the above-mentioned measures. For the next 15 years, we saw some developments, and major strides in the field of gender and women studies and development. But the end was nowhere near. To assess and reorganize, the UN held its fourth World Conference on Women in Beijing, China in 1995. This was another significant landmark for the global agenda for gender equality. The conference culminated in 'The Beijing Declaration and the Platform for Action', which was adopted unanimously by 189 countries. Going a step ahead from its predecessors, the declaration set strategic objectives and actions for the advancement of women and the achievement of gender equality. The conference identified 12 critical areas of concern in relation to women. The main themes identified included poverty, education and allied training, health, violence and conflict, economy, power and decision-making, media, environment, and the issue of the girl child. The Beijing conference was structured on the shoulders of the political agreements reached at the three previous conferences, and consolidated five decades of legal advances aimed at securing the equality of women with men in law and in practice[3].

These four conferences pushed for countries to study, design,

---

[2]United Nations, 'World Conference to Review and Appraise the Achievements of the United Nations Decade for Women, 15-16 July 1985, Nairobi, Kenya', https://tinyurl.com/yh8rv5h5. Accessed on 27 August 2024.
[3]UN Women, 'World Conferences on Women', https://tinyurl.com/2s38rxnv. Accessed on 27 August 2024.

enact and implement laws and policies that were for the agenda of gender equality at the national level. For instance, in India, the government of the day under Prime Minister Rajiv Gandhi established the Department of Women and Child Development as a part of the Ministry of Human Resource Development[4]. In 2006, under the Manmohan Singh government (UPA-I), the department was upgraded to Ministry of Women and Child Development[5]. Under the ambit of this department (later ministry), the idea was to empower women, ensure their independence, help them attain their right to live as equal citizens, and participate towards the development of the country.

As a nodal ministry for the advancement of women and children, it formulates plans, policies and programmes, enacts/amends legislation, and guides and coordinates efforts of both governmental and non-governmental organizations working in the field of Women and Child Development. In addition, the ministry is also responsible for implementing certain innovative programmes for their main target audience. These programmes cover welfare and support services, training for employment and income generation, and awareness generation and gender sensitization. They play a supplementary and complementary role to the other general developmental programmes in the sectors of health, education, rural development, etc.[6]

The clear mandate of the State to support the cause of gender equality and freedom of women, coupled with the legal protection of the Constitution and an array of laws (both criminal and civil), should ideally be enough to push for the larger agenda. *Ideally.*

---

[4]Government of India, Ministry of Child and Development, https://tinyurl.com/2ju9ca8r. Accessed on 27 August 2024.
[5]'India's Report on the Implementation of Beijing Declaration and Platform for Action in Context of the Twentieth Anniversary of the Fourth World Conference on Women and the Adoption of the Beijing Declaration and Platform for Action 2015', https://tinyurl.com/39rmpybb. Accessed on 27 August 2024.
[6]Ibid.

Yet, as we discuss this issue in 2024, we must not forget that these modern times have also compounded and increased the nature and range of issues women face today. There is a visible increase in the numbers of cases pertaining to violence against women, their numbers in the job market are plummeting, and there seems to be an atmosphere of discord prevailing between the genders even today. This is not to say that no progress has been made. In the context of education, health, employment, violence and economic participation, the country has experienced some growth, but it is visibly not enough to reach our Sustainable Development Goals (SDGs) or even to realize the principles enshrined in the Constitution of India.

While policies and legal frameworks have been put in place to assist and achieve gender equality, grave fault lines continue to persist. The reason is that while on the one hand, the educated and political class makes policies and laws, it often tends to miss the emotional, psychological and social reasons for the sorry state of Indian women. Therefore, knowledge gaps emerge at the policy implementation stage. These underlying themes form the core through which we can understand why women continue to remain on the fringes of the public sphere, underperform in their economic potential, and face unequal representation.

KEEPING HER AT BAY

Indian society, like the larger global society, functions on a deeply divided idea of private-public sphere. The former is designated as exclusively a woman's arena while the latter is dominated by men, indicative of the sexual division of labour that, for centuries, has been damping the social and political development and economic growth of India along with many other countries. However, there have been pushbacks.

Like the efforts of the global community, India too had its leaders and laws that tried to amend the situation. The likes of

Savitribai and Jyotiba Phule, Fatima Sheikh, Periyar, Raja Ram Mohan Roy, Annie Besant, Mahatma Gandhi and many others initiated a range of movements. Their ideals and work found their imprint enshrined in the Constitution. The man at the helm of the Constituent Assembly, Dr B.R. Ambedkar, along with his like-minded peers, spearheaded the project of writing one of the most remarkable constitutions ever. Babasaheb's views about the status and condition of women pushed for structural reforms in Indian society. In a speech at the All-India Depressed Classes Women's Conference in Nagpur in 1942, he remarked that he measured the progress of a community by the degree of progress which women achieved[7]. His statement provides us with a litmus test that we can put to use at any given moment in history to assess where we are in terms of women empowerment. He, along with several other leaders of the time, was of the opinion that the Indian woman was being forced to underplay her potential. He believed that through the means of education, women would be able to break their shackles and become truly independent.

Dr Ambedkar's ideas have resonated with many others who came after him. Advocating women's education, Amartya Sen, winner of the 1998 Nobel Prize in Economics, is of the opinion that women's education plays a crucial role in facilitating radical social and economic changes: 'I think gender inequality is not the natural human condition. But the idea that somehow women have to be in an inferior position—or not quite such dominant position—is really wholly artificial for me.'[8]

Stalwarts like Annie Besant, Raja Ram Mohan Roy, Ishwar Chandra Vidyasagar, Savitribai Phule, Pandita Ramabai, and D.K. Karve dedicated their lives to overcoming social barriers

---

[7]Ambedkar, B.R., 'The Rise and Fall of Hindu Woman: Who was Responsible for It?' in *Dr. Babasaheb Ambedkar Writings and Speeches*, Vol. 17-II, Education Dept, Government of Maharashtra, Mumbai, pp. 109-129.
[8]Sen, Amartya, 'Feminism is an issue of humanity', UNU WIDER, https://tinyurl.com/mrys66yv. Accessed on 27 August 2024.

and uplifting women's status through education. Their efforts bore slow but impactful results as there was a shift in attitude from pre-Independence to post-Independence Indian society. Since India gained Independence, there has been a significant increase in the overall literary rate from a meagre 18.3% in 1951 to almost 73% in 2011. During the same period, female literacy rate has gone up from 8.86% to 64.3%, while male literacy rate has increased from 64.63% to 80.9%. The rural–urban divide also indicates the percentage of women in higher education in rural areas to be significantly lower at 50.6% compared to urban area enrolment of women at 76.9%[9] [10].

This is because past governments have launched an array of social schemes to promote the cause of education for all, especially women. The Right to Education Act 2009, schemes such as 'Beti Bachao, Beti Padhao', and pioneering initiatives of civil society such as 'Educate Girls' are aimed at increasing enrolments and retention of girl children in schools. Yet, in relative terms, it is a cause for worry that even after 76 years of Independence, we have still not been able to get 100 percent of girls to be in schools.

The social and traditional approach to women being groomed as homemakers or caregivers, leading to high drop-out rates from schools, is central to the problem. Despite access to education being free for female students from economically disadvantaged families, additional costs of materials, transportation, hostels and tuitions are unaffordable to many, especially at higher levels of education. The persisting issue of women's safety is another reason why girls are unable to access education and are forcefully married early even today. As per the report of the National Family Health Survey data of Government of India, more than 45.6%

[9]"Population Census, 2011", https://tinyurl.com/4k2tmk48. Accessed on 27 August 2024.
[10]Government of India, Ministry of Statistics & Programme Implementation, *Women and Men in India-2017*, 'Literacy and Education', https://tinyurl.com/7u7ytvus. Accessed on 27 August 2024.

girls are married at the age of 18 years[11].

The lack of a supportive ecosystem providing awareness of career options, scholarships and personalized guidance at the right time also act as a deterrent to women's education. These challenges are well known and are being addressed by several stakeholders to the best of their ability. Yet, in order to expedite female literacy and encourage women to acquire higher education based on their potential, mentoring and counselling should be taken up as the topmost priority.

However, this not to say that progress has not been made. The Gross Enrolment Ratio (GER) in Higher Education has grown from 24.5% in 2015–16 to 28.4% in 2020–21. The GER for male and female at all-India level is 28.3 and 28.5, respectively. The GER for SC male is 25.8 and SC female is 26.0. The GER for ST male is 21.4 and ST female is 20.9. For categories 'All' and 'SC', the female GER is greater than the male GER[12]. The idea is to increase this ratio; a target has been set to raise the overall women's enrolment ratio to 30% by 2025.

After the USA and China, India has the world's third largest higher education system as per a World Bank Report[13]. Over the years, in India, women's enrolments have been increasing in the field of science—historically a male-dominated field. There has been a rise in the enrolment of women in undergraduate programmes in pure sciences, from 7.1 % in 1950–51 to 51.7% in 2019[14]. We have several examples of women researchers and

---

[11]Government of India, Ministry of Health and Family Welfare, 'National Family Health Survey (NFHS-5), 2019-21, India Report', https://tinyurl.com/3489p5ru. Accessed on 27 August 2024.

[12]Government of India, Ministry of Education, Department of Higher Education, New Delhi, 'All India Survey on Higher Education, 2021-2022', https://tinyurl.com/59hk9234. Accessed on 27 August 2024.

[13]Reddy, A. Amarender, & Gayathri Vaidyanathan, 'India's Higher Education Needs a Paradigm Shift', *The Wire*, 28 Feb 2019, https://tinyurl.com/265nmbhx. Accessed on 27 August 2024.

[14]Burke, Ronald J., & Mary C. Mattis, *Women and Minorities in Science,*

scientists who have made sterling contributions to the field of science. Tessy Thomas, hailed as the 'Missile Woman of India', played a pivotal role in India's ballistic missile defence programme; Indian aerospace engineer Nigar Shaji was the project director of Aditya-L1, India's first solar mission; Gagandeep Kang, a renowned Indian microbiologist and virologist, was the first Indian woman elected as a Fellow of the Royal Society; Janaki Ammal, the renowned botanist known for breeding a new type of sugarcane, was appointed the first Director of the Central Botanical Library; and Anna Mani, the first Indian woman to be appointed Deputy Director-General of the Indian Meteorological Department are just a few notable women scientists who have left their indelible imprints on the sands of time. However, in the field of engineering and technology, women's enrolment growth rate has been slow.

To overcome challenges posed by the traditional education system in India, the option of distance learning is also largely available for women. Distance learning is now much more accessible thanks to technology intermediation. Such a mode of learning could help women who wish to get back to work or who are unable to pursue higher education in colleges but are keen to acquire formal qualifications. Private providers also offer a plethora of e-learning programmes that are predominantly aimed at professional development. These programmes help those who are aware of their relevance and are either supported by their employers or self-funded. However, there is a need to rethink how distance learning could result in transformative impact on the empowerment of women and enable them to be part of the workforce in much larger numbers.

Technology, Engineering, and Mathematics: Upping the Numbers, Edward Elgar Publishing, 2007.

SHRINKING PURSE

However, making progress in the education sector would be meaningful only if we are able to translate it into economic and employment growth and opportunities. While the potential for women's participation in the economy is immense, the World Economic Forum's Global Gender Gap Report 2023 shows India ranking 127th out of 146 countries in terms of gender gap[15]. The index measures gaps on four broad parameters—economic participation and opportunities, educational attainment, health and survival, and political empowerment. While India is faring better on last three factors, its poor score on 'economic participation and opportunities' for women accounts for its low rank in the global list. Therefore, as substantiated above, as more and more women pursue their educational aspirations, the need for restructuring the market to include the female workforce has become the need of the hour.

The report estimated that women in India contribute 17% of the national GDP, as against the global average of 40%[16]. India ranks 120th out of 131 countries in female labour force participation rates (FLFPR). The economic opportunity resulting from more women being part of the workforce thus benefitting every nation has been highlighted by several studies. For instance, a study undertaken in 2017 by McKinsey Global Institute noted that there was potential to add up to $12 trillion to the global GDP if India increases its women participation in the workforce[17]. As per this report, in India if the participation of women becomes equal to that of men, India's GDP could increase by 60% by

---

[15]World Economic Forum (WEF), 'Global Gender Gap Report 2023', 20 June 2023, https://tinyurl.com/52nserxy. Accessed on 27 August 2024.
[16]Ibid.
[17]McKinsey & Company, Global Institute Report, 'Women Matter: Time to Accelerate—Ten Years of Insights into Gender Diversity', October 2017, https://tinyurl.com/ahs9xdpa. Accessed on 22 August 2024.

2025. The discussion about the role of women in society in the Indian context assumes further significance in view of the goal envisioned by Prime Minister Narendra Modi for the economy to touch $6.69 trillion by 2030, from its current status of $3.51 trillion[18].

Indian women's participation in the workforce has been a matter of concern for many. That is because the trends of the economy show that when the economy is doing well and job opportunities are available, the rates of women participation in workforce have been falling over the years. Over nearly two decades, India's female labour participation rate has dropped from 32% in 2005 to 19% in 2021. The status of women from minority communities, the majority of whom are Muslims accounting for 12% of the population, also calls for closer examination[19].

Although the number as a share of their population is still lower than that of non-Muslims, there has been an increase in Muslim women acquiring higher education in 2017–18 compared to 2007–08, from 6.7% to 13.5%[20]. Work participation among Muslim women in 2001 was 14.10%, while in 2011 it was 14.80%, which shows that the participation growth rate is almost negligible[21].

Women employment in the corporate sector has also seen a decline over the years. The World Economic Forum's Global Gender Gap Report 2023 noted that the share of women in professional and technical roles has declined to 29.2%. The share of women in

---

[18]"Narendra Modi sets ambitious economic goals for probable third term", *The Economic Times*, 4 April 2024, https://tinyurl.com/ycy6dwwu. Accessed on 27 August 2024.

[19]Chakrabarty, Roshni, 'Female labour participation declining in India: Why are women not working?', *India Today*, 11 June 2023, https://tinyurl.com/dutfu8ne. Accessed on 27 August 2024.

[20]Barman, Sourav Roy, 'Steady uptick in Muslim girls going to schools, colleges', *The Indian Express*, 13 February 2022, https://tinyurl.com/3ar4fcpx. Accessed on 27 August 2024.

[21]Lahiri, Deepanjali, & Dr Shadab Ruha, 'Muslim women in India's workforce: Where are they?', IDR, 30 July 2021, https://tinyurl.com/4fwp5u2. Accessed on 27 August 2024.

senior and managerial positions is merely 14.6%, with only 8.9% firms with top female managers. Of the top 100 companies listed by the Bombay Stock Exchange (BSE) in India, 91 companies have only one woman director. S&P 500 companies have only 5.8% women CEOs. Furthermore, there is a huge gap in the pay scale offered to men and women. Globally, India is among the bottom ten on the gender pay-gap indicator, as the estimated earned income of Indian women is only one-fifth that of men[22].

However, there is a catch in the curve. There have been important changes observed in women's workforce participation rate. Based on Periodic Labour Force Surveys (PLFS) 2017–18 to 2022–23, the overall labour force participation rate (LFPR) by the current weekly status (CWS, where the reference period is one week) of those aged 15–59 has increased from 51.5% to 58.3% between 2017–18 and 2022–23[23]. This increase in LFPR is primarily on account of the rise in the count of working women in rural areas who have opted for self-employment. Especially post-Covid-19, male members of the family have had to migrate to cities in search of jobs and women in rural areas have become income earners based on individual capabilities. Most of these jobs are related to agriculture and labour-oriented assignments.

India's low female labour force participation is a complex social phenomenon, observed in all strata of society, in both rural and urban locations irrespective of their educational qualifications. Social and family constructs are such that women are deprived of even the ability to have their own identity and build successful careers for themselves. Those who are able to break away from

[22]Mallikarjuna, K.G., & N.T.K. Naik, (2014), 'Indicators of Women Economic Empowerment', *International Journal of Humanities and Social Sciences*, 3 (3), pp. 67–74.
[23]Press Information Bureau, Government of India, Ministry of Statistics & Programme Implementation, 'Periodic Labour Force Survey (PLFS) Annual Report 2022-2023 Released: Increasing Trend in Labour Force Participation Rate and Worker Population Ratio; Constant Decrease in Unemployment Rate', 9 October 2023, https://tinyurl.com/r8nsdu8t. Accessed on 27 August 2024.

traditional constructs due to education and the opportunities that come their way are small in number. The majority of women not being part of the workforce also means that these women are contributing their efforts to services that are *not entitled* for compensation, namely the care economy. There are others who receive meagre compensation by doing predominantly labour-oriented tasks which do not offer social security benefits since these jobs are outside the purview of legislative framework.

The reasons for women not taking up jobs or discontinuing their careers are centred around the responsibilities they are expected to fulfil on the home front. Quality of life is another key determinant for deciding about women working and the choice of sectors. The number of women who have exited from the workforce stands at around 20 million for the period 2004–05 to 2011–12[24]. Patriarchal norms, monetary expectations mismatch, rural–urban transitions, lack of childcare support, safety concerns and misaligned supply and demand factors are also key reasons for women dropping out of the workforce.

To fix these, as a starting point, policies supporting women's transportation to and from work, congenial work environment at the workplace, work-from-home options as well as safety of children and working mothers would be necessary to attract women to consider joining the formal sector and building careers. It is equally important to create jobs that are conducive for women in rural areas instead of the current labour-oriented options predominantly offered in agriculture by the informal sector.

Apart from opportunities for employment, microfinance is an important tool for empowering women. The portfolio of microfinance institutions (MFIs) touched almost rupees four lakh crore during the third quarter of 2023, according to the self-regulatory organization Microfinance Industry Network

---

[24]Population Census 2011, https://tinyurl.com/4k2tmk48. Accessed on 27 August 2024.

(MFIN) report[25]. According to a 2021 report by the National Bank for Agriculture and Rural Development (NABARD), over 70% microfinance beneficiaries in India are women[26]. With microfinance, women who traditionally lack access to banking and credit services tend to benefit and are able to start business ventures. This results in women being increasingly confident due to their financial independence, enjoying an enhanced status in society, taking an active part in decision making, besides reduction in violence against women. Above all, a change of mindset towards working women from immediate family members and policymakers should be a priority for ushering in transformation in families.

SHE MUST LEAD

By 2024, we are presented with a plethora of studies conducted by private, public and civil society enterprises that have shown the immense capability of women to lead the show. Additionally, we also know that from an economic perspective, the idea of entrepreneurship has been the backbone of the Indian economy through the ages. It gained importance and enhanced support from the government since liberalization in the '90s. Lately, it has gained further momentum due to the focus of the government on supporting entrepreneurship with the view to create jobs and provide a boost to the economy.

According to the Sixth Economic Census released by the Ministry of Statistics and Programme Implementation, women constitute around 14% of the total entrepreneurship, i.e. 8.05 million of the total 58.5 million entrepreneurs in India. Furthermore, the share of women in the non-agriculture sector

---

[25]'NBFC-MFIs largest provider of micro-credit: Report', *The Economic Times*, 12 June 2024, https://tinyurl.com/2xty4upz. Accessed on 27 August 2024.
[26]NABARD, 'Status of Microfinance in India 2021-22', https://tinyurl.com/4mu7m9nv. Accessed on 27 August 2024.

constitutes about 65% of all women entrepreneurs, amounting to 5.29 million women[27]. Bain's analysis suggests that while accounting for enterprises masquerading as women-owned enterprises, in reality, the proportion of businesses truly owned and operated by women is less than 20%[28]. According to the MasterCard Index of Women Entrepreneurs 2020, India ranked 52nd out of 58 countries in terms of women's ability to thrive as entrepreneurs[29]. This indicates the potential for further growth and support for women entrepreneurs in India.

Women entrepreneurship is being promoted aggressively through several schemes of the government[30]. In addition, specific venture funds have been set up to support women entrepreneurship. A good example of this is Arise Ventures, a venture capital firm set up by Ankita Vashisht that has funded more than 30 ventures that are women-owned start-ups involving technology, consumer products and sustainability solutions[31].

Entrepreneurship is the outcome of self-motivation, previous experiences, understanding the supply-demand gap and possessing the ability to fulfil the needs. In reality, most micro enterprises are created by women due to the inability to find jobs that meet their monetary requirements. As a result, independently or as part of self-help groups (SHGs) they form, they face several challenges in making their businesses successful. While SHGs

---

[27]Government of India, Ministry of Statistics & Programme Implementation, 'HIGHLIGHTS OF THE SIXTH ECONOMIC CENSUS', https://tinyurl. com/6xrdzjwk. Accessed on 27 August 2024.

[28]IBEF: India Brand Equity Foundation, 'WOMEN ENTREPRENEURS SHAPING THE FUTURE OF INDIA', 4 January 2022, https://tinyurl.com/r9phtmfe. Accessed on 27 August 2024.

[29]Mastercard, 'Mastercard Index of Women Entrepreneurs 2020', https://tinyurl. com/wbbpc296. Accessed on 27 August 2024.

[30]Bidnur, Vijay Vyankatesh, & Anjali Avinash Kalse, 'A REVIEW ON WOMEN ENTREPRENEURSHIP IN INDIA-PROBLEMS, PROSPECTS AND GOVERNMENT SUPPORT', July 2023, https://tinyurl.com/j9n6v57h. Accessed on 27 August 2024.

[31]Tejaswi, Mini, 'Bengaluru Entrepreneur to float $1bn venture fund', *The Hindu*, 7 March 2022, https://tinyurl.com/5e72hn52. Accessed on 27 August 2024.

started gaining momentum in the '70s, today, over 72 million women comprise nearly 6.6 million SHGs[32].

Despite the number of SHGs growing substantially, access to market and finance are two interconnected challenges most women entrepreneurs in this segment face. While banks and non-banking financial companies (NBFCs) are flush with funds, as part of their loan-sanctioning process, they often find women do not own any asset. Hence, many of them are unable to access credit. Situated in rural locations and lacking the network, many women micro-entrepreneurs face difficulty in finding customers[33]. Insufficient knowledge of market trends and demands, lack of confidence, lack of support from the family, socio-cultural barriers, poor product packaging, lack of awareness of legal, safety and hygiene parameters, lack of contemporary skills in product design and finish are some reasons that make it hard for women micro-entrepreneurs to expand beyond their immediate vicinity and sustain their businesses.

In order to promote and scale women entrepreneurship in rural and urban locations, out-of-the-box approaches would be required. In each state, there should be a concerted effort to make at least 100 SHGs hugely successful, with adequate digital, marketing, domain, packaging and capital support to make them icons that others could emulate in due course. Market access in cities and places with tourist footfalls reserved for women entrepreneurs would create motivation and the urge to scale up. Capital access should be provided on easier terms for deserving women who have the potential to succeed. Since risk-taking appetite in most

---

[32]Khaitan, Shreya, 'Women's self-help groups in rural India have pushed past obstacles and boosted household incomes', *IndiaSpend.com*, 25 October 2020; retrieved from Scroll.in, https://tinyurl.com/ar4asvmy. Accessed on 27 August 2024.

[33]Ganesh, Uma, 'Adopting Digital Proficiency to Shape Women Entrepreneurs of the Future', in *ReThink ISB Management*, 5 May 2022, https://tinyurl.com/j2pxb6tj. Accessed on 27 August 2024.

women is low, governments should come forward and assume risks in select cases to collaborate with women entrepreneurs and demonstrate the pathways to success. As in the US, where for defence projects, women-owned enterprises are given priority in bidding for defence technology-led solutions, and convert them into usable public-domain solutions, in India too, a similar approach to promote women entrepreneurial potential could be of immense help.

At the higher end of the knowledge spectrum, STEM (Science, Technology, Engineering and Mathematics) offers a myriad set of opportunities for talented women who are keen on entrepreneurship. STEM fields straddle a spectrum of industries covering robotics, artificial intelligence, aerospace, computer science, renewable energy, and several applied fields as well. These industries being technology-dependent and innovation-driven, women who have a penchant for experimenting with new ideas should be able to gain the attention of these businesses with the sheer strength of their concepts, and their acumen in implementation of their breakthrough ideas which would address the gaps in the market. Of the funding that takes place in India, only 6% flows towards a company with a woman founder/co-founder as per the report shared by Google in 2022[34]. This percentage further reduces to 1.5 while considering only women founders[35]. The global male-to-female entrepreneur ratio is 10:7 as per the Global Entrepreneurship Monitor Report[36].

However, there are some excellent examples of STEM Indian women entrepreneurs—Parul Ganju (co-founder Ahammune), Kiran Mazumdar-Shaw (Biocon Limited), and Upasana Taku

---

[34]Rekhi, Dia, 'Only 1.5% of total funding goes to Indian startups with women funders', *The Economic Times*, 14 June 2022, https://tinyurl.com/27fvm9vy. Accessed on 27 August 2024.
[35]Ibid.
[36]GEM: Global Entrepreneurship Monitor, 'GEM 2020/2021 GLOBAL REPORT', 2021, https://tinyurl.com/2u74vbv5. Accessed on 27 August 2024.

(Mobikwik), who have established their ventures as pioneers in their respective domains. They have managed to tap into capital resources as required from time to time, based on their ability to communicate the potential of their products and services to address market gaps to potential investors with confidence and clarity. The strong foundation they have in STEM principles and business dynamics are helping them build world-class ventures. In order to magnify their successes and attract larger number of women to become entrepreneurs, closer linkages with the government, academic institutions and venture capitalists would be required alongside training, exposure and mentorship of those who have foundation academic qualifications in STEM. The impact they could create would be across the globe in all sectors that are starved of quality talent and innovation, and which would be willing to support such initiatives.

FOURTH DIMENSION

Like the growth of entrepreneurial options, digital technologies have opened up a world of opportunities for everyone across the world. Newer technologies and digital transformation have opened up new avenues for economic empowerment of women, offering them opportunities for professional development and participation in the workforce on equal footing with their male counterparts, thus enabling them to get connected to the world at large and to express themselves freely.

Digital technology has created multitudes of income-earning opportunities which women are able to tap into, and with the flexibility of working from anywhere, especially post-Covid-19. Women have discovered the new world stage they are now able to access. Working part-time, flexi-time, remotely are options made available by organizations across the world to women based on their family commitments, professional expertise and their interests.

According to research carried out by the Observer Research Foundation to study the gender gap in India's digital access, three key factors are responsible[37]. First is the rural–urban digital divide, which translates to women in rural areas being less likely to own mobile phones due to lower broadband penetration in such areas. Second is the income-based digital divide between households that prevents equal access to digital technologies. Lastly, regressive social norms and discrimination at the household level prevent women from enjoying equitable access to digital devices and technology, further exacerbating the gender divide.

For rural women, unequal access to technology is, however, slowly disappearing with the help of digital technology paving the way for everyone to be part of the network for all their needs. There are several examples of successful initiatives being implemented for empowering rural women. Some unique success stories include WeChimni, the pioneering initiative of GTT Foundation to skill rural women in various arts and help them market the products to corporate India through the e-commerce platform, e-Mahila, a project being implemented under the ASARE Scheme by the KSWDC (Karnataka State Women's Development Corporation) to provide all possible services to the rural public through rural women, and Nabanna Information Network for Women, a UNESCO project that is built around innovative use of databases, intranet portals for the benefit of poor women.

Broadband access and extending network across the length and breadth of the country are being addressed by the government. Significant changes are expected over the next few years with change in technology, and the investment required is likely to come down. As far as the resources required to access mobile devices is concerned, several private sector players are coming up with attractive low-cost models. With large-scale manufacturing

---

[37]Observer Research Foundation (ORF), Nikore, Mitali, 'India's gendered digital divide: How the absence of digital access is leaving women behind', 22 August 2021, https://tinyurl.com/4m4x8uj3. Accessed on 27 August 2024.

of mobile devices in India taking off, there would be increase in adoption rates.

India has also benefitted significantly from the outsourcing of business processes and technology-related services. The tech industry has been welcoming women in large numbers, at a scale never experienced before in any other country. Women graduating with degrees have been able to launch into attractive tech careers and create a niche for themselves. Women make up 36% of India's tech workforce[38]. While this percentage is much better than the overall female share (24%) of India's total workforce, a deeper analysis indicates that over 51% of entry-level recruits are women, over 25% of women are in managerial positions, but less than 1% are in the C-Suite. Participation of women in the workforce drops drastically as one starts looking up the corporate hierarchy.

Although the tech industry offers jobs that are suitable for women and enable them to balance their family and work priorities, resulting in several success stories, women still face several challenges that hinder their career advancement. The tech industry is still predominantly male-dominated, with women experiencing lack of equity in opportunities with regard to male counterparts. Women face other challenges too such as lack of equitable salary, harassment at work, lack of training and professional development opportunities, lack of career progression at the same pace as their male counterparts, and are, therefore, unable to break the glass ceiling[39].

Some corporates are cognizant of these challenges and have taken several initiatives focused on supporting and retaining

---

[38]NASSCOM, 'India's Tech Industry: Women for the Techade', https://tinyurl.com/38jwy8fd. Accessed on 27 August 2024.
[39]SkillSoft, 'SKILLSOFT'S 2022 WOMEN IN TECH REPORT INDIA REGION: Learn How to Close Organizational Gaps and Arrive at Meaningful Solutions to Empower Women in Tech in India', 2022, https://tinyurl.com/ycksfvwj. Accessed on 27 August 2024.

women at the workplace, including training, mentoring, flexible working hours and experience sharing by role models and peers. There have also been successful programmes to bring back women who had exited from the workforce, and have had career breaks, by finding suitable opportunities for them and by bridging the gap for the current skills required.

Another factor that requires attention in the Indian context is the large number of low-paying jobs created on the basis of low-level digital skills. With the increasing deployment of AI and generative AI, there is a strong likelihood that many tasks that are routine and repetitive in nature will become automated, and may lead to loss of jobs. According to the report published by International Monetary Fund 2018, female workers in low-skill clerical and sales jobs are most at risk of being replaced by automation in the developed world[40]. In India, automation of housework and emergence of the 'gig' economy can further marginalize women workers. While we may have to be prepared for this, it is important to bear in mind that automation and AI would also create new jobs. Therefore, programmes aimed at upskilling the current workforce and also equipping new entrants with the right digital skills would be necessary to take advantage of the continuous digital transformation journey.

Digital financial inclusion is being promoted aggressively by the government to fight against poverty and gender inequality, thus supporting the attainment of the UN's SDGs. However, with limited access to digital technology and digital financial services, women face difficulties in tapping into available funds[41]. In the last few years, the opening of bank accounts for all and

---

[40]Brussevich, Mariya et al., 'Gender, Technology, and the Future of Work', IMF Staff Discussion Note, October 2018, https://tinyurl.com/22ttb6mh. Accessed on 27 August 2024.

[41]Scott, Kerry et al., 'Freedom within a cage: how patriarchal gender norms limit women's use of mobile phones in rural central India', *BMJ Journals,* BMJ Global Health, 2021, https://tinyurl.com/2dd3svt4. Accessed on 27 August 2024.

implementation of Aadhaar cards have made it easy to provide financial support through banks. Digital connectivity, access devices and dependable stable networks are still to be addressed in rural locations, but with ongoing efforts, we are experiencing constant improvements. Therefore, digital technology could be considered a strong catalyst for socio-economic transformation and empowerment of women.

TOP-DOWN CHANGE

Given the significance of the 2030 Sustainable Development Agenda globally, gender equality and empowerment are no longer a choice but essential ingredients for countries to benefit from for enhanced economic growth. In this context, India adopted the concept of Gender Responsive Budgeting in 2005–06 which uses the budget as an entry point to apply a gender lens to the entire policy process from planning to implementation stage[42]. Since then, several other countries have included gender perspective in their planning process.

According to Janet G. Stotsky, gender budgeting gives scope to understand gender-differentiated impact of fiscal provisions, programmes and policies[43]. Even before the formal process of adopting gender budgeting, Indian policy framework had some focus on gender and had budget allocations and reviews based on goals set for gender-specific initiatives. 'Mission Shakti' aimed at strengthening interventions for women's safety, security and empowerment during the 15th Finance Commission from 2021 to 2025; the agenda highlighted by NITI Aayog for 2018–2020 has

---

[42]Bansal, Rohit, & Shivangi Singh, 'Role of Skill India in Women Empowerment', in SKILL INDIA: A Catalyst to Nation Building. pp. 66-71, Empyreal Publishing House, 2020, https://tinyurl.com/7zw6e6ns. Accessed on 27 August 2024.
[43]Stotsky, Janet G., 'Gender and Its Relevance to Macroeconomic Policy: A Survey', IMF Working Paper WP/06/233, 2006, https://tinyurl.com/4ftwb5wa. Accessed on 27 August 2024.

also adopted gender-responsive budgeting as a tool for promoting gender equality and ensuring adequate budgetary provisions through gender-responsive planning and budgeting processes[44].

Planning and budgeting are precursors to excellent implementation and outcomes. Apart from policy-driven measures, we also need to focus on bringing about a qualitative change in our social environment. Various stakeholders at the grassroots, particularly men, need to be sensitized about women-specific concerns and priorities so that the implementation process is energized and propelled to address the mammoth challenges which could be transformed into an enviable opportunity for the nation as a whole.

As the nation takes positive strides towards becoming an attractive fountainhead for innovation, technology, economic prosperity and transformation, the world is looking at India for future survival and growth. The critical success factor for India which is blessed with demographic dividend is to develop and nurture its talent pool, of which 50% is women. Therefore, it is no longer a question of concessions to be made to women for their emancipation; women's empowerment has become an economic necessity and a national priority. In this agenda, it has become imperative for corporates, NGOs, academic institutions and researchers to come together to recognize the strengths and the success stories of women so far, and put in place plans to overcome the challenges faced. This journey will not be an easy one as it has to understand the mindset of women and society at large as it develops the framework for supporting women to succeed. The journey with the right approach in itself and the impact at each milestone could create a lasting impact for mankind.

---

[44]Mission Shakti, General Budgeting Scheme, Government of India, Ministry of Women and Child Development, https://tinyurl.com/zs4d9zy8 . Accessed on 22 October 2024.e

1

IN THE ANCIENT RUINS—GENDER NORMS, THEN AND NOW

Eika Chaturvedi Banerjee
Founder, Eikam Resonance

Human beings, like other species, have had the innate ability to transmit their *know-how* and *know-why* to successive generations. However, unlike most members of the animal kingdom, human beings do not depend solely on evolution or the mutation of the DNA. Instead, they have developed language and memory, curated artefacts, and enshrined principles that have determined, and continue to dictate, the terms of our culture. Enshrined in these collective memories are stories and narratives, all of which are available to us today, thanks to our habit of maintaining records. Thus, our past holds the key to our modern-day problems. While a plethora of differences existed in ancient knowledge systems, they also had striking similarities. One such similarity that has been recognized as a dominant narrative across civilizations and ages is the discourse on women and their closest ally, Mother Nature.

The ability of nature and women to be at the helm of reproduction has endowed and empowered both with a powerful weapon. They are two pillars on which the very existence of humankind reposes. In ancient belief systems, female agency was worshipped—the woman was central to everything society held dear.

Moreover, there was (and perhaps continues to be) an interesting correlation between the three Ws—Wisdom, Wealth and

Women—that were central to survival. There are ample references and sources, practices and patterns that show how women have remained at the centre of entire civilizations through their unique history, economics, politics and culture. To this day, Hindus worship Goddess Laxmi and Saraswati to safeguard their wealth and knowledge. Christians hold Mother Mary in high regard, and Muslims continue to revere Khadija and Fatima. Represented in different colours and invested with different powers, women in different faiths have always been the source of nurture, strength and influence. Such notions existed in native philosophies, and broadly defined the nature of State and society.

Having recognized the significance of feminine power and its inherent ability to both create and nurture humanity, it is perplexing how the dominant narrative has largely marginalized women. Female figures have been restricted to the background, and their aura or power has been neglected. Dominated and controlled by the male point of view and voice, our past remains captivated in twisted and tainted narratives. In such narratives are assumptions that women of strength and power exist only in our mythology; that this is how society has always been. Nothing could be further from the truth.

By way of a brief introduction, this essay tries to focus on the ancient Sanatan Dharma, and a society based on its principles. Here, we find a unique story, one that allows us to examine the male-female dynamics, using a more inclusive and revealing understanding of gender interactions that was common thousands of years ago.

In Sanatan Dharma, and in Indian philosophy, the gender principle is believed to encompass all creation. It mandates a male and a female agent to vibrate, pulsate, fuse, combine, and unite, for creation to happen, like the pistil and stamen—the male-female polarity—for a flower to reproduce and create more pollen, or like the polarity of the positive anode and the negative cathode on a diode for electricity to flow. Even hermaphrodites produce both male and female gametes to reproduce. Between these dichotomies, society has always negotiated the roles it assigns to each gender. Over time, however, the balance has been lost, leading to what can only be termed as catastrophic inequalities.

To negotiate socially-assigned gender roles, and our relationship with gender-based leadership, we needed to first appreciate the concept of gender, its significance and expression.

The Samkhya Darshan, one of the earliest schools of Indian philosophy, blends the principles of polarity and gender in the most evocative manner. The duality of *Purusha*, the 'male' consciousness, is brought alive through *Prakriti*, the 'female' nature or matter. *Purusha* is consciousness, awareness, the universal principle; *Prakriti* is the potency that brings about evolution and changes in the empirical universe, much like the principle of the male noun and the female verb. *Purusha* Brahma, the creator, creates through the *Prakriti* of Saraswati, Goddess of Wisdom. *Purusha* Vishnu, the preserver, preserves through the *Prakriti* of Lakshmi, Goddess of Wealth. *Purusha* Shiva, the disruptive destroyer, destroys through the *Prakriti* of the powerful Shakti, Goddess of Wrath.

GENDER ROLES ACROSS THE GLOBE

Contrary to our understanding of mythology, real-world experiences present a very different picture. Access and control of resources is largely restricted to men while women have to depend on external agencies to survive. The reason we see a struggle and flux at so many levels for ownership of wealth and wisdom between the sexes is due to a natural breakdown of ancient rules that recognized in equal measure the importance of both women and men.

The issue is that socially, we impose our perceived gender roles on our sex. So rigid is the system in place that it is dismissive of even scientific temperament. It ignores the fact that gender and sex are two distinct aspects of a human being—sex is the manifestation of our physical bodies, while gender is the representation of our masculine/feminine energy from within. In fact, Carl Jung, Swiss psychiatrist, psychotherapist, psychologist and pioneering evolutionary theorist, identified these expressions as *anima* (the unconscious feminine side of a man) and *animus* (the unconscious masculine side of a woman). The terms 'man' and 'woman', commonly refer to the physical manifestation of the 'masculine' and 'feminine' bodies[1] [2].

These physical manifestations of 'man' and 'woman' have varying definitions and expectations, serving specific yet different purposes in societies. There are different premiums on the look, feel and function of these masculine and feminine manifestations.

For instance, in Middle Earth, the central longitudinal swathe of Earth comprising the old lands of Europe and Africa, the premium on the physical expression of being a man or a woman was with regard to their fertility, birthing and parenting capabilities. That is where studying our ancient myths and folklore unpacks our beliefs, biases and interpretations by exploring our blood memory and civilizational DNA.

On similar lines, European and African lore celebrated motherhood. The dominant mythological and social iconography is of the sacrificing woman and mother role. Similarly, Matryoshka dolls (Russian nesting dolls), Sergei Papa Bear (symbolises guardianship) and Santa Claus are all celebrations of the female/male form in their parenting roles. The Chinese Mooncake festival celebrates the legendary woman's devotion to her husband in the face of threat, and the Japanese Hinamatsuri or Doll Festival celebrates the transition from girlhood to womanhood. Another common theme running across these cultures is the strength women were equipped with, even in stories from their mythology.

[1]Jung, C.G., The Archetypes and the Collective Unconscious, Routledge, 2nd Ed., 1991; Jung, C.G., *Four Archetypes*, Routledge. 3rd Ed., 2003.
[2]Bair, Deidre, *Jung: A Biography*, Back Bay Books, 2024.

In oral history, parenting was considered a virtue for both sexes and women were considered to be centres of powers.

On the contrary, in more modern, 'newer' ideas, the depictions have changed. Owing to multiple factors such as changing economic realities, social upheavals, wars, and global annexation of cultures, the narrative has changed slowly and steadily. The premium on physical expression was split between a feminine energy resonating with the weaker, 'damsel in distress' phenomenon, while the masculine energy acted as the saviour of all. The ascent of this psychological dichotomy is imperative to our understanding of modern-day gender identities.

These Jungian archetypes that emerge from the Western civilizational schema are about the male as the provider and the hunter, and the female as the provided and the 'kept'. The iconography of the male hero winning conflicts and rescuing the 'imprisoned/kidnapped' princess has, in fact, continued to play out in popular media and movies. The premium is on the female being chaste and pure, and on the male being the macho hero. These themes continue to dominate modern-day cultural tropes as well. Girls are voiceless and choiceless, and mere trophies in the end. It is easy to correlate that with the prize date on the 'prom' night or the bride in virginal white. The physical expression of gender is only relevant to the female's purity and her need to be rescued.

In the Indian subcontinent in particular, the understanding of gender manifestation is fascinating. On the lines of nature versus nurture, Indian spiritualism treated nature and its resources such as trees, rivers, mountains, grass, stones, cows, all as mother substitutes. There is no real need to deify a female from the human species solely as birth giver. When we began to adopt Western ideas without much reflection, an inherent hypocrisy set in. This led to the worship of motherhood, but also to crimes and manipulations against women at large. Virginity was seen as a virtue and a tool for manipulating the lives of women. What we see in these troublesome dichotomies is the underlying religious iconography, and the folklore, both most revealing of the premium on the human male/female expression.

Such an approach questions the role the physical manifestation of the man/woman plays in this part of the world. Curiously, our ancient scriptures and related stories, including our present-day rituals and symbols, convey the same idea—the physical manifestation of the human male/female form is for the purposes of physical intimacy and consummation. This union of the male and the female form is a celebration. Besides the scriptures, even temple architecture celebrates intimacy and the pleasure human bodies derive from each other. There are *apsara*s, celestial beings, and the *yaksha*s and *yakshini*s, whose sole purpose of existence is to provide physical pleasure. Gods and goddesses have their independent identities and powers. They have consorts and partners, sometimes even multiple ones. They exult in their unions.

This understanding is incredibly contextual and relevant to the three moot points of ancient Indian wisdom. First, the interest in the male/female physiology/physical manifestation is relevant only for physical intimacy and in desire as the origin of all creation. Beyond that, the gender of the form is irrelevant. Second, it emphasizes sex as being a biological fact, and the notion of gender as a mental and social construct. Sex resides in the body, gender in the mind, and the intellect or *buddhi* which is a part of the Divine, is not an embodiment of either.

Thus, while there is ample evidence to support that even within our culture, originally the male/female engagement had a physical connotation, social forces, structures, and exchange of ideas with other societies have heavily influenced our understanding of this engagement. The quest for power and domination has superseded our traditional knowledge, and continues to pose as the original thought on the position of women in Indian society. We, as a nation, have co-opted the global gender idea.

GENDER AND LEADERSHIP

The tradition-versus-modernity debate has given rise to some of the most obvious conflicts in the context of Hinduism. We are caught between our worship of the divine feminine on the one hand, and the prevalent gender violence and discrimination against women on the other.

While we have tried to partly decode our understanding of gender roles, let us attempt to understand our relationship with power, faith, and leadership before we can fathom their interplay.

Geert Hofstede developed the framework for cross-cultural psychology, to study national cultures through power distance. This index is defined as 'the extent to which the less powerful members of organizations and institutions (like the family) accept and expect that power is distributed unequally'[3]. A higher degree of the index indicates that hierarchy is clearly established and executed in society, without doubt or reason. A lower degree of the index signifies that people question authority and attempt to distribute power.

India scores very high on the power distance index. According to deductions of the hierarchical collective, India has respect for age, stature, and social order. There is acceptance of, and submission to, the 'higher authority/power'. There is a well-defined construct of the phenomena of the universe that we comprehend and understand. Then there is that which happens in the cosmos, but which is beyond our ken, yet. Still, as surprising as it may seem, our ancient knowledge offers a counter-argument.

With regard to Sanatan Dharma, the Bhagwad Gita speaks of the concept of *Kshetra/ Kshetragya*, which urges us to examine our own loci of control, that which is within our *Kshetra*, the

---

[3]Hofstede, Geert, 'The 6-D model of national culture', https://tinyurl.com/5ya5az5y. Accessed on 27 August 2024.

insentient, and act on it, and then witness the rest to *Kshetragya*, the sentient[4].

The theory of karma also explains the ideas of free will and destiny, and the balance of accounts between everything happening to us in the present as a consequence of our past actions/thoughts/emotions, our own past karma, the *prarabdh* that is the balance of our past that needs to be settled in our present lifetime. This then becomes our destiny, our fate for this lifetime, that which needs to be accepted and settled. Then there is the *agami*, the karma we accrue in this present lifetime, which has to be settled in this lifetime and the future ones. This is where our free will comes in. We have the choice to accrue our own thoughts/deeds/actions/emotions. We can exercise this choice.

There is an inherent belief in the justice of the ultimate karmic audit, that everyone lives with the karmic ledger of their own *sanchita*, their own pots of personal eternal karmic balance—the ruler and the ruled; the rich and the poor; men and women; leaders and their followers.

Women, in particular, have been conditioned over time to believe that their control on wealth and finances, hence voice and choice, is conditional and optional, whereas for a man it is primal and fundamental. This facilitates the justification for women to bow out from fighting fiercely for external positions, and to succumb to the role of the all-absorbing nurturer. This is where the seeds of the unquestioning acceptance of our lives lie. With these seeds in our collective unconscious, watered by the historical experience of being colonized, subverted and submitting to power, we have come to believe in our faith-based survival and function.

While this stepping back is a global phenomenon that

---

[4]Prabhupada, A.C. Bhaktivedanta Swami, *Shirmad Bhagwat Geeta Yatharoop*, Bhaktivedanta Book Trust, 2019; Yogananda, Paramahansa, *God Talks with Arjuna: The Bhagavad Gita*, Self-Realization Fellowship, 2nd Ed., 2004; Aurobindo, Sri, *Essays on the Gita*, Sri Aurobindo Ashram Publications Department, 9th Ed., 2001.

helps understand women's unequal access to wealth, there are some differences in culture. The Hindu submission to power structures and leadership is based on the subliminal acceptance of the concepts of karma and dharma. This, combined with our understanding of sex as a simple physical manifestation of the *sharira* or human body, actually makes the Bharatiya civilization **gender agnostic to leadership**. The sex of a leader or of a god is irrelevant. What is important is the powers they have, the leadership they offer, and the hope and faith they inspire.

This holds true of a monarch, or of an elected leader in governance.

In contrast, the relationship between gender and leadership is a complex one in the newer world. Gender roles exist as power play between the 'knight in shining armour' and the 'damsel in distress'. Combined with the challenging conflicts of accepting leadership and authority, it is eventually the concept of the 'woman in leadership roles' that gets compromised. It is hardly surprising that in the corporate world, industry captaincy, or among democratically elected heads of state and governance, there is little or no representation of the feminine gender. The civilizational DNA, the context or archetype of the woman in power, are completely missing

In contrast, in this part of the world, comfortable with gender-agnostic leadership, women have occupied leadership roles forever—as heads of state, and as heads of business houses. Power structures and bloodlines hold far greater sway in the determination of leadership positions, than considerations of gender. Daughters and sons are groomed equally for succession, whether in business or in politics. In the West, power is still considered the domain of a male heir, either direct or indirect.

In India specifically, the challenges to women in leadership roles are not external or contextual. We already have the context and the comfort of women in power. We celebrate the Goddess in her various forms for nine days, twice a year, where every aspect of her nature and nurture is explored and venerated. It is in our collective dharma to facilitate and empower the feminine energy, and we do need constant reminders to do so.

THE WAY FORWARD: THE KARMA-DHARMA AXIS

Systemic shifts need seismic movements, especially since these concern nearly half the total population. Alternatively, if every member of our society can operate at their best capacity with their best vision, we will have a society punching far above its weight and heft, with the whole being truly greater than the sum of its parts.

This is where the twin pillars of dharma and karma come into play, raising the conscious awareness of our actions, thoughts and emotions, and of their consequences on various spheres of our existence and relationships. If we can bring in the following levels of awareness and acceptance into our consciousness and into the deliberation of our choices, we would have amped up our own impact:

- **Me/Svadharma:** Activate the blood memory of our complete human selves, with gender being only one part of our identities at the bodily level, literally. Accept our bodies, embrace our emotions, and express ourselves from the absolute truth of our own intellect.
- **Mine/Aparadharma:** Engage with those immediately around us as people beyond their positions and the roles they occupy, beyond their gender, age, race, religion, education, position.
- **Humankind/Paradharma**: At the organizational/societal/ industry level, normalize human engagements and roles, beyond gender stereotypes and conversations on race and religion. Celebrate love in all its expression. Exult in our human selves at home and at work, and in all the spaces in between, at all times.

Maybe it is indeed time for us to live the eternally circular truth of the two *mahavakya*s or great sayings:

Tat Tvam Asi—That which You are
Aham Brahmasmi—I am the Infinite Divine within myself[5].

---

[5]'What Does Aham Brahmasmi Mean?' Yogapedia, 21 December 2023. https://tinyurl.com/56sb9mzw. Accessed on 23 August 2024.

2

WOMEN'S EMPOWERMENT— GLOBAL AND NATIONAL VIEWS FROM ECONOMISTS

Dr Ajit Ranade and Dr Ejaz Ghani
Economists

PART 1
WOMEN'S PARTICIPATION IN THE MODERN ECONOMY

Dr Ajit Ranade

In October 2023, the Nobel Memorial Prize in Economic Sciences was awarded to Claudia Goldin, the Henry Lee Professor of Economics at Harvard University. The citation says that she was awarded the prize for enhancing our understanding of women's labour market outcomes. This terse statement does not do full justice to her large body of work which spans several areas affecting the role of women in the economy. Her most intensive and definitive study is of women's labour force participation and outcomes over 200 years of American history.

Many of her findings and conclusions, drawn from American data, are applicable to most other countries, including India, despite the cultural and geographical differences. The major areas Goldin has touched upon, and to which many other researchers and scholars have also contributed, include explaining the gender gap in wages—how this has evolved and what explains its persistence; why women's participation in the labour force, i.e. for paid work, and its evolution continue to be low in some countries; the interplay between marriage, fertility and women's labour supply; the role of education in career pathways of women, and lastly, the evolving reduction in occupational segregation.

Each of the four areas highlighted by Goldin form the basic starting point of our enquiries into the realm of women studies, labour, and their role in the economy, growth, and change in our societies. Historically women's labour was primarily in the home or in family businesses. For generations, their contribution has been considered as a 'matter of fact', taken for granted, making them rather invisible in the eyes of a world and society that looks at hard data to determine productivity. Thus, their work has neither been measured nor counted in the aggregate national economic output.

In primitive societies and at a time when agriculture and allied sectors formed the main source of national income, women had some negotiating power. Farms were the means of livelihood and, by extension, the kitchen that has been accepted as the 'natural realm' of women was at the centre of our household economy. Thus, on the micro and macro level, women were able to make some room for themselves and their contribution was recognized.

Tides changed and by the end of the eighteenth century, new scientific and technological advancements ushered in a new economic system. As industrialization progressed, it gave way to capitalism and factories became sites of economic growth. Working in factories meant more stress on physical labour and long working hours. Men became the natural choice of workers for factory owners. Women did participate and work in factories and as domestic servants, but were considered as alternative labour—in case men were not available. The modern economy, since its inception, was moulded and run on a system that did not take women's labour into serious account. The participation of women in the formal economy is a phenomenon that has evolved only in the past century and half.

It has been a rather slow race but by the twentieth century, women had stepped out of their homes and were demanding a larger say in the way their society, politics, and economics were working. Women proved their capabilities, especially in the war years when men went to fight and the so-called 'second sex' stepped up and took up jobs that were historically categorized as 'men's jobs'. Not only did women enthusiastically serve and perform, they became the engines that ensured economies did not collapse while the men were away. However, their contribution was yet again sidelined in the post-war era. As troops returned to their native lands, they were also expected to return to their jobs. Consequentially, women were asked to go back to their realm of expertise—the home.

However, the seeds of economic independence were sown and once the global tumult had somewhat calmed down, post 1960s, women's participation in the workforce increased dramatically, influenced by higher educational attainment, changes in family dynamics (especially in Western societies) and evolving social and cultural norms. The widening reach of higher education was crucial since it allowed women to enter professions such as teaching, nursing, and eventually law, medicine and business and financial services. Accumulation of human capital in the form of training and skills is a key factor for women, and the return on their investment in human capital has increased over time.

This historical trend has been captured by economists, sociologists, and even psychologists. Goldin and others have pointed out that as an economy develops over time, the U-shape of the participation of women in the labour force emerges. With economic development, the economy goes from being agrarian to industrial and finally services-dominated. In the agrarian phase, women work on farms alongside their menfolk. With industrialization, the work is less flexible, more rigid, in the factories and on assembly lines. Hence, the participation of women drops. Conversely, with more economic advancement, the services sector dominates, and women are able to participate in greater numbers.

Through her research and extensive study on the subject, Goldin was able to quantify large data sets and provide us with a rather crisp road map. Her thesis culminated in a U-shape graph depicting high participation in the early stage, followed by low participation during the industrial phase, and high participation again when there is more prosperity. The female labour force participation rate (FLFPR) can be as high as 85%–90% in advanced economies.

IN THE NAME OF SOCIETY

The U-shape of women's participation in the workforce can be seen from the angle of family income and social roles and norms. The patriarchal mindset that has plagued the global society for centuries is one of the major determinants of women's workforce participation. The attitude of carriers of patriarchal values insists on the sexual division of labour in the name of maintaining a balanced and functional society.

As family income rises, women pull back and tend to look after household work and childcare. For rich and very rich households, the workforce participation rate goes up again. This is the U-shape with respect to household income. In many countries, the female workforce continues to represent an untapped potential that can greatly enhance the national output and economic prosperity. Lower female labour force participation along with the still persisting gender wage gap is a double whammy. As famously said by a former head of the International Monetary Fund (IMF), if women's participation rate becomes equal to men, and if the pay gap is reduced to zero, national output can jump by more than 20%!

Then there is social stigma. If a woman is working for pay outside home, there is a stigma attached to it. It implies that the 'man of the house' is either lazy or unable to earn enough for his family. This stigma has been observed across different cultures, including in India. Thus, social stigma might also prevent women's participation in the workforce, especially for middle-income families.

The interplay of marriage and social norms also might have a decisive influence. It is quite common to hear a comment such as: 'My daughter is in a temporary job, but as soon as she gets married, she will quit.' It is as if a job is simply a temporary arrangement before marriage and motherhood. Indeed, Goldin's and other people's work has documented how in olden times, nearly 60% of an adult woman's prime working age was spent in either being pregnant or nursing a child. Just look at our grandparents' generation, which tended to have people with a dozen siblings or more. Imagine the plight of those mothers.

All this changed, thanks to family planning, postponing marriages and spacing out pregnancies. Also, the total fertility rate, i.e. the average number of children born to a woman in her prime age, dropped sharply. The special role of contraception in increasing FLFPR is also highlighted in Goldin's work. Her work also covers women's struggle against discrimination in the workplace, and their fight for equal pay.

BABY STEPS

It is also worth remembering the economic strategy of the former prime minister of Japan, Shinzo Abe, which was nicknamed Abenomics. Abe's campaign promise before his party's stunning victory in December 2012 was to bring Japan out of its deflationary funk into strong and sustainable economic growth. His three arrows consisted of expansionary monetary and fiscal policies (the first two arrows), and structural and economic reforms (the third).

This third arrow consisted of deregulation, trade liberalization, tax reform and industrial restructuring.

An important component of the third arrow was 'womenomics', getting more women into the workforce and in positions of leadership. Women have long been considered the most 'underutilized' resource of the Japanese economy, a point often underscored by Abe. Japanese women are highly educated on average, and indeed have a higher college enrolment rate than men. Yet, female labour force participation rate in Japan has been among the lowest among OECD (Organisation for Economic Cooperation and Development) countries. Government survey showed 63% women quit their jobs disappointed by their career prospects. Seventy per cent women are not able to return to the workforce after the birth of their first child. The reasons include non-availability of quality childcare centres. Female participation remains crucial for Japan, since its population is declining and also ageing rapidly. The elderly will make up 40% of the total population by 2060, and the ratio of working to retired persons will be 1:1 by 2050. Unless women participate in much greater numbers to expand the workforce, the pension and tax burden will be crushing, and will affect economic growth. If female labour force participation is on a par with other industrial nations, Japan's per capita output would be higher by 4%. Female participation in Japan is lower by as much as 25% compared to male participation. If this were on parity with male participation, then Goldman Sachs' estimates suggest Japan would gain eight million workers, and its gross domestic product (GDP) would be higher by 14%.

It is precisely because of such dismal numbers and a 'low base' that the benefits from increasing female participation are immense to Japan. Realizing this, Prime Minister Abe put in place numerical targets and tangible metrics in his 'womenomics' strategy. He initially aimed to have 30% of leadership positions for women in government and business. He also initiated massive investment into state-funded high-quality childcare centres all across Japan, but mostly in metropolitan regions.

LONG WAY TO GO

Beyond education, skilling, pay parity and Board positions, India's agenda should also include providing women leadership positions in political life. The recent violent experience in Nagaland, where the local community refused to let women enjoy 33% reservation in local governments, shows how far we have to go. This resistance to even constitutional mandates shows that there is as much a cultural hurdle as an economic policy hurdle to achieving progress for women. But as Japan's 'womenomics' indicates, numerical targets do help us get started.

∽

PART 2
INDIA'S CHALLENGE

DR EJAZ GHANI

Economic growth is an inherently gendered process, and gender-based inequalities are huge barriers to shared prosperity (United Nations, 2019). A central driver of economic growth over the past century has been the increased role of women in society. This growth has come in many forms: the removal of political and cultural barriers to the participation of women in the labour force, and reduced discrimination in education, wage differentials, and management practices that prevent talented women from reaching leadership roles.

India has taken several steps to promote gender equality, including ratifying human rights treaties and establishing a National Commission for Women. The Indian Constitution's

Preamble, Fundamental Rights, Fundamental Duties, and Directive Principles all enshrine the principle of gender equality. The Government of India designated 2001 as the 'Year of Women's Empowerment' and legislators established the National Policy for the Advancement of Women. In 1993, India ratified the Convention on the Elimination of All Forms of Discrimination against Women (CEDAW). States have also amended their laws to ensure equal inheritance rights for sons and daughters. For example, in 2005, the Hindu Succession Act was amended to secure Hindu women's inheritance rights at the federal level.

INDIA'S ECONOMIC PICTURE

India has experienced immense economic growth since its independence in 1947, but women and men do not share this growth equally. Women's economic participation remains dismally low, with only 23% of women in the labour force in 2021, compared to 72.7% of men, resulting in a staggering gender gap of nearly 50 percentage points. Despite several efforts, gender disparities have remained deep.

Structural transformation programmes supported by IMF and World Bank have accelerated economic growth but failed to make a significant contribution to increased female participation in jobs and reduce gender gaps in wages. For example, consecutive women earnings reports in the past years place female earnings at an average of only 40% of those of men in self-employment, followed by 64% of men in casual wage jobs, and 76% of men in regular wage jobs. India's gender balance in entrepreneurship and jobs remains among the lowest in the world. Improving this balance is an important first step for India's development and its achievement of greater economic growth and gender equality.

Ideally, trade liberalization and competitive forces should have turned employment outcomes in favour of females because firms that discriminate against women are competed away from the market unless they change their hiring strategy. However, empirical evidence suggests that market competition has failed to bridge the gender segmentation in India. Gender disparities have remained deep, especially in the manufacturing and services sectors in India. Some southern states, like Karnataka, Kerala and Tamil Nadu, have shown an improving trend in gender parity and business ownership by women in the manufacturing sector. However, female establishment ownership rates remain extremely low in states like Bihar, Haryana and Gujarat. Deep gender disparities in female ownership rates in the manufacturing sector are also evident across major cities.

India's services sector, a fast-growing and more dominant sector, has also failed to reduce gender disparities in the start-up of new enterprises. Female enterprise ownership shares in services barely reach 10% in states with the highest female ownership rates, like in Kerala, Tamil Nadu and Andhra Pradesh, and remains much lower in states like Rajasthan, Bihar, Orissa and Uttar Pradesh, at less than 6%.

India is the fastest urbanizing country in the world. Empirical evidence shows that female enterprise ownership rates in major cities tend to be higher than overall state averages. Gender disparities remain worse in rural areas due to poor infrastructure and restrictive family norms that become constraints to starting a business. Women-owned enterprises, therefore, do seem to benefit from strong agglomeration economies in case of both manufacturing and services sectors. Urbanization has not reduced the gender gap either in cities or in rural areas. The share of female-owned businesses has declined with the increase in distance from major cities in India, as has female employment share in the services sector.

Has India experienced any convergence in gendered participation across states? Not yet. Rather, states with higher income have continued to display higher growth in shares of female-led plants, and the gap in female-led plants has widened between the leading and lagging states within India.

Gender discrimination affects many aspects of women's lives, including career development, mental health, and the workplace. Efforts to reduce gender disparities need to be scaled up. We will examine why India's structural transformation has failed to achieve gender equality. What can be done to promote gender equality, jobs and growth? There is an urgent need for rigorous analysis that can guide policymakers on how to approach, measure and respond effectively to closing gender gaps while building stronger economies and improving long-term human welfare and shared prosperity.

TRANSLATIONS OF STRUCTURAL REFORMS

Gender-focused structural transformation can address root causes of gender inequalities by removing structural barriers, changing laws and policies, and adapting systems and services. These changes can challenge harmful gender norms, roles and relations, while working towards redistributing power, resources and services more equally. Economic theory suggests that growth may improve gender equality directly by raising women's employment, and indirectly by reducing poverty, thereby causing poorer families to discriminate less against females in intra-household allocations. India and many developing countries around the world have implemented structural reforms—supported by regional and global multilateral institutions—ranging from better macroeconomic policies, trade and regulatory reforms, investments in human and physical infrastructure, and so on.

Structural transformation has generated higher economic growth but not yet improved gender equality in India. Empirical evidence shows that although structural reforms have made India the fastest-growing large economy in the world, gender inequality has remained deep-rooted in the Indian economy.

Female labour force participation rates have been declining during the last two decades, and remain well below several Sub-Saharan African countries[1] [2]. The UN Global Gender Gap data from 2023 shows that women's economic participation and opportunity is worse in India than in 127 of the 146 countries studied. Women are underrepresented in economic and political leadership positions and paid less when they perform the same or equal-value jobs as men. Women face the highest incidence of poverty, the worst health conditions, and highest likelihood of being victims of violence, and as girls, are also exposed to the possibility of child marriage, teenage pregnancy, and child domestic work.

The disconnect between structural reforms and gender gap may be due to gender policies being overlooked in structural reform programmes. In recent years, the focus of structural policy reforms on gender equity has increased. India provides a good data point for examining the links between structural transformation and gender equity, as it is simultaneously enthusiastic about promoting women's participation in government but also a laggard in regulating gender issues in the workplace.

A gender lens was applied in India to different drivers of economic growth, using an enterprise survey of more than 900 districts in India. Enterprises provide a micro lens to the drivers of growth and structural transformation in India. Unfortunately, it found that India's structural transformation has failed to make a significant contribution to increase female participation in jobs and to reduce gender gaps. The share of females in manufacturing employment has not increased significantly; more female workers are finding the services sector a better (or more accessible)

[1]Najeeb, Fatima, Matias Morales and Gladys Lopez-Acevedo, 'Analyzing Female Employment Trends in South Asia', World Bank Policy Research Working Paper 9157, February 2020, https://tinyurl.com/4t2pz98r. Accessed on 9 September 2024.
[2]*Global Gender Gap Report 2023, Insight Report June 2023*, World Economic Forum, https://tinyurl.com/459zcpn7. Accessed on 9 September 2024.

employment avenue than manufacturing. Despite huge structural reforms to promote growth, gender-based segmentation has not subsided in India.

Women-owned enterprises in India remain concentrated in low-paying industries, and this concentration has only increased over time. Statistics suggest a strong negative relationship between average industry wages and the share of female-led plants in the unorganized manufacturing sector. This negative association between the share of female-owned plants and average industry wages is also prevalent in the services sector but is not as strong as in the manufacturing sector.

An examination of the gender pattern by industry shows that tobacco products, ready-to-wear apparel and textiles attract the largest count and share of women entrepreneurs, perhaps because these industries are known to impose relatively lower requirements in terms of physical labour. Among the services, education, sewage, refuse disposal, sanitation and financial intermediation services attract the largest share of female proprietors. Broadly, these are also industries that have attracted the largest count and shares of female employees.

In India, the gender of the enterprise owner overwhelmingly predicts the gender of the employees. Industries that have higher rates of female entrepreneurship and employment are also broadly industries that have the highest segmentation in terms of female employees being matched to female owners. People seem to prefer working with others of their own gender—this is also true for male-led plants. Some industries, like transport equipment, radio, television and fabricated metal products are among the most segmented in manufacturing, while in the case of services, male-led plants in water transport, land transport and research and development tend to employ the largest share of male workers.

IMPACT OF COMPETITION ON GENDER DISCRIMINATION IN INDIA

India has undergone massive competitive changes since the turn of the millennium. This has perhaps been a result of a conscious strategy of restructuring the economy through a wide variety of reforms, such as the massive trade liberalization episode of the 1990s, the large-scale investment in highway infrastructure in the 2000s, and more recently, domestic reforms that dismantled reservations of products for smaller plants. These macro reforms are known to have enhanced economic activity and improved allocative efficiency and productivity at the firm level.

If gender disparity in India is a result of discriminatory hiring practices in the labour market, then economists, dating back to Gary Becker, would argue that competition should drive out such discrimination. The idea behind this theory is that people prefer to work with their own 'types'. In lax environments, or when firms have market power, managers may engage in discriminatory behaviour to hire their own 'type' and still be able to remain in business. However, competition is thought to put a brake on the scope of discrimination and crony capitalism. If a firm is in a fierce battle for survival, then it must optimize to stay in business, and firms with managers who are willing to give up (or never had) tendencies to discriminate among male and female employees will be more likely to succeed.

Evidence from the United States suggests that following deregulations in the banking sector, discrimination within banks and among product markets declined due to greater competition. However, a systematic study on the impact of pro-competitive reforms on gender discrimination and/or segmentation in developing countries is rather scarce. The limited research that does study the 'gendered' impact of competition in developing countries mainly investigates the effect on female labour force participation rates, sectoral employment patterns and wage inequality. Most studies on developing countries have employed trade liberalization as a competitive force to study changes in gender discrimination thereafter. A few studies in the context of developed countries have also focused on domestic banking reforms.

We examined the impact of such reforms on gender segmentation (*see references*). Using establishment-level data from India, we examined the impact on gender-based outcomes and segmentation in both manufacturing and services emanating from a range of pro-competitive reforms including not only India's mostly exogenous trade liberalization episode, but also industry-specific domestic reforms and infrastructural reforms.

India is a very important laboratory for studying these effects. First, the country has a history of discrimination, broadly speaking, be it by gender, caste, or otherwise. Moreover, this matters for India's economic growth and development. For instance, Khera (2016) finds that an improvement in public provisions (such as better water facilities, sanitation development, and access to electricity) which increases female labour participation by 1.5% would lead to a 1.4% gain in GDP. Lawson (2008) estimates that India's per capita income could be 10%–13% higher than under the baseline scenario of unchanged gender inequality in 2020 if the gender gap decreases by 50% from its 2008 value. The widely followed crimes against women in India and the growth of female political set-asides speak to this important struggle of mainstreaming gender parity in India's growth narrative.

Second, a striking feature of the Indian data is that one knows the gender composition of the workforce. Most notably, we are not aware of large-scale data set studies that are able to unite the owner's gender, employee gender, and localized competition in the manner we examined. In case of the unorganized sector manufacturing and services sector establishments, one also knows the gender of the business owner. This provides exceptional details about gender-based employment patterns that stretch over a long period of time. This offers a very rare opportunity to study gender-based outcomes, especially in the setting of a developing economy. As establishments also have geographic and industry identifiers, one can make very precise assessments of discriminatory behaviour. For example, we can examine whether gender discrimination is prevalent in leading or lagging regions and states. How does this relate to the local education of the workforce or the quality of physical infrastructure in these regions?

India shows a clear pattern of gender segmentation in both manufacturing and services. For example, in the unorganized manufacturing sector, about 90% of employees in female-owned business are female, while this share is 81% in the case of the services sector. Furthermore, the extent of gender segmentation in India's female-owned as well as male-owned businesses has increased over the years. Beyond these core results, we also note that since 2001, the share of female entrepreneurs and their resulting employment has increased in the informal manufacturing sector. For the services sector, these statistics are, however, much lower in level as well as in growth terms. Finally, although the share of female employment is slightly lower in services than in manufacturing, it has shown dynamic growth.

These broad patterns mask the varying trends in female entrepreneurship, employment, and gender segmentation across leading versus lagging regions as well as among industries within manufacturing and services. Our state- and industry-level descriptive statistics suggest that states and industries with higher female entrepreneurship shares are also the ones with higher female participation shares in employment. Further, there is a positive association between female involvement in ownership or in employment and gender segmentation in female-led businesses. In general, the magnitude of this correlation is found to be stronger in unorganized manufacturing than in the organized services sector. Among the correlates of female activity, we find that participation of women in both manufacturing and services is greatly influenced by larger working-age populations and female-to-male gender ratios in the local economy. Technology plays a vital role in reducing gender segmentation in the services industry relative to that in informal manufacturing. Across the board, we find a relatively higher importance of district-level local infrastructure in determining female participation and in reducing gender segmentation among male-led plants.

It is possible that some other factors, beyond competition, are leading this trend. To test the micro impact of increased competition on gender segmentation, we exploit the spatial and industry-level variation in reforms where certain districts (e.g. in Golden Quadrilateral or GQ highway upgrades) or specific industries (e.g. in tariff liberalization or de-reservations) were differentially affected. We begin with utilizing the spatial variation in the design of a major infrastructure project in India. The GQ project that upgraded 5,846 kilometres of roads connecting many of India's major industrial, agricultural and cultural centres not only heightened economic activity for Indian manufacturing but also facilitated a more natural sorting of certain industries from nodal districts into peripheral locations. The upgrades also encouraged decentralization by making intermediate cities more attractive for manufacturing entrants. Importantly, and the subject of ongoing research, the upgrades are also associated with better allocative efficiency in the organized manufacturing sector (Ghani, Goswami and Kerr, 2016a).

Our descriptive results, however, do not find any impact of such competitive forces on gender segmentation among districts located in proximity to the GQ highways. By comparison, we find a decline in gender segmentation among non-modal districts lying away from the highways, which is rather opposite to what the theory would predict. In a subsequent experiment, we switched to exploiting the industry-level variation in the pro-competitive trade liberalization reforms. Beginning in 1991, trade reforms opened up the Indian economy by substantially reducing tariff rates on many products. These mostly exogenous reforms allow for an industry- level long-difference analysis of trade-based competition. For empirical identification, these reforms offer ample variations internal to India. For example, trade deregulations took place at different times for various products. This staggered timing in trade reforms across a range of products provides enough room to use an econometric tool to identify the stimulus in competition across industries. Our results suggest a very limited correlation of tariff changes to participation of women in Indian manufacturing. Nonetheless, we do find that a reduction in trade protection is associated with a decline in segmentation among male-led plants.

We examined the consequences on gender segmentation of enhanced competitive forces due to the elimination of products reserved for small-scale industries (SSI). With the aim of promoting SSI, the Government of India embarked on a policy of reserving products exclusively for production by smaller plants. Starting with the third five-year plan (1961–66), this list of reserved products progressively became larger over the years up until 1997. Since 1997, India has witnessed a five-year reservation policy and gradually most products were de-reserved by 2007. Our work reveals that industry-level de-reservations were positively associated with overall activity, in general, and with female activity, specifically.

Like trade reforms, de-reservation reforms are also associated with a decline in segmentation among male-owned businesses, while they are associated with an increase in segmentation among female-owned plants. This multi-dimensional analysis has immense relevance for policy. For instance, cutting across the spatial dimension, we note that certain locational traits such as leading versus lagging states generate higher levels of gender segmentation, but they do not respond differently to investments in infrastructure.

Furthermore, we find that certain district traits such as local infrastructure and technology usage play an important role in mitigating gender segmentation in India. This work on the impact of pro-competitive reforms on gender segmentation points to the possibility that not all policies are equally effective in reducing discrimination. For instance, we find null effects of reforms that enhance competition in a spatial context. Specifically, districts located in proximity to the GQ highways did not witness an increase in activity of women or a reduction in segmentation post-upgrade. By comparison, industry-specific pro-competitive reforms, such as trade liberalization and product de-reservation, are associated with a decline in segmentation among male employees and an increase in participation among women. The efficiency of the state underlies these features, and these traits govern their effectiveness in promoting competitive workforces.

India's workforce remains highly segmented by gender. Said differently, there is an extreme inclination of female-led establishments to hire female employees, and likewise the tendency of male-owned plants to have a primarily male-dominated workforce.

IMPACT OF POLITICAL REFORMS ON GENDER GAP IN INDIA

While India is a huge laggard, it is also a leader in political reforms to reduce gender gap. India pioneered women's political representation in 1993 with the 73rd Constitutional Amendment Act, reserving a third of seats in local Panchayat elections for women. India was the first country in the world to implement political representation of women in local elections. India already has four decades of experience with the political reservation for women in local elections.

The world can learn from India about how political reforms can be used to reduce gender gap. We examined the effects of political representation of women in local elections in most states that implemented the Act. A massive growth was seen in new women-owned establishments with associated employment of approximately 40% after political reservations were implemented. Political representation in Rajasthan and West Bengal led to more investment in drinking water and roads in response to complaints by local women. Political participation of women strengthened the administration of state transfer programmes, local public goods such as educational and medical facilities, the overseeing of local infrastructure (water, sewage, roads, etc.), and the monitoring of civil servants.

Political representation of women not only reduced social prejudice, oppression, and exploitation of women in local power structures, it also became a new driver of economic growth. Economic growth came in many forms: removal of cultural and political barriers to the participation of women in labour markets, reduced discrimination in wage differentials, and changes in management practices that have promoted talented women to leadership roles, among others.

Given the huge benefits from political representation of women in local elections observed over the last four decades, India is now planning to scale up women representation from local to higher levels. The Indian parliament has passed a Women's Reservation Bill—Nari Shakti Vandan Adhiniyam—which will reserve one-third seats in the lower house of parliament and state assemblies for women. The Bill needs to be aligned with the redrawing of the boundaries of parliament and state assembly constituencies and increased population of India. Its implementation should not be delayed, as India has a long history of implementing political representation of women.

CAUSES FOR PERSISTENT GENDER DISPARITIES IN INDIA

Is it poor infrastructure, limited education, and gender composition of the labour force and industries? Or is it deficiencies in social and business networks and a low share of incumbent female entrepreneurs? We used detailed micro-data on the unorganized manufacturing and services sectors to explore the drivers of gender gaps across districts and industries.

We found that a district industry with more incumbent female employment has a greater female entry share. Among district-level traits, a higher female-to-male sex ratio, a higher working-age to non-working-age population ratio (demographic dividend), better-quality infrastructure, and more stringent labour regulations appear important. The relative female entry rate declines with high population density. Education and female literacy rates are not associated with gender differences in manufacturing.

Infrastructure correlation is the most policy-relevant. Inadequate infrastructure affects women more than men, perhaps because women often bear a larger share of the time and responsibility for household activities. It is notable that while the within-district infrastructure access is prominent, access to major cities is not found to influence gender balance. Additional analysis finds that transport infrastructure and paved roads within villages are especially important. Travel in India can be limited and unpredictable, and women face greater constraints in geographic mobility imposed by safety concerns and/or social norms. Better transport infrastructure may alleviate a major constraint for female entrepreneurs accessing markets.

The agglomeration metrics suggest that female connections in labour markets and input-output markets contribute to a higher entry share. A one-standard deviation increase in either of these incumbent conditions correlates with a 2%–3% increase in the share of new entrants that are female. This compares to a base female entry ratio of 21%. Most of the basic district-level linkages observed for manufacturing continue for services. Somewhat surprisingly, a higher female entry ratio is not associated with a greater female sex ratio in the district, but female literacy rates and general education levels are more predictive. This link may be due to services being more skill-intensive than manufacturing in India. Stronger incumbent female-owned businesses again predict a greater female entrepreneurship in service industries.

What about agglomeration's effects on gender balance? The agglomeration metrics suggest that female connections in labour markets and local buyer/seller (input-output) markets contribute to a higher entry share. Proximity to customers and suppliers reduces transportation costs and, thereby, increases productivity. These results support the conclusion that female entrepreneurship in India follows from incumbent female-owned businesses in a district/industry that encourage subsequent entry. The strength of local input-output conditions is important, and their effects appear to be driven primarily by the presence of other local female-owned businesses.

THE WAY AHEAD

Gender equality is a fundamental human right, and gender equality is the central driver of a higher and more inclusive growth. Low female labour force participation and occupational segregation due to gender lead to inefficiencies and misallocation of talent that, if addressed, would boost incomes, and stimulate growth. Long-run GDP per capita would be almost 20% higher if gender employment gaps are closed[3]. Gender equality in leadership

---

[3]Pennings, Steven, 'How much would GDP per capita increase if gender employment gaps were closed in developing countries?', World Bank Blogs, 4 March 2022, https://tinyurl.com/yc6ctz2e. Accessed on 9 September 2024.

positions could not only increase economic growth, but also improve social and environmental outcomes.

India needs a comprehensive strategy to reduce deeply embedded gender gaps that have persisted. The first pillar of a gender transition path should be to scale up education to reduce the huge gender gap at schools and colleges. The second pillar is to integrate the country's growth strategy with its gender strategy—India's growth agenda should focus more on closing gender gaps in access to economic opportunities, earnings and productivity. The third pillar is to scale up the political representation of women. India has already made huge progress in increasing women representation in local Panchayat elections; this could be scaled up to assembly and parliament elections. A faster implementation of the new Bill will boost India's GDP by nearly $1 trillion. Increased political representation of women will improve investments in both physical and human infrastructure.

There is great potential for reducing gender disparities and increasing economic growth by improving investments in physical and human infrastructure (especially in rural areas and tier-two cities), strengthening the links between formal and informal sectors through the digital revolution and technological advances, and promoting gender networks in local businesses. Female networks in labour markets and input-output markets need to be encouraged to promote more women entrepreneurs. Inadequate infrastructure affects women more than men, as women face greater constraints in geographic mobility imposed by safety concerns and/or social norms. Therefore, states with better transport infrastructure have alleviated one of the major constraints for female entrepreneurs in accessing markets.

Reducing the time required for unpaid household responsibilities also requires scaling up investments in infrastructure. These investments are useful not only for women, but also for businesses and the economy. Lack of access to certain types of infrastructure services (such as water, electricity and sanitation) have a greater impact on women who bear a larger share of the time and responsibility for household maintenance and childcare activities. Better electricity and access to water reduce the burden of women in providing essential household inputs for their families and allow for more time to be directed toward entrepreneurial activities.

Empowering half of the potential workforce has significant economic benefits beyond promoting gender equality. While achieving economic equality sometimes requires tough choices (such as progressive taxation) that may discourage effort, the opposite is true here. Unlocking female empowerment and entrepreneurship will promote a broader dynamic economy and economic growth.

For India to become a world-class economy, women entrepreneurship will need to play a bigger role in economic growth and development. Despite recent economic advances, India's entrepreneurial gender balance remains among the lowest in the world. Improving this balance is an important step for India's development and its achievement of greater economic growth and gender equality. Gender networks clearly matter for entry into entrepreneurship and these linkages and spillovers across firms can depend a lot on common traits of business owners. Likewise, interactions between the informal and formal sectors may not be as strong as interactions within each sector, and these linkages need to be strengthened through increased gender networking.

3

NARI SHAKTI AND SOCIAL HARMONY FOR A COMPASSIONATE INDIA

Dr Raghunath Mashelkar,
Dr Vijay Kelkar and Abhay Vaidya
Pune International Centre

The image of the Indian woman as one of shy and meek femininity has evolved over centuries due to a confluence of cultural, historical and socio-political factors. Understanding this requires a deep dive into the transformation of social norms and values through the ages.

Indian society has been predominantly patriarchal, with men holding the primary power and women being relegated to subordinate roles. This system promoted the ideal of a docile and obedient woman, aligning with the interests of maintaining male dominance and control. Yet, just two words are enough to characterize the strength of Indian women over millennia: fortitude and resilience. While fortitude is 'courage shown by somebody who is suffering great pain or facing great difficulties,' resilience is 'the capacity to withstand or to recover quickly from difficulties; toughness.'

For centuries, the Indian woman has suffered enormously in a caste-driven, male-dominated, patriarchal society. As a result, she has always had an inferior status, whether at home or outside. She has suffered inequality and has been denied the freedom to pursue her goals and ambitions. Time and again, she has been treated harshly and cruelly, denied education, and forced to submit to numerous abhorrent practices such as Sati, in the name of culture and religion.

Over centuries, literature, the arts, and later, media have played a pivotal role in shaping social norms. The portrayal of women in classical literature, folklore and films often accentuated traits such as modesty, sacrifice and domesticity, reinforcing these stereotypes in popular consciousness.

Traditional Indian culture placed great emphasis on the preservation of family honour and values. Women, as bearers of family honour, were expected to conform to ideals of modesty and chastity. Besides, socialization practices also taught the girl child from a young age to be soft-spoken and compliant.

Paradoxically, ancient Indian thought glorified and deified women, as is evident in the uninterrupted march of Indian civilization over the last four to five millennia. Devdutt Pattanaik, the popular author and commentator on Indian mythology, points out that women have been worshipped as symbols of power. Ancient seers depicted power not just as physical power for the victory of good over evil, but also included the pursuit of knowledge and the creation of wealth. Therefore, says Pattanaik, the fearsome Goddess Durga, also worshipped as Kali, is flanked by Lakshmi, Goddess of Wealth, and Saraswati, Goddess of Learning in Indian mythology.[1]

Ancient Indian wisdom also recognized that the strength of women complements the strength of men, depicted through the image of Ardhanarishwar—*Ardha Nari Eshwar* ('God is half-man, half-woman').

For millennia, Indian values such as empathy, compassion, tolerance, 'live and let live', have been upheld as much by religious

---

[1] 'Devdutt Pattanaik on Women in Hindu Mythology', the Shift series, 8th March 2019, https://www.youtube.com/watch?v=-Fa7Wyirgd0. Last accessed on 23 July 2024.

leaders and sacred texts, as by mothers narrating to their children the story of Lord Ram and Sita, along with other unforgettable stories from the epics and Indian mythology that depict the strengths and weaknesses of human beings. These values form the bedrock of social harmony in India.

The Indian psyche has also been shaped by the forces of history as waves of invaders plundered India over centuries, and were eventually absorbed into Indian society. Indian pluralism thus has a solid foundation that can neither be denied nor easily destroyed.

EDUCATION AND EMANCIPATION OF WOMEN

Emancipation of the Indian woman through education and economic empowerment is an ongoing process. Over the last century, women have accomplished extraordinary feats in multiple domains, be it within or outside the country. From Dr Anandibai Joshi—India's first female doctor of Western medicine—to social reformers and freedom fighters such as Annie Besant, Sarojini Naidu (the Nightingale of India), Aruna Asaf Ali and Kamaladevi Chattopadhyay, and modern-day icons such as Irom Sharmila— the Iron Lady of Manipur, Narmada Bachao Andolan crusader Medha Patkar, social activist Aruna Roy, corporate leader Indra Nooyi, and missile scientist Tessy Thomas, several Indian women have demonstrated remarkable courage, resilience and dedication in their crusade for social justice, and to bring about positive changes in society.

Despite societal tendencies to overlook their contributions, Indian women have continuously run the wheels of the country. They manage households, excel in professional arenas, and are the backbone of social and economic progress. Self-help groups in rural India, primarily led by women, exemplify grassroots leadership, fostering community development and financial independence.

Their contributions, often unsung, form the bedrock of India's growth and prosperity. Thus, the true image of the Indian woman should be one that celebrates her strength, resilience, and relentless spirit, acknowledging her role not only in historical and religious contexts but also in the ongoing narrative of India's progress.

To a large extent, this emancipation resulted from the opening up of education for the girl child, which coincidentally happened in the city of Pune, barely 100 years before India's Independence.

IN QUEST OF COEXISTENCE

Social harmony—the peaceful coexistence of people in society in the pursuit of collective well-being—is a recurring theme at Pune International Centre. In our previous book, *India's Pathways to Success: Winning in the Next Decade* (2023)[2], we highlighted the significance of social harmony for a large and complex multi-religious, multi-ethnic and multi-cultural nation like India, all of which needs to be reiterated today.

It is our belief that as we continue to strive for a society built on the principles of cooperation, compassion and respect for human dignity, the contributions of women will remain indispensable in realizing our shared aspirations for a better future.

Social harmony and economic prosperity go hand in hand. In this essay, we have spoken of some inspiring women leaders who fought for, championed, and created social harmony. More importantly, we have shown the extraordinary attributes common to all these women that made their stupendous achievements possible.

While building the power of our Nari Shakti, these inspiring exemplars and their exceptional attributes can serve as the beacon

---

[2]Ghani, Ejaz, Ganesh Natarajan and Abhay Vaidya (2023), 'Sustainable Livelihoods and Social Commitment', in Ganesh Natarajan and Ejaz Ghani (Eds.), *India's Pathways to Success: Winning in the Next Decade* (1st Edition), Rupa Publications.

for building the harmonious Bharat@100 of our dreams.

There is a lesson in all this for men too. Just as Jyotiba Phule extended his fullest support to his wife Savitribai, as did Usman to his sister, Fatima bi, men must be by the side of the women in their lives to empower and strengthen Nari Shakti, and in the process, our nation. Mahatma Gandhi, a staunch advocate of women's rights and social equality, had many powerful quotes about the important role of women in fostering social harmony. He felt that to believe women are the weaker sex is an injustice; if strength were to be judged by moral power, women exceed men in every regard. For him, the philosophy of non-violence, truth and true power was spearheaded by women.

Women have played a crucial role in fostering social harmony throughout history by championing peace, justice and equality. Gandhi's belief that women were more capable of taking bolder decisions for the cause of non-violence has time and again been proven right. Globally, there are several examples of women who have corroborated this belief much more than men.

Internationally, leaders like Eleanor Roosevelt, former First Lady of the United States, who played a pivotal role in drafting the Universal Declaration of Human Rights, worked tirelessly to promote global harmony and human dignity. In India, Sarojini Naidu, a renowned freedom fighter and poet, was instrumental in the country's struggle for independence, advocating communal harmony and women's rights. In Liberia, Ellen Johnson Sirleaf, Africa's first elected female head of state, led remarkable efforts to reconcile a nation torn by civil war, emphasizing peacebuilding and national unity. These women, among many others, have been beacons of hope and agents of change, demonstrating that social harmony thrives under inclusive and compassionate leadership.

Often, the voices of women advocating peace, justice and reconciliation have helped us rise above chaos and led us towards a more harmonious and just future. It is important to recognize the enormous power behind the quiet strength and determination of women that can hold society together by strengthening the fabric of peace amidst chaos and conflict.

CELEBRATIONS ON THE SIDELINES

But this contribution by women to society, this aspect of Nari Shakti, has not been celebrated as much as it should have been. This essay focuses on the denial and ignorance of the role women have played as champions and creators of social harmony, at times against great odds.

Historically, women have been pivotal in promoting intercultural understanding and reconciliation. The pioneering work of social reformer Savitribai Phule, her childhood friend Fatima Sheikh, and Jyotiba Phule's aunt Sagunabai Kshirsagar, in promoting education for the girl child deserves particular attention. In 1848, barely 100 years before India's Independence, these three brave women who suffered and stood up to social contempt, went on to establish 18 schools for the girl child in Pune. They were supported in this cause by the colonial British government and a small group of well-meaning Brahmins, notably Tatya Saheb Bhide, who offered the premises of his Bhide Wada to open India's first school for girls on 1 January 1848[3].

When Savitribai Phule and her illustrious husband and social reformer, Jyotiba Phule, were forced to vacate their home in Pune for defying social norms, they were given refuge by none other than Fatima bi (in all likelihood, the first Muslim lady teacher of India) and her brother Usman. The historic dawn of women's education in India is also one of the many shining examples of social harmony at the grassroots where a Hindu and a Muslim family came together to initiate positive social change, and were

---

[3]Gupta, Reeta Ramamurthy, *Savitribai Phule: Her Life, Her Relationships, Her Legacy*, HarperCollins India, New Delhi, 2023.

assisted by a handful of right-thinking Brahmins, thus overcoming caste barriers too, in eighteenth-century India.

In troubled times, often it is women's compassion, empathy, resilience and nurturing spirit that have guided us towards reconciliation and healing. In fact, many such inspiring figures have won the Nobel Prize. Leymah Gbowee, the 2011 Nobel Peace Prize laureate, led a women's movement in Liberia that played a crucial role in ending the country's civil war[4]. Through grassroots activism and collective action, Gbowee and her fellow women effectively pressured political leaders to engage in peace negotiations, demonstrating the power of women in building bridges across divides and fostering reconciliation.

Women have been key contributors to community building and social cohesion. In many societies, women are the primary caregivers and nurturers, responsible for instilling values of compassion, cooperation, and empathy in future generations.

Wangari Maathai, founder of the Green Belt Movement in Kenya, and winner of the 2004 Nobel Peace Prize, empowered rural women to plant trees and participate in environmental conservation efforts[5]. By mobilizing women at the grassroots level, Maathai not only helped mitigate environmental degradation but also fostered a sense of solidarity and collective responsibility within communities.

Shirin Ebadi, Iranian human rights lawyer and the 2003 Nobel Peace Prize laureate, has been a fearless advocate of justice and equality in Iran[6]. Despite facing harassment, intimidation and persecution from the Iranian government, she has continued to defend the rights of women, children and political prisoners,

---

[4]The Nobel Prize, Leymah Gbowee—Biographical, https://tinyurl.com/3y8557eb. Accessed on 10 May 2024

[5]The Green Belt Movement, Wangari Maathai biography, https://tinyurl.com/4peyxkdk. Accessed on 9 September 2024.

[6]The Nobel Prize, Shirin Ebadi—Facts, https://tinyurl.com/mryhvk3f. Accessed on 9 September 2024.

demonstrating remarkable resilience and determination in the face of great adversity.

Time and again, women have been instrumental in taking up the cause of marginalized and oppressed groups, amplifying their voices and championing their rights.

Rosa Parks, often referred to as the 'mother of the freedom movement', set off a wave of protests and activism when she refused to give up her seat on a segregated bus in Montgomery, Alabama[7]. Her act of resistance catalyzed the civil rights movement in the United States, and inspired countless individuals to stand up against injustice, illustrating the transformative power of women's courage and leadership in advancing social equality and harmony.

Corazon Aquino, known as the 'Mother of Philippine Democracy', led the peaceful People Power Revolution in the Philippines, which toppled the authoritarian regime of Ferdinand Marcos in 1986[8]. As the first female president of the Philippines, she worked towards healing the wounds of Marcos' dictatorship, and promoting national unity by embodying the power of peaceful resistance in achieving political and social change.

These extraordinary women leaders exemplify the transformative impact women can have on society even in the most challenging circumstances. Through their courage, perseverance, and unwavering commitment to social justice, they have inspired generations of activists and change-makers to strive for a more peaceful, inclusive and harmonious world.

In short, from advocating peace and reconciliation to nurturing communities and amplifying marginalized voices, women have globally played indispensable roles in shaping a more inclusive and equitable world.

---

[7]History.Com Editors, 'Rosa Parks ignites bus boycott', in History, 9 February 2010, https://tinyurl.com/7utzryft. Accessed on 9 September 2024.

[8]Lo, Barnaby, 'Filipinos Mourn "Mother of Democracy" Cory Aquino', *CBS News*, 5 August 2009, https://tinyurl.com/np9xbhsn. Accessed on 9 September 2024.

Let us now look at the role women have played in shaping India. In post-Independence India, women have scaled extraordinary heights in multiple domains, be it within or outside the country. Indeed, several Indian women have demonstrated remarkable courage, resilience and dedication in their fight for social justice and efforts to bring about positive change in society and ensure social harmony despite facing numerous challenges and obstacles on the way.

WOMEN LEADERS IN SOCIAL HARMONY

In India, women's contributions to the growth and development of our democracy and society have been sidelined. Several inspiring examples from pre-Independence India are often forgotten by readers of history today, despite the fact that these remarkable women played a pioneering role in India's struggle for freedom.

Annie Besant, a prominent social reformer, women's rights advocate, and political leader during the pre-Independence era, fervently campaigned for women's suffrage, workers' rights, and Indian nationalism. She used her platform to raise awareness about and mobilize support for social change.

Sarojini Naidu, the Nightingale of India, was a gifted orator and charismatic leader who played a pivotal role in India's struggle for independence. Her impassioned speeches and poetry galvanized the masses, fostering unity and resilience in the face of colonial oppression, while strongly advocating women's rights, social reforms and communal harmony.

Aruna Asaf Ali, a fearless freedom fighter and activist, played a crucial role in India's struggle for independence. Defying British authorities, she risked her life to participate in civil disobedience movements, inspiring others to resist oppression and fight for liberty.

Kamaladevi Chattopadhyay was a pioneer in social reforms and women's empowerment, promoting rural development and communal harmony, and advocating social justice and cultural preservation.

In post-Independence India, several women have carried forward their legacy. Among them is activist Sampat Pal Devi, who inspired the creation of the Gulabi Gang, a powerful women's rights movement in rural India[9] that fought against gender-based violence, caste discrimination and social injustices, empowering women to assert their rights and challenge oppressive systems.

Another notable figure is Irom Sharmila, the 'Iron Lady of Manipur', who undertook a 16-year hunger strike to protest against the Armed Forces (Special Powers) Act (AFSPA), 1958[10]. She advocated for the repeal of the Act, promoting peace, justice and reconciliation in conflict-affected regions.

Among the more illustrious names is Mother Teresa, the 1979 Nobel Peace Prize laureate, known for her selfless dedication to serving the poor and the marginalized. She founded the Missionaries of Charity, which provides care and support to the sick, orphaned and dying in India and around the world[11].

Another prominent social reformer and politician, Rajkumari Amrit Kaur was instrumental in advancing women's rights, healthcare reforms, and social welfare policies in post-Independence India, working towards building a more equitable and inclusive society[12].

Indian women were never ones to restrict their abilities. Medha Patkar founded the Narmada Bachao Andolan (NBA) and has been a leading voice for the rights of displaced communities affected

[9]Desai, Shweta, 'Gulabi Gang: India's women warriors', *Al Jazeera*, 4 March 2014, https://tinyurl.com/32yfhbtj. Accessed on 9 September 2024.
[10]Explained Desk, 'Explained: Irom Sharmila and her struggle against AFSPA', *Indian Express*, 13 May 2019, https://tinyurl.com/bde73zy8. Accessed on 9 September 2024.
[11]Spink, Kathryn, *Mother Teresa: A Complete Authorized Biography*, HarperSanFrancisco, 1997.
[12]Constitution Of India, Constituent Assembly Members, 'Rajkumari Amrit Kaur 1889-1964', https://tinyurl.com/yht684k7. Accessed on 9 September 2024.

by large-scale development projects, advocating social justice, environmental conservation, and sustainable development.

For those who claim that women are physically and mentally weaker, or unfit to govern, Indian women have given a steady response. Kiran Bedi, the first female Indian Police Service (IPS) officer, was a trailblazer in law enforcement and prison reform, promoting transparency, accountability and social justice within the criminal justice system.

Aruna Roy, a social activist, is the founder of the Mazdoor Kisan Shakti Sangathan (MKSS), a grassroots organization advocating transparency, accountability and social justice in governance. She empowered rural communities to demand their rights and entitlements through grassroots mobilization and participatory democracy.

All these women leaders, who have been in the public glare, have won public acclaim for their phenomenal work in fostering social harmony.

UNSUNG HEROES

But there are also women who have been 'unsung heroes', who have done phenomenal work contributing to social harmony.

Dr Raghunath Mashelkar instituted the Anjani Mashelkar Inspiration Award to celebrate such unsung heroes.

Flavia Agnes won the award in 2019[13]. By overcoming personal challenges of an abusive marriage, she became a gender justice warrior and since then, has been advocating legal reforms to create social harmony through social reforms. She has been championing the movement for women's empowerment through her organization Majlis, which provides expert legal opinion and support to women and children who have experienced

---

[13]INTERNATIONAL LONGEVITY CENTRE-INDIA, 'ILC Awards 2019', https://tinyurl.com/yvxpy98d. Accessed on 9 September 2024.

abuse. She has provided litigation support to over 50,000 women and legal advice to another 150,000, most of whom are from underprivileged and marginalized backgrounds. Thus, through Majlis, she is contributing to social harmony by ensuring access to justice and empowerment for women from all walks of life.

Dr Keerthi Bollineni is another remarkable woman who won the award in 2022[14]. Her journey has been marked by profound personal losses and hardships, including the untimely death of her husband and daughter. She had to endure social ostracism and abusive relationships. She confronted violent attacks, threats from various quarters, and political pressures. Despite these challenges, she remained undeterred, bolstered by her unwavering commitment to protecting women's dignity and rights, and creating social harmony.

Dr Bollineni recognized the pervasive issue of gender-based violence, exacerbated by the Covid-19 pandemic, and took proactive steps to address it. By establishing Vasavya Mahila Mandali (VMM), and initiating the Mahila Mitra programme in collaboration with the Vijaywada police, she spearheaded community-based interventions aimed at sensitizing law-enforcement agencies and the public alike on gender-based violence and the importance of gender equality.

Her leadership extends beyond direct interventions. Through VMM, she has formed a group of change-makers who are actively engaged in grassroots efforts to combat domestic violence and provide support to survivors.

Dr Mashlekar has also been associated with the Jamnalal Bajaj Awards as a member of the jury for a couple of decades. He has been Chairman of its Advisory Council since 2019. These awards are given to those who propagate, promote and practise Gandhian values to bring about transformative social inclusion.

---

[14]'Keerthi to receive Anjani Mashelkar Inspiration Award', *Hindustan Times*, 20 December 2022, https://tinyurl.com/bdzc6mkj. Accessed on 9 September 2024.

There is a special category for women. Some of the awardees have spearheaded major social transformations, leading to social harmony. Here is an inspiring case.

Sister Lucy Kurien won the Jamnalal Bajaj Award for Development & Welfare of Women and Children in 2021[15]. She exemplifies the essence of compassionate leadership and commitment to social harmony through her work for women's and children's rights. In 1997, she established Maher, meaning 'Mother's Home', to provide a safe home for destitute women and victims of violence and abuse, providing them with shelter, care and dignity. Sister Lucy and her team's tireless efforts led to the expansion of Maher's activities. She started from one small home near Bhima Koregaon. This was extended to nearby villages and cities including Ratnagiri, Miraj and Satara in Maharashtra. Today, Maher operates 24 different outreach projects. Since its founding, Maher has provided care and shelter to over 5,000 children and over 5,900 women.

Currently Maher has 46 short-stay and long-stay homes in Jharkhand, Kerala and Maharashtra. In total, Maher houses hundreds of street children, destitute women (including several mentally ill women picked from the roadside), as also aged/ mentally ill destitute men. Maher also provides local communities of Dalits and indigenous 'tribals' with water wells and pumps, solar cookers, basic supplies, and day-care centres for their children who otherwise would have no educational opportunities.

The ultimate dream of social harmony is creating a 'casteless' society. Maher provides a 'caste-free zone' where people of all castes sit side by side and eat together. Sister Lucy is an exemplar in demonstrating the first principles of spreading social harmony across the nation.

---

[15]Bajaj Beyond, Jamnalal Bajaj Awards, 'Lucy Kurien—Recipient, JBA 2021', https://tinyurl.com/m4259xys. Accessed on 9 September 2024.

COMMONALITIES

What is common to these remarkable women leaders who have championed and led social harmony? What special qualities enabled them to navigate the complex social and political landscape, mobilize support, and effect meaningful change, ultimately advancing social justice and promoting social harmony?

There are ten common tenets that these women leaders embody.

First, all these women leaders demonstrated a deep sense of compassion and empathy for the marginalized and oppressed, driving them to take action and advocate their rights.

Second, they showed extraordinary courage in the face of adversity, standing up against injustice and oppression even at great personal risk.

Third, resilience and perseverance defined their efforts. Despite setbacks, they never lost sight of their goals.

Fourth, they amplified their voices through various mediums, bringing the plight of these women to the centre-stage, providing support and resources, and fostering self-reliance and agency.

Fifth, these women leaders possessed a clear vision for a more just and equitable society, inspiring others to join their cause and work towards common goals.

Sixth, unwavering determination and razor-sharp focus was a hallmark of their character.

Seventh, they embraced diversity and inclusivity, recognizing the importance of unity and solidarity across different social groups and identities.

Eighth, adaptability and flexibility in their approach allowed them to innovate and experiment with new strategies and tactics to achieve their objectives.

Ninth, they possessed the convening power to foster collaboration and cooperation among various stakeholders, building coalitions and alliances to amplify their impact and effect systemic change.

Tenth, and most importantly, they upheld the highest ethical and moral standards, leading by example, and earning the trust and respect of their followers and supporters.

These ten tenets have enabled these extraordinary women to champion social harmony. From Mother Teresa's selfless dedication, Rajkumari Amrit Kaur's tireless advocacy, Medha Patkar's resilience, Kiran Bedi's trailblazing transparency, and Aruna Roy's grassroots empowerment to countless unsung heroes, these women have inspired generations to strive for a more inclusive and equitable world.

SOCIAL HARMONY AT THE HEART OF INDIA

Inter-religious conflicts constitute the dark side of India's reality; the intermingling of cultures over centuries and the resultant multi-religious, multi-cultural and multi-ethnic character of Indian society is its brighter side, hallowed by the birth of major world religions such as Hinduism, Buddhism, Jainism and Sikhism. The spirit of social harmony stands embedded in the Indian DNA and is, therefore, a part of our identity and character. Religious pluralism and social harmony are thus deeply ingrained in the Indian psyche. Sant Kabir and Sai Baba of Shirdi, who have a following of millions, preached religious harmony, and so did rulers from Emperor Ashoka (*c.* 268–232 BCE) to the seventeenth-century king Chhatrapati Shivaji Maharaj.

Hinduism, in its most ancient form, propagated the idea of oneness of the soul in all living beings, and of *Vasudhaiva Kutumbukam*—the concept of the entire world as one family.

The values of religious pluralism and tolerance that are foundational to India were articulated eloquently by Swami Vivekandanda in his historic 1893 speech at the World Parliament of Religions, Chicago: 'I am proud to belong to a religion which has taught the world both tolerance and universal acceptance. We believe not only in universal toleration, but we accept all religions as true.'[16]

Indian culture, language, cuisine, literature and virtually everything that comprises Indian society is a syncretic amalgamation infused with the spirit of liberalism, secularism and communal harmony.

Every child in India needs to internalize these values transmitted by our forebears from generation to generation to help India emerge as a real Vishwaguru (world teacher). Who else is better poised to do this with unblemished love, care and compassion, if not our very first guru—our mother.

Shri Krishan Kant, former Vice President of India, had given a speech at an award function of the All India Management Association in 1998, when one of us (RAM) received the JRD Tata Corporate Leadership Award. These were the Vice President's inspiring words:

> The best symbol of female values that has been created by nature is in the form of 'mother'. Mother is 'creativity' and 'innovation' personified in solving human problems in the family. She represents excellence, morality, equality not in material terms but as a living cultural symbol practising these values. Out of all the management experiences in business, industry, public service and society, mother is the best manager nature has created. Mother's instinct has sustained Mother India. It is more specific than the word 'culture' itself. The growing alienation between man and society, which modern-day management practices have to contend with, may find its solution in the management practices which derives strength from the way mother manages her family in small and big ways, i.e. Mother Culture!

---

[16]Art Institute Chicago, 'Swami Vivekananda and His 1893 Speech', https://tinyurl.com/yk77f2x3. Accessed on 9 September 2024.

The crucial point to note is how he highlights the growing 'alienation' while underscoring the power of a mother to create an 'alignment'. Indeed, that is the power of Nari Shakti—to convert 'alienation' to 'alignment', the very essence of social harmony.

FINAL WORDS

The growth of Indian society, which is essential for economic and political progress, depends on how we treat our women. Empowering women creates a fairer and more inclusive society, allowing everyone to reach their full potential. This leads to a better-educated society, more people working, and new ideas, all of which help the economy grow. Politically, when women are respected and given equal chances, they can take part in making important decisions, leading to more balanced and effective policies. How we treat women reflects the overall health of our society. By focusing on gender equality, India can ensure that everyone, regardless of gender, can succeed and help build a stronger, more vibrant future.

4

SUCCEEDING IN A MAN'S WORLD

Arundhati Bhattacharya
Chairperson & CEO, Salesforce India

It has been almost a decade since I retired from more than 40 years of service as the top official of State Bank of India, India's largest bank. My tenure made several headlines, turned heads, and forced people to take note that in the 218 years of existence of this esteemed organization, I was the first woman to have ever led it from the front. Yes, that is more than *two centuries.*

Thus, the reception of my book *Indomitable: A Working Woman's Notes on Work, Life and Leadership* (2022) made sense to me. My story resonated with readers, who often cite it as inspirational for not just women but for everyone looking to build a career that blends conventional success and unconventional choices in the modern business world. However, my story is not very different from that of any young or middle-aged woman or man today who is trying to balance their personal lives as they pursue their goals.

In all honesty, during my school years in Bhilai and Bokaro, I never dreamed I would grow into a business leader, one who would be honoured with a few national and global awards. But here I am today, always grateful, and seeking opportunities to share and give back. Years have passed since I started out as a probationary officer. Yet, even today, across the globe, and in particular in our society, a greater number of obstacles are placed in the paths of women as they step out and engage with the world. Women's boundaries and limits are both decided for them and more than often, we ourselves accept, without a doubt or question, the ceiling that has been set for us.

This patriarchal mindset pervades all spheres of life, and makes it easier for men to be successful as defined traditionally— professionally and financially. This is not to say that men do not have their own struggles. Patriarchy harms both, and this realization is necessary to forge ahead together. True progress will require the participation of everyone, not just women or other isolated gendered groups. Henceforth, drawing from my own journey, what I share here is a practical guide for employers, and more importantly, for the Indian career woman, to facilitate success in an environment where the odds are not in her favour.

There is no denying that we have come a long way. From an era when even the question of educating girls was considered a taboo, India is at a point in history where females in higher education increased by 32% in 2021-22[1]; the numbers are equally encouraging at the entry levels across sectors as well[2]. But this heartening trend weakens just around the time women are ready to take on mid-management roles. In my 47 years as a working professional, I can count on the fingers of one hand the companies in India that have upheld a gender parity agenda through the ranks.

The picture is slightly more encouraging at the topmost tiers where after years of government reforms, especially after the introduction and implementation of the Companies Act of 2013, Section 149 (1), the number of women board members

[1]Press Information Bureau, Government of India, Ministry of Education, 'Ministry of Education releases All India Survey on Higher Education (AISHE) 2021-2022', https://tinyurl.com/ywxsw7uu. Accessed on 23 August 2024.
[2]Rathore, Manya, 'Employability among female graduates across India in 2017, by industry', STATISTA, 12 September 2022, https://tinyurl.com/2fuxvszh. Accessed on 23 August 2024.

increased from 1 in 20 to 1 in 5. Sadly, the representation is still far from parity[3]. This perplexing landscape reflects global trends. For nine years in a row, research conducted by McKinsey on women in workplaces in the United States and Canada has identified that the problem is not the glass ceiling, but the broken bottom rung of the ladder[4]. In 2023, for instance, research found that for every 100 men promoted from entry to managerial level, only 87 women were promoted in what has been an unchanging trend.

The above-mentioned trends do not exist in a vacuum. An overpowering presence of rigid social and cultural norms play a vital role in shaping our psyche. For centuries, women have been stuck in a vicious loop wherein they are restricted to the private sphere, enforcing a gendered division of labour which continues to be reinforced at every stage of their lives, allowing for restrictions to be imposed on their aspirations.

Patriarchy instils in women, from birth, the need to prioritize others over our own choices, and family over work, irrespective of our aspirations and talents that, in turn, leads to young girls and women unquestionably accepting the widely-held belief that they are *supposed* to take care of the home and that their realm is limited to the private sphere, thus making them complicit in their own subjugation. For many women, and men, their societal and familial conditioning affects their behavioural and economic outcomes. The roles and norms imposed on women in our households leave a lasting impact on the psyche of girls and young women, causing them to step back from their careers. When a woman is indecisive on this matter, chances are she

[3]Vohra, Neharika, WOMEN ON BOARDS IN INDIA: NUMBER, COMPOSITION, EXPERIENCES AND INCLUSION OF WOMEN DIRECTORS, IIM Ahmedabad and FICCI, 2020, https://tinyurl.com/mrmf485u. Accessed on 23 August 2024.
[4]McKinsey & Company, Krivkovich, Alexis et al., 'Women in the Workplace 2024: The 10th-anniversary report', https://tinyurl.com/55jm4jv5. Accessed on 23 August 2024.

may be guided by her personal support system who are likely to share and reinforce the same beliefs—of choosing her family over her career.

CORPORATE MESSAGE, SOCIAL CALL

Nobel Prize-winning economist Dr Claudia Goldin refers to this societal conditioning as the 'residue of history'[5] and has established through research that the gender pay gap can no longer be explained just by differences in education and choice of occupation but kicks in after the birth of the woman's first child. This is now known as the 'motherhood penalty'. In India, research published in early 2023 by the Ministry of Labour and Employment showed that nearly 5 in 10 women who were not in the labour force attributed their decision to leave to having to focus on childcare and personal commitments at home[6]. Over the decades, this societal phenomenon has created an inaccurate impression among employers—that women cannot be expected to shoulder key responsibilities in the workplace.

An important step to dismantle this self-perpetuating myth has to be taken by those around the woman, including the government, educational institutions, employers, families and communities. However, the decisive, and more important, step has to be taken by the woman herself. When women are able to overcome the historic differentiation between genders, a more equitable environment is created.

Let us take a look at the differences across sectors. The Women in India's Startup Ecosystem Report (WISER) published in 2023 found that start-ups have 32% of women in managerial

[5]Smialek, Jeanna, 'Claudia Goldin Wins Nobel in Economics for Studying Women in the Work Force', *The New York Times*, 9 October 2023, https://tinyurl.com/mu5mupkc. Accessed on 23 August 2024.
[6]https://tinyurl.com/bdf3zvxr. Accessed on 22 October 2024.

positions compared to 21% in corporate firms[7]. At the CXO level too, start-ups are doing better, with 18% of women in leadership roles compared to 5% in traditional corporations. The difference is even more marked in start-ups with women founders which have 2.5x more women in senior roles compared to male-founded start-ups.

Most well-known firms understand that women need greater support to negotiate life situations. Hence, they have policies in place such as paid maternity leave, return-to-work programmes, childcare support and the soft and hard infrastructure to help women navigate later-life challenges like caring for elderly family members, and menopause. But this empathetic approach comes in a manner that is detrimental to the woman's career graph.

For instance, women who return from sabbaticals taken for parenting lose seniority. This may demotivate talented female professionals from returning to full-time work or from gunning for the top job. So, while the support now being offered to women recognizes that women value the fulfilment and financial independence that come with a professional life, it does not acknowledge their highest aspirations. But such a policy shift may create resentment among other employees. This can be addressed by fostering a stronger sense of empathy. The challenge is *how do we do this*?

As the popular idiom goes, where there is a will, there is a way. The answer lies in communicating a strong social message at the workplace that both men and women are holistic beings. Men are also conditioned by societal expectations to place work above all else. Effective and consistent communication through our channels and policies must influence men to rethink this philosophy, encourage them to prioritize their families and friends, and take time off for caregiving and personal interests. And our

[7]Jaswal, Mansi, 'Women-led startups rise to 18% in past five years: Report', *Livemint*, 30 October 2023, https://tinyurl.com/5bndntwt. Accessed on 23 August 2024.

actions must back the messaging. For instance, Scandinavian countries insist that both parents take a minimum of a few months' leave from childbirth onwards until the child is in full-time school. This type of social communication unequivocally indicates that parenting is a shared responsibility, and will work towards removing any stigma men may feel about wanting to spend time with their children.

Similarly, we must also help our female employees understand and believe that they are not just primary caregivers whose careers are a secondary source of income for the family, but individuals with dreams, needs and wants like anyone else. This balanced approach will ensure that men understand what women are dealing with as they juggle diverse responsibilities, and shall ensure that women feel supported enough to chase their dreams without fear. Reminding men and women that we are after all holistic human beings with the same vulnerabilities and dreams helps build a bridge of empathy, thereby breaking the negative cycle that causes women to fall out of the workforce.

EQUITY AND EMPATHY

In my observation, there are two categories of (decision-makers in) companies. One category is convinced that more needs to be done to provide women with equitable access to career growth. The second camp questions this, arguing that it might be less than worthwhile to expend energy and resources to alter something so deeply entrenched in our minds. Companies that adopt communication and policy to emphasize that all employees are holistic people with the same needs and wants, will drive an important attitudinal shift in the working world that will help the first camp advance its cause more easily, thereby providing robust evidence to the second camp that these policy changes are indeed well worth the investment. This can help in immediately addressing any perception differences that exist.

The long-term approach is to create a culture of empathy and responsibility-sharing, which will enable a climate of equity to prevail. A key route to providing this equity is to empower women to remain in the workforce by fostering an environment that facilitates flexibility. In 2022, 82% of working women respondents in a survey stated that they wanted greater flexibility at work, and possibly more crucially, more than 7 out of 10 respondents said they had rejected a role, quit, or considered quitting a job due to lack of flexibility in policies[8]. The Covid-19 pandemic caused havoc in many areas of our lives, but the silver lining emerged in the form of work-from-home. With this, hybrid and flexi-time became accepted ways of working; the fear that people will not be productive if they do not come into office has been done away with. We now know for sure that many roles can be effectively carried out away from office. This is the right time for organizations to build robust policies to extend this to women and even others who need it. A counter-argument to the effectiveness of work-from-home options for women is that their caregiving responsibilities prevent them from logging in during traditional working hours. There is a simple solution that can even deliver business benefits.

Women are freed up from domestic duties in the afternoons, evenings, and even late nights. Companies can help them use these chunks of time to carry out tasks, such as research and routine paperwork, that do not require synchronizing with others, or even tasks that require collaborating with international markets early in their business day. This not only boosts opportunities for women who are unable to work traditional hours but also extends the hours of productivity for the organization. It will also keep women's professional skills well-honed when personal responsibilities slow their conventional career progress. Ultimately,

---

[8]Rathore, Manya, 'Opinion of workplace flexibility among women in India in 2022', STATISTA, 13 May 2024, https://tinyurl.com/msdte6pm. Accessed on 23 August 2024.

flexi-work creates a beneficial situation for everyone involved. But everything comes with a catch or a downside.

There is a possibility that this flexibility may be taken advantage of by those who can come to work during the traditional full hours. In other words, women who do not need this facility may use it just because it is an available option, creating resentment among others. To prevent this, the objective behind why this is offered must be clearly communicated. Transparency and clarity in communication from the company make working women appreciative of the support and ensure they use it responsibly. There may be some disadvantages attached to flexi-work, such as not being included in important meetings or considered for promotions. Embedding sensitization programmes for managers and team members as an important part of building a culture of greater empathy will tackle this. Therefore, flexi-time presents a win-win scenario for both women and the company. Businesses gain access to a talented pool outside traditional working hours, potentially tapping into the talent of capable women who can contribute productively and meaningfully to the workplace even if commitments at home prevent them from coming to the office or working during regular hours. To further support the argument, companies that have withdrawn this flexibility post the pandemic have seen their women employees resign en masse, including some who had spent decades with the organization. Against this larger backdrop of supportive policy and greater empathy, I recommend a few mantras that a professional woman can put into practice to forge ahead in a man's world.

EIGHT MANTRAS TO SUCCEED

In 1978, psychologists Pauline Rose Clance and Suzanne Imes shared a groundbreaking study introducing the 'Imposter Phenomenon,' an internal sense of intellectual phoniness that

150 high-achieving women experienced despite their substantial professional accomplishments[9]. Not surprisingly, they attributed this to early family dynamics and societal stereotyping. This is now more commonly referred to as Imposter Syndrome. A 2023 KPMG survey discovered that 75% of executive women in corporate America have personally experienced imposter syndrome at certain points in their careers[10]. Eighty-five per cent believe imposter syndrome is commonly experienced by women, and 74% of executive women believe that their male counterparts do not experience feelings of self-doubt as much as female leaders do. Eighty-one per cent believe they put more pressure on themselves than men do, in order not to fail.

So, while the notion of a 'man's world' may be slowly fading, it is not happening fast enough. Across the globe, women's internal dialogues and how they engage with the outside world continue to be powerfully shaped by unfavourable systemic factors since their very early years.

To counter this, a woman has to radically rethink how she views herself, how she handles her daily interactions, and how she makes her way through an environment that may at times be harsh and at times ignore her. Below are eight guiding mantras I gleaned from my decades-long experience in the business sphere that will empower women to thrive in this evolving world. These mantras are not meant to be a rigid set of rules, but rather sparks to inspire action. They acknowledge the complexities women face—from internal doubts to external obstacles—and offer practical strategies to overcome them. Every woman's professional

---

[9]Clance, P.R., & S.A. Imes (1978), 'The imposter phenomenon in high achieving women: Dynamics and therapeutic intervention', *Psychotherapy: Theory, Research & Practice*, 15 (3), pp. 241–247, https://tinyurl.com/2hkze8pt. Accessed on 23 August 2024.

[10]Paulise, Luciana, '75% Of Women Executives Experience Imposter Syndrome In The Workplace', *Forbes*, 3 August 2023, https://tinyurl.com/565y54yy. Accessed on 22 October 2024.

journey is unique, fashioned by her own aspirations and values. She can use these mantras as a part of her foundation to meet the work goals she desires.

DELUSION OF INDISPENSABILITY

This is an oft-repeated reminder for women that is relevant across cultures. With our conditioning to hold ourselves accountable for all matters on the family front, we bring it to our work as well. In the quest to become 'superwomen', we end up spreading ourselves too thin. The belief that 'if I don't look into this, it will not get done' creates a need to control minute details. Honestly, that is a delusion. Women have to prioritize, just like their counterparts, in order to keep up their energy and efficiency. They should delegate responsibilities at home and at work, supporting the team, family members and house help as they take over tasks, by placing confidence in them while they learn from mistakes.

While building this support system, women must ensure that everyone, including managers and clients, knows whom to reach out to or how to reach them when the need arises. Within a short period of time, people at home and at work will be able to cover up for the woman's absence very effectively. The most famous and mildly amusing instance of this is ex-PepsiCo CEO Indra Nooyi asking her children to check with her staff about playing video games when they finished homework, because she was busy with meetings. This strategy of smart delegation will give a woman greater energy to focus on the most important task of the day that needs their attention, whichever that may be. It will also afford her the bandwidth to travel more for work, and make time to recharge herself through relationships and personal interests, making her a better professional, manager, spouse, parent, daughter and more.

POWER OF BEING PRESENT

Guilt underscores a woman's every action. This deeply ingrained belief that pushes her to overextend herself also haunts her when she succeeds in delegating. She may begin to believe that she is no longer needed, gradually withdrawing from the spotlight or participating less. Another reason for this is the hesitation a woman may feel in male-dominated environments. There is a direct way to address this issue. A woman should give complete attention to whatever she has prioritized that day, be it at work or at home. She should focus on contributing, resolving issues, and leaving the situation better than she found it. At home, a woman should not take away credit from family members and the help who have been holding the front. But there is a tendency to make the woman feel guilty for proposing improvements but not being present when the situation was building up. A woman should recognize that this is more often than not a gendered accusation. At work, she may find herself in a room full of men discussing an important strategy using metaphors from what are considered male bastions such as motorcycles, automobiles or contact sports. She should not allow herself to be excluded in this way and insist on sharing her inputs through comparisons drawn from the same areas if she is comfortable, or in any manner that is familiar to her and understandable to all.

This quietly assertive approach will constantly signal to family members, colleagues, clients and other external teams such as suppliers and agencies, that a woman is dependable and brings valuable perspectives to the table. It will help do away with guilt on the home front, and also build confidence among those in a woman's professional sphere that when she is present, she will help get the job done, effectively undoing the stereotype that women cannot be relied upon for key responsibilities as multiple factors hold them back from participating completely.

WE ARE A FAMILY!

While the workplace is increasingly comfortable with ambitious women, this may not always be the case on the home front. Traditional value systems can still cause some family members to believe that focusing on a career is an irresponsible choice for a woman, taking her away from family, which should be her main focus of attention. This may lead them to place obstacles in her way and make things hard for her. To a degree, being fully present when with them as discussed earlier will resolve this, but it may take some more effort to win their support. A woman can take a beat to understand where such family members are coming from, rather than reacting with anger. Then consistently, gently and firmly reinforce to them the considerable positives the family gains from her career, takes pride in her success, a reliable source of income for better financial security for everyone, and an essential role model for young people of all genders in the house to look up to—that anyone can achieve anything and everyone shares all responsibilities.

This view is data-backed by a comprehensive study conducted by Harvard Business School Professor Kathleen McGinn, her team and international colleagues across 29 countries in the 2000s[11]. The findings published between 2015 and 2018 revealed that daughters of working mothers are more likely to take up supervisory roles and earn better. Men who grow up in such families take up more responsibility on the home front. And children of working parents are happier on an average.

---

[11]Gerdeman, Dina, 'Kids of Working Moms Grow into Happy Adults', *Harvard Business School: Working Knowledge*, 16 July 2018, https://tinyurl.com/238s23f6. Accessed on 23 August 2024.

BOLDER WITH BOUNDARIES

Women by nature, especially Indian women, have been told over millennia that modesty is a great virtue. We may not know it, but we have a collective unconscious that tells us that it is immodest to talk about our achievements or ask for what we deserve (even while writing the first paragraph of this essay, I was wondering whether I was being immodest!). Of course, humility is key to sustainable achievement and success, and grabbing the limelight from others who deserve it is not a redeemable quality for anyone. However, as women, we need to make the distinction between these traits and the ability to speak up when needed. A woman should not shy away from stepping up to take credit for any success that is rightfully hers. Also, she should speak up when there is blatant discrimination against her or her female colleagues.

The most famous example is the multi-talented Sudha Murty who broke stereotypes to study engineering as a lone woman in a class of 150 students. While at the Indian Institute of Science, Sudha came across a recruitment advertisement from Telco, a Tata Group company, inviting applications from young engineers. A line in the advertisement said 'Women candidates need not apply.' This triggered Sudha to write to the man himself. J.R.D. Tata took cognizance of Sudha's anger at such blind discrimination, and she was soon invited to Pune for an interview, with all expenses paid. Sudha thus became the first woman engineer to be hired by Telco. Since then, she has continued to serve as an inspiration for generations of Indian women trying to make it in a man's world. While today blatant instances of discrimination are few and far between, we should not hesitate to call those out and the more subtle ones that still persist. The calling out needs to be done in a manner that doesn't put an 'activist' tag on the person. Normally, this can be achieved if the calling out provides a solution while stating the problem.

FROM ADVERSITY TO OPPORTUNITY

There is no debating that patriarchy seeps into all areas of life and work, making it harder for women to progress toward their goals. It is good that now there is an increasing awareness of this among women. This realization is equipping us to convert obstacles into stepping stones.

Harking back to the 1970s, Kiran Mazumdar-Shaw was refused employment as a brewer by leading alcohol manufacturers in India, simply because she was a woman. She responded by setting up her own biotechnology company, Biocon, and the rest of the story is well-known. Today, there is no dearth of examples of Indian women who start their own companies because the formal working world cannot support them when they need flexibility. Internationally, a new study co-led by Tiantian Yang, Assistant Professor of Management at the Wharton School, found that professional women are more likely to start their own businesses to beat the motherhood penalty. And these one-woman businesses grow into successful concerns that generate employment for many[12].

IN THE DRIVER'S SEAT

No matter what a woman does, there will be someone telling her it cannot be done. This might even be other women because patriarchy leads us all to subconsciously believe that we can tell women what to do. A woman should be aware that this bias may be at play when she is given advice. She also needs to be wary of stereotypes perpetuated in the media or in her personal circles, whether it is the high-achieving female CEO showcasing every

---

[12]Yang, Tiantian, 'Premium or Penalty? Differential Effects of Gender and Race on Internal Promotions to Top-Management Positions', Mack Institute for Innovation Management, The Wharton School, 5 October 2024, https://tinyurl.com/4d8hftkr. Accessed on 22 October 2024.

win or the woman who sacrificed everything to take care of her family. Most of us do not fall into either extreme category and also do not know the reality in the lives of some of these women who are held up as examples.

This mixture of a larger awareness, self-knowledge and self-confidence is crucial as we negotiate spheres not yet prepared to engage with women who want complete agency over their own choice. If a woman does not want to take a sabbatical as a new mother, she should not take it. In my case, I had to make the difficult decision of sending my very young daughter back to India in the late '90s since I had no extended support system to care for her in New York, where I was posted. It was a heartbreaking decision.

Later, I chose to give my interviews for promotions, though I was attending to my ageing parents and mother-in-law. It was not an easy choice at that time, but something in me said that it was the path to tread. However, I have to add that navigating these dilemmas was easier for me since I have been blessed with a family that supports my choices both in spirit and in action. This is also not to say that every woman must make the same choices. If a woman feels she is not ready for bigger responsibilities, even if there are no external factors that managers or family members can discern, she should evaluate why she is experiencing this hesitancy, and not feel pressured, even if she works in a company that has many successful senior women leaders.

After all, as we dismantle patriarchy, we do not have to create new stereotypes while shattering old ones. Every woman is her own person. She can and should create her own definitions of how she takes care of her family and succeeds professionally. Some of these unique paths women choose are not always covered in the media as huge success stories, but they are equally important as holistic examples for all genders. These journeys can be found in our families, communities, and in the trajectories of colleagues we are close to, who share their personal convictions with us.

When there is no crisis, a woman manager should get people to buy into her vision, work out the roadmap, and then step back and give them the space to deliver. However, during a crisis at work, she has to lead from the front. Courage is not about being fearful. It is all about stepping up even when one is afraid, and knowing that as one steps up, fear recedes. Barring rare instances where personal and professional crises occur together, she has to be on the spot. She should work through everything and provide input. This balanced style of leadership will win her the continued trust of her team. But there is a larger purpose as well.

History has chronicled legendary women like Rani Lakshmibai, who represented unwavering determination and an unyielding spirit to defy societal boundaries, shatter norms, and prove that courage knows no gender. Today, Indian women like the champion boxer Mary Kom are blazing winning trails in global sporting arenas, asserting that we can triumph anywhere. But many young women are still struggling to fight off the conditioning that women need to be led, especially during difficult times; they grow up seeing such scenarios around them. More likely than not, they are in a woman leader's immediate environment, placing the onus on the woman leader to prove to them that this belief is not true.

CATERING TO OUR BIOLOGICAL MACHINERY

Due to our biology, we experience a range of physical and emotional ups and downs. Whether it is post-partum depression, gynaecological issues such as endometriosis, or menopause, each woman experiences each of these differently. Pregnancy is a choice, but each time can be more or less challenging for women who have two or more children. Many women are likely to experience miscarriages during their reproductive years. Menopause is not a choice. Rather, it is a stage of life that is likely to require additional support from a woman's doctor, her personal circle and her employer. Some studies[13] establish an association[14] between gynaecological conditions and stress, but these are only signals that we should manage stress wisely, not signals to give up on our dreams. However, this volatility that is inherent in our biology is yet to be as openly discussed as it should be. There are certainly policies at work that acknowledge it, but more needs to be done. There is also a traditional sense of shame associated with it, worsened by extreme images in the media of women who do not seem to be bothered by these concerns, have completely overcome them, or are completely overwhelmed by them. The truth is more nuanced. There are likely to be times in a woman's life when she will need help from medical specialists or mental health professionals, and the greater support of her family. There is no stigma in seeking this and even letting your employer know if necessary. A woman might pull out of these difficult situations by the dint of her resilience, with minimal support, but such an approach could dampen her energy and enthusiasm for her work and relationships. But seeking expert help and sharing the burden with a trusted circle will ensure she rides out the rough phase with her spirit intact, emerging as a wiser, kinder person.

These eight actionable points are gleaned from my own learnings over four decades and together constitute a proven formula to succeed in a man's world. I agree that these are simple to understand but not easy to implement. Most women are aware that they should negotiate the working world in a confident and courageous manner, not allowing anyone to dictate their choices and speaking up when needed. But they worry that this will

[13]Reis, Fernando M. et al., 'Is Stress a Cause or a Consequence of Endometriosis?', *Reprod Sci.*, 2020 Jan; 27 (1): 39-45, Epub 2020 Jan 6, PMID: 32046437, https://tinyurl.com/2cu2988k. Accessed on 23 August 2024.

[14]Basu, Barnali Ray, Olivia Chowdhury & Sudip Kumar Saha, 'Possible Link Between Stress-Related Factors and Altered Body Composition in Women with Polycystic Ovarian Syndrome', *Journal of Human Reproductive Sciences*, 2018 Jan-Mar; 11(1):10-18. PMID: 29681710; PMCID: PMC5892097, https://tinyurl.com/5h7823tw. Accessed on 23 August 2024.

create a backlash because what is considered smart, ambitious behaviour for a man is not always appreciated in women, be it at home or at work. A woman must be prepared for some pushback in the face of confident behaviour. However, whilst never picking personal battles, she should never lose sight of the fact that she is rightfully asking for what she deserves.

GOING BEYOND THE MANDATE

Some readers may recall Jennifer Palmieri's clarion call that every woman has the 'power to change the world by changing the way she behaves in it.' Palmieri, who was part of Barack Obama's White House team and worked with Hillary Clinton during her presidential campaign, remains in the public eye, and has shared her journey and learnings in a well-received book, *She Proclaims: Our Declaration of Independence from a Man's World*[15]. Advancing the mandate in the public and private sectors, having spent most of my career in the public sector before a second innings in a leading private company, I would like to share a few observations about gender equity across the two landscapes.

The private sector has 18% women employees, with the IT, textiles and consumer services sectors leading the way with 34%, 33% and 27% women employees, respectively, according to The Udaiti Foundation[16]. The foundation's analysis has also identified that private firms with <500 employees have women in 23% of key leadership roles, but the number drops steadily to 11% as the size of the company increases[17]. Meanwhile, the FY 2022–23

---

[15]Palmieri, Jennifer, *She Proclaims—Our Declaration of Independence from a Man's World*, Grand Central Publishing, Hachette Book Group, USA, 21 July 2020.
[16]The Udaiti Foundation, 'Close the Gender Gap', https://tinyurl.com/4wrmykd2. Accessed on 23 August 2024.
[17]Das, Yudhajit Shankar, 'More women in office now, but what about leadership roles?', *India Today Business*, 14 December 2023, https://tinyurl.com/28jkujv9. Accessed on 23 August 2024.

Public Enterprises Survey[18] reported that women constituted 8.88% of total employees in Central Public Sector Enterprises (CPSEs). Around 4 in 10 women employed in the public sector are in managerial and supervisory roles. The reader is shrewd enough to interpret the numbers. However, as someone with an insider's perspective across both sectors, I noticed that the public sector leadership often waits for government directives to advance the cause of gender equity.

From my personal experience implementing programmes to facilitate equity for women, such as sabbaticals for parenting, I urge decision-makers in the public sector to be more proactive and innovative. It is possible to identify and implement gender equity programmes that already fall within one's remit. With careful examination, one is likely to find that existing frameworks offer many such opportunities that can be tapped into without a push or mandated changes initiated by people even higher up in the echelons. Another simple example from my time as a senior banking leader is the banking sector converting two half-working days on Saturdays to full holidays every month. This gave women and, in fact, all employees more time with their families and is now an established practice in the Indian banking sector.

Coming to the private sector, I find that some firms have been trailblazers in the area. They genuinely care about achieving gender equity in the workplace, and understand the larger positive ramifications such as sustainability, greater creativity, improved decision-making, and finally a boost to the bottom line. Policies like extended paid leave and flexi-work for mothers and fathers of young children, a transparent pay structure to reduce the gender pay gap, and unconscious-bias workshops are among some of the initiatives designed daily to further the cause.

---

[18]Government of India, Ministry of Finance, Department of Public Enterprises, 'Public Enterprises Survey 2022-23', https://tinyurl.com/28cbbusn. Accessed on 23 August 2024.

Concerningly, however, there are companies in the private arena that do not progress beyond government-mandated requirements and some tick-box exercises, despite having the resources and the awareness required to hire and nurture women professionals. Given the absence of constraints, it will serve them well as employers, and in the pursuit of profitability, to pay greater attention to this pressing concern and remedy it. Building a fairer future together across the formal working landscape, we have to up the ante on gender equity. Here is why.

A recent survey (86-a) of Gen Z professionals across India found that 61% of those surveyed said they would accept less money from a workplace that values mental health and inclusivity. Fifty-seven per cent wanted a strict work-life balance, while 42% cited a menstrual leave policy as a must-have, and 44% wanted effective harassment policies. Fifty-nine per cent wanted a workplace that treated everyone fairly. The research findings also revealed that young women continue to feel the workplace is skewed against them. Consider innovations like mentorship programmes and reverse mentorship programmes spanning genders which can open up new perspectives. In 2006, I was on the verge of giving up my banking career, but my mentor, Mr M.S. Verma, who was earlier chairman of the bank I worked in, guided me towards a different decision, the outcomes of which we see today. Ensure that women employees are consulted on initiatives designed to provide them with equal opportunity. Make sure there are mechanisms to keep a woman safe when she has to speak up against discrimination.

Keep in mind that men are not women's adversaries and are battling their own pressures and conditioning. Many men today are manifestly supportive and encouraging of not only women at home but also of women at their workplace. And they must be comprehensively supported in their allyship efforts. It may not always be easy for men to be allies with women in the workplace. But men can do different things to be effective allies.

Being an ally means more than just offering support; it requires challenging traditional norms and fostering an environment of partnership and growth. Today, companies are adept at building data platforms to monitor every dimension of a business. If a company hasn't already, it is time to develop and use a similar monitoring platform to track the impact and outcomes of gender equity programmes. The platforms should capture data of every granularity and level to tell senior management at a glance how the various initiatives are doing in terms of retaining women, upskilling them, and preparing them for the roles they desire. Not just that, these platforms should capture feedback and satisfaction levels to be used for constant improvement. There isn't more to be said about why a company, no matter its size and sector, should zoom in on its gender equity strategy to empower women to succeed in a world that remains unfair to them. There is abundant evidence that greater participation of women in the workplace will not only empower women but also drive progress for all as well as economic prosperity for the nation[19].

I have shared my mantras for succeeding in a man's world. Inspiring role models abound. But a woman does not have to be daunted by their levels of achievement. Every woman in the workplace can shape her own journey of independence. And I have discussed strategies for how employers and employees can come together to achieve gender equity. With nine companies in the global Bloomberg Gender Equality Index, the journey has just begun for corporate India[20]. Let us race toward making it everyone's world.

---

[19]'India will manage 8% growth by 2030 if more women join workforce, says report', *Livemint*, 26 October 2023, https://tinyurl.com/2fz2nm96. Accessed on 23 August 2024.
[20]Sturgess, Donna, 'Driving innovation within the company: Is your team switched off?', *People Matters*, 4 May 2009, https://tinyurl.com/yubcbhh9. Accessed on 23 August 2024.

5

THE LIGHT AT THE END OF THE TUNNEL: *EDUCATING* A GIRL

Safeena Husain
Founder, Educate Girls

Knowledge is power, and far too many women in India today lack power, voice, and choice. And behind every woman who has been denied knowledge, behind every woman who remains unable to read and write, there is a girl who was denied education.

In all my years of work, travelling across the northern and central states of India, and before that, spending time in communities on the margins in South America and sub-Saharan Africa, I have never met a girl who does not want to go to school. I have never met a girl who chooses to stay at home, look after younger siblings, cook, clean, work in fields, and prepare for marriage, as a child.

Every girl I have ever met wants to go to school.

I am who I am because of my education, an education that also came at a cost and was secured in spite of personal challenges. But it is an education that is mine and has enabled me to harness a power I can channel to ensure that every girl is able to access her right to quality education.

Since Independence, education has been every child's inalienable right. Progress has been made through successive National Education Policies in 1968, 1986 and after a prolonged gap, most recently in 2020. In 2009, the Right to Education

(RTE) Act was also a watershed moment, and in the post- RTE era, together with the added global impetus of the Millennium Development Goals, that sought to ensure universal access to primary education for all, India's enrolment rates are now the highest they have even been. Never in history have more children been enrolled in schools.

Despite this, school remains a distant dream for millions of girls in India who live on the margins and are held back by a mindset that still considers that a goat is an asset and a girl is a liability. In that all-important balance sheet of life, girls are devalued and goats are prized. Across the country, particularly in remote rural communities, the prospect of marriage and motherhood trumps independence and choice, and an estimated 30 million girls[1] of school-going-age are still not in school.

In this essay, I want to make the case that at the heart of an education and skilling system that successfully builds a society that is open, equal and just, lie both balance and participation. And to achieve this, we need an equal focus on girls and boys, with an intentional investment in equity to make up for historic exclusion and a deeply entrenched mindset that holds girls back. Additionally, we need community-led approaches to change behaviours and social norms that again prevent our education system from truly serving our planet and all our people.

So what is the state of play? Well, a girl's right to education is yet to be fully realized for large communities across our country and the root causes of the problem can be explained through three P's: poverty, patriarchy and policy. When these three P's intersect, there is an explosion of out-of-school girls.

Poverty is a significant driver in girls' inability to participate in the education system, with families seeing education as a huge opportunity cost and requiring girls to either work to earn or

---

[1]Educate Girls' own calculations are based on data from https://tinyurl.com/yey2a4vj. Accessed on 23 August 2024.

work at home to enable both parents to earn. At the same time, patriarchal norms may prioritize marriage over education, a mindset that fails to recognize a girl's right to choose and pursue an education. And when we talk about rural, remote and tribal areas, awareness of and access to the government's schemes is patchy at best. Policies may be in place, but accessibility is poor.

Today, millions of girls are denied their right to education simply because of their gender. They lack agency—the ability to make choices and decisions about their lives—due to enduring barriers and systems that undermine their fundamental rights. Therefore, ensuring accessible education for girls is not only about providing knowledge but also about cultivating their agency. By empowering girls through education, we equip them with a voice and enhance their agency, enabling them to shape their own futures and contribute meaningfully to the lives of those around them.

Education and skilling are not yet fully participative processes in India and girls cannot achieve this potential alone. Just as a woman empowered by education becomes an agent of change in her community, the school and its wider network of relationships must work together to support her education. This includes teachers, peers, families, and communities, all of whom play a crucial role in breaking down barriers through collective action and creating an enabling environment where every girl can thrive. When communities play an active role in education, the Right to Education becomes a reality for all.

In working at both the individual and the community level, let me show you how we can support the government's education system through local solutions, and local ownership of the education that communities wish to see for their children. For me, all this has to start with ensuring that every last girl is able to go to school, study and complete as a minimum their 10th-Grade certificate. And, in doing this, we will be better equipping not only every girl, but also the next generation.

SO, WHO AM I TO TELL YOU THIS STORY?

I was born and grew up in Delhi, and was the first person in my family to travel overseas to study. I was privileged enough to study, live and work in the UK and the USA, but I realized that I needed to return home. The seed was planted on a trip I made in the year 2000 when the non-profit I was running took me back to India to Mussoorie, in Uttarakhand. I was to meet the team that was setting up a medical clinic and as I was flying through Delhi, I picked up my father and took him along for the trip.

On the first day, we walked into the village and one of the more confident women, who greeted us, pulled back her veil and asked my father how many children he had.

'Here she is. My only child. My everything!' he said with a smile that concealed nothing and revealed everything—pure love and pride.

On hearing this, some of the women started crying and expressed deep sorrow for my father, as if it was a curse to have a daughter as your only child.

This incident stuck with me, and as I thought about all the girls born in that village where the mothers themselves saw their daughters as a burden they wished they weren't carrying, something started to burn within me. It was the realization that this was what I had to do. As a daughter of India, I had to advocate for these girls, for my sisters. Being a girl was a chance of fate. Being a girl was a blessing and should be a destiny. But until everyone believes this, girls will face exclusion from a life that is rightfully theirs. I had visited a village in remote rural Uttarakhand, and there on the margins, I had seen first-hand that the biggest problem girls faced was mindset. And this is what I committed to tackle.

Educate Girls, the organization I founded in 2007, is built on the premise that a) education is an equal right for every girl and every boy, no matter where they live or who they are, b) girls face a history of exclusion, a discriminatory mindset that continues to place hurdles in their path to education, empowerment and independence, and finally, and c) girls' education can have a huge multiplier effect. An educated mother is more likely to educate her own children, breaking the cycle of poverty and illiteracy, benefitting both the next generation of girls, and boys, and contributing not only at an individual level but also at the national level to a world where justice, peace, and a sustainable future are all possible. Since we started work, we have mobilized over 1.8 million girls for enrolment into the government school system, and supported the education of close to 2.2 million children. We have worked across four states of India, in thousands of villages and schools, and mobilized a team of over 23,000 village-level volunteers. On this journey, we have learnt strategies and approaches that shape our work today and will enable us all to understand what is truly needed to make education and skilling more balanced and participatory.

HOW TO FIND EVERY LAST GIRL?

As I explained, at the heart of the problems still facing girls in India today are marginalization and mindset. Exclusion from access to schools is no longer universal, but hotspots remain where a concentration of girls live on the margins of their village, on the margins of society and on the margins, economically. The first task at hand is to find every one of these girls.

As an economist by training, I am passionate about data and evidence. When we first started work, I went to the government who provided me with their list of 'educationally backward districts' in India where the gender gap was greatest; nine of these districts were in Rajasthan. Equipped with this list and the support of the government, I knew where I needed to start if I wanted to find out-of-school girls. We then met district education officers and were given their lists of girls not going to school, but with sometimes arbitrary school catchment areas and incomplete lists, we soon discovered that girls were being missed, and many girls remained invisible.

The first key strategy in our approach was, therefore, to conduct a census-like door-to-door survey that remains the backbone of our work today. Once a district and a block had been identified through publicly available data, Educate Girls recruited a team. We went to every village, drew a map, and then knocked on every door to find and include every girl in our list. By working from a list, we were sure to have an inclusive approach to enrolment. We were ensuring that we were going to the margins and not missing a single family. Once we knew who was out of school, our work began to create the strategy to enrol every girl and ensure she went to school. In our 16-year history, we have knocked on the doors of over eight million households and ensured that every girl was counted, and that every girl *counts*!

As time went by, we started to see that the problem was more concentrated than we had originally thought. We started to see that in certain areas, 50% of the out-of-school girls were found in just 10% of the villages, and 23% of villages had no out-of-school girls at all. This information led us to the conclusion that if we could accurately predict where to find the areas where the most out-of-school girls were living, we could precision target our work, conduct the door-to-door survey in half the number of villages and still find the majority of out-of-school girls. Essentially, if we could go where the need is greatest, we could enrol many more girls, with a similar budget within a shorter time frame.

Together with data scientists, we built a machine learning (ML) algorithm to help us learn from our previous surveys, and by combining this historical programme data with public data (such as the 2011 census and DISE—District Information System for Education—data set), we could teach an algorithm to identify villages in new geographies where we can expect to find the most out-of-school girls. Using these predictions, we were able to create heat maps that identified geographic clusters of villages, or hotspots with the highest density of out-of-school girls.

Technology and data have played a critical role in our work. Over time, we evolved from using paper lists to feeding our survey data into a performance management system using GPS tracking and smartphones. And through this combination of comprehensive surveys with the use of predictive analytics, we have been able to grow our work and find more girls faster within our limited resources. But the secret of our success lies in this unique combination of the digital and the human. And herein lies the next lesson to share.

GROUNDWORK

What is pioneering about our approach is that it combines sophisticated technology such as machine learning and geo-tagged surveys using smartphones to find out-of-school girls, with readily available village resources: young, energetic, mission-aligned men and women with deep community knowledge. The digital and the human! Both of these are critical to the successful enrolment and retention of girls in school. The use of technology has dramatically improved our targeting and efficiency, but it has had to go hand in hand with the 'boots-on- the-ground' work of a team of village gender champions, or Team Balika.

Girls are out of school because they live on the margins, they are outside school catchment areas, they are forgotten and fall off government lists, they are invisible, forced to work to support their families economically. But girls are also out of school because of mindset and this is where our second key strategy comes in—an army of gender champions who work as volunteers across all our villages to challenge a mindset and change behaviours so that girls enrol in schools and learn.

While technology and specifically artificial intelligence (AI) have played an indispensable role in identifying clusters of out-of-school girls (which in turn informed strategies to increase accessibility, cost-effective resource allocation), it is the participation from communities that ensures the viability of our programme. It was back in 2011 that we first started to realize that we were creating a movement, not just delivering a programme! So, we launched Team Balika—our team for the girl, with the powerful message: 'My village, my problem and I am the solution!' In every village where we work, we recruit a member of the community to volunteer with us and advocate for all the girls who are out of school.

What is unique about our volunteers is their outrage and their tenacity—they have personal experience and understanding of the mindset that devalues a girl and keeps her out of school. Through the Team Balika movement, we have seen over 23,000 young people inspired to work for girls, because they have their own knowledge and experience of gender discrimination in their families. Some Team Balika members are young women who had to fight for their own education. Some are brothers, husbands or fathers of girls who have been excluded, or of women who remain dependent even today because of lack of education or skills.

'I work for girls' education because of my mother,' one of our Team Blaika volunteers once told me. 'She was exploited at the bank and lost part of her savings just because she couldn't read. I fought for my own education; I will educate my daughter and ensure that no girl in my village is kept away from school!'

Another dedicated Team Balika volunteer is Sanjay. Reflecting on his childhood, he remembers the stark contrast in experiences between him and his sister. He received the love and attention of his parents and grandparents, and his sister did not. He was served good food, his sister had to eat last and what was left over. He played outside while his sister had to stay indoors and do all the housework. He went to school; his sister wasn't allowed to study and was married off at a young age. Today, when Sanjay meets his sister, it breaks his heart to see her so dependent on her husband. Since she can't read or write, she can't travel alone, take a bus, fill basic forms, read a newspaper or dial a phone number. He feels angry with himself for not standing up for his sister when they were growing up. But now he channels that anger, that energy, into girls' enrolment, and ensuring that every girl in his village has the opportunity to go to school.

With these lived experiences, youth like Sanjay, in their quest for purpose, have been and continue to be dynamic agents of change, altering the mindset in their communities and changing behaviour. They are not just solving the problem 'for' the community; they are solving it 'with' the community for lasting change. So, real transformation is fuelled by the collective strength of the village

It is stories like these that are at the heart of our work to challenge the mindset and change community behaviour. Families are persuaded to change their mindset, girls are enrolled in school and persuaded to aspire to complete their education, through powerful stories of change.

One such story is of Durga. She grew up in a family of seven children. Durga's father worked hard, but living on the margins. The slightest problem was amplified. When the floods came, there was no money to repair the house. When Durga's sister fell ill, there was no money for medical bills. Loans trapped the family in debt. Durga and her sisters had to work with their father in the fields or take on domestic chores so Durga's mother could supplement the income herself through daily-wage work.

When Educate Girls' Team Balika Pooja visited the house, at first she faced resistance. The school was far, the opportunity costs seemed too high. Durga's father, Sanjay, did not think education was the right thing for his girls. It took a couple of months of visits, but deep down, despite his traditional beliefs, Sanjay came around to the idea of education for his daughters as well as his sons. When Pooja told him a powerful story of a girl in their village who had completed her education and was now working in the local Kasturba Gandhi Balika Vidyalaya (KGBV), a girls' school, this inspired Sanjay to allow Durga and her sisters to enrol in the residential school themselves and study.

Today, Durga is studying for her Auxiliary Nursing Midwifery (ANM) exams and is already working as a community nurse. When she has time, she also puts in some hours in her village, speaking to parents and persuading them to keep their girls in school after 8th Grade and complete their education.

Pooja was a neighbour of Durga and her father. She was a trusted friend and became an advocate for Durga. She knew what a local solution could be and the kind of story that might persuade her father—the ultimate decision-maker who could decide her future. I started off trying to do this job myself but as an outsider, this was not the right role for me. I talked to the wrong people, misunderstood village dynamics, and very soon realized that a village can solve its own problems, with the right tools and the right approach.

Volunteers receive intensive training, ongoing mentorship and support in order to help them identify the best strategies for enrolling girls who are currently working or kept at home. They are overseen by a cadre of field staff, again locally hired, to manage the teams and on an ongoing basis adapt the implementation plans to village-level realities. Strategies involve sitting with families and village elders, challenging damaging social norms, and presenting clearly the benefits of and rights to an education. All this is underpinned by each volunteer's deep knowledge of their own village and their own communities. Without this, we were failing.

Community members need to feel part of the solution; they want to hear stories from people they know and trust, and from people who know and understand their realities. Village meetings strengthen this collaboration and draw the communities in, imparting a sense of ownership. These gatherings raise awareness about the importance of girls' education, and distribute responsibility among various stakeholders, ensuring a unified effort towards a sustainable change of mindset.

IT TAKES A VILLAGE

Once we have found and enrolled girls in school, supplementing the school curriculum is critical as, all too often, girls have missed out on important stages of their education, they are enrolled late, and receive no support at home from their parents. These girls are very often first-generation learners. Our curriculum *Gyan ki Pitara*, delivered by our Team Balika volunteers within the school day and in collaboration with government school teachers, supports every child in the classroom to learn critical micro-competencies that will ensure their progress and build their core skills in foundational literacy and numeracy. The curriculum is designed in such a way that it promotes gender equity and inclusion, and both boys and girls benefit from content that transforms stereotypes, attitudes, norms and practices by challenging power relations, rethinking gender norms, and raising critical awareness about the root causes of inequality. Enrolling and staying in school has much to do with feeling engaged, succeeding, learning and participation. Girls join Girl Councils (*Bal Sabha*s), take on leadership roles in school committees, and learn to have a voice, agency and confidence.

We impart life-skills education (LSE) by integrating it into Bal Sabha, a democratically elected girls' council, and it becomes part of the learning curriculum. This creates a student-centred learning space where girls discover their passions, weave together diverse learning experiences, and work on projects with peers. This approach empowers girls through ownership and choice, motivating them to actively engage with the school community.

Spanning 15 weeks, this programme equips adolescent girls with essential skills such as problem-solving, decision-making, and interpersonal communication. They further develop their confidence through leadership training, public-speaking workshops, and communication exercises. By establishing Bal Sabhas and implementing the LSE module, we are giving young girls opportunities to collaborate with each other to participate in developing skills that will help them make decisions that affect their lives.

By focusing on every child in the classroom, boys and girls learn together, and all benefit from the additional support. School Management Committees are reignited and helped to create school improvement plans, and our Team Balika volunteers lead village meetings to ensure that parents, teachers and the village leadership all participate together in the development of the school and the enrolment and attendance of all the children. If a boy is not attending school, he too will benefit from the systems that have been put in place to engage the whole village in the enrolment and attendance in school of its children.

When parents are more engaged in their children's education and have an opportunity to see and participate in the school community, change is more sustainable. During the Covid-19 pandemic when we had to teach outside in order to remain socially distanced, very often parents for the first time witnessed their girls' happiness and confidence at learning. An African proverb concludes: 'It takes a village to raise a child.' That is exactly what we have found as we built community participation in driving change for girls and their education.

SECOND CHANCE

We have been working now for 16 years and things have changed. We have seen the number of out-of-school girls in our earliest districts drop significantly. We have been encouraged to learn from the government's own data that in these communities, wider indicators are now better than national averages when it comes to women's literacy levels, reduction in child marriage and improvement in family planning.

An analysis of the past three rounds of National Family Health Surveys (conducted by the Government of India) reveals that, on an average, the first eight districts where we worked have outperformed other districts of Rajasthan in five out of six educational and health indicators. This has set a remarkable benchmark of progress in years of schooling, reduction in child marriage, and improved family planning. On an average, in eight districts, there was an additional increase of three percentage points in the number of women (aged 15 to 49) with 10 or more years of schooling, compared to the state average of 8%. And, on an average, across these districts, there was a decline of seven percentage points in the occurrence of child marriages among women aged 20 to 24, surpassing the state average decline of 10%.

Despite encouraging data, just recently I was back in Rajasthan and visited a remote village, far from the city and public services. In a couple of hours, we trekked out of the village, up 45⁰-inclines through valleys and over hills, and of the girls we met, not one of them was going to school. They had all enrolled in primary school, but before taking their 8th-Grade exams, they had dropped out.

'School is far.'

'There is too much work to do at home, collecting water, cooking, looking after the goats.'

'I have to look after my mother's shop when she isn't there.'

Their brothers were in school, but these girls had not set foot in a classroom now for three years. I climbed a mountain to meet these girls, and realized that this is now the next mountain we at Educate Girls have to climb if we are to ensure that every girl can lead an independent life with choice and agency.

An estimated 91 million girls in India, aged 15 to 29, are not in education, employment or training. In recent years, we have seen female labour force participation of only 33%[2]. Girls

---

[2]International Labour Organization, 'Labour Force Statistic Database (LFS)

face barriers that are different from those of boys, particularly in adolescence. Till today, despite efforts to halt the practice, an estimated 1.5 million girls[3] under 18 are married each year, and the path to marriage and motherhood stands in the way of girls reaching adulthood with the skills and education they need.

Addressing the issue of inaccessibility in education sometimes entails taking education directly to the doorstep. This is particularly crucial when catering to adolescent girls and young women who have either been out of classrooms for years or who have missed schooling altogether. A camp or proximity model is successful in such cases, as it allows those aged 15 to 29 to easily congregate in a relative's or trusted local person's house, eliminating the travel barrier that often kept them away from secondary education in the first place.

This model also eliminates traditional distinctions between teacher and student where student-centred activities and self-learning exercises are guided by a *prerak* (compassionate adult tutor) who supports their preparation for the crucial 10th board examinations. The environment becomes a judgement-free and intimate community where girls and young women learn from and encourage each other, promoting both individual and collective growth. For some, bonds of sisterhood formed here are particularly strong, giving them a sense of belonging and personal community that was alien to them before. Ultimately, this empowers them to become active participants in their own education and future.

The solution to ensuring that balance is restored and girls are able to participate in sustained secondary education and skilling lies in taking education to where they are. Efforts to

---

ILOSTAT', World Bank Group I Data, https://tinyurl.com/434rvrhm. Accessed on 23 August 2024.
[3]UNFPA-UNICEF GLOBAL PROGRAMME TO END CHILD MARRIAGE, India, Country Profile, 2021, https://tinyurl.com/2udk4yfw. Accessed on 23 August 2024.

enrol girls in primary school will help us solve this problem in the long term. It will also be critical to support schools to deliver an education that promotes gender equity and inclusion, transforming the next generations' understanding of gender norms. But in addition, we need to ensure there is a system for girls to access a second chance at completing their 10th-Grade certification through distance learning and the government open schooling system.

Shenaz is a truly inspiring woman in her late twenties. She left school at 12 and sat with me recently in our tutor programme near Pali, where she has joined her 14-year-old daughter Salma in studying for her 10th-Grade exams. At 29, she was now availing of a second chance. The two of them took part in a role play where they played the role of a daughter persuading her father to allow her to go to school. As Shenaz spoke the words on her crib card, I noticed a tear roll down her face. She explained to me later how the role play could have been written about her. Her own failed struggle to complete education played out exactly as it did in our story; she had been deeply moved, as had I by her honesty and her reignited ambition.

Shenaz is unusual given her age, but she is an illustrative example of the 91 million young women who have not completed their education, who may have become wives or mothers when still children, who were denied their right to an education because of the patriarchal mindset that sought to dictate their future and deny them a choice.

The majority of girls in our second chance programme, Pragati, are aged 18 to 22. They come to a study centre, sometimes a community space, at times a room in a school, sometimes even the home of the prerak. Over a period of five months, they receive guidance from our team and peer support from others in their group, as they navigate the curriculum content and study, and learn about exam techniques whilst being guided through the process of enrolling and taking their open schooling exams.

Girls who have been out of school for a number of years and now want a second chance have an uphill struggle, particularly when girls drop out at 8th Grade. The Right to Education Act does not yet extend beyond 8th. Despite more focus of government investment in National Rural Livelihood Mission for girls over 18, there is still an expanding 'invisible middle' with girls aged 14 to 18 disappearing if they are not in school.

The government open schooling system should be a viable option, but it is fractured in many states. Even in states like Rajasthan where the open schooling system is functioning, girls living on the margins are often unaware of the opportunity, do not know how to enrol for it, and are not used to self-study, or preparation for exams, let alone know how to choose subjects and think through options. Problem-solving, critical thinking, aspiration-building, digital literacy, communication skills are all capabilities that often elude girls who have been forgotten by the system.

Our focus on 10th-Grade pass is driven by the fact that this credential truly unlocks so much for young people; without it, so many doors remain shut. Continued education in Industrial Training Institutes (ITIs) and polytechnic institutes all require a minimum 10th-Grade certification. To take out a simple loan to start a business post-skilling, a young person needs to be a 10th-Grade pass. For entry-level jobs with the government, whether that is with the railways as a typist, the ICDS as an aanganwadi worker, a court clerk, the police force, etc., a 10th-Grade certification is required. Tenth-Grade pass is basically a stepping stone for financial independence and a future.

MULTIPLIER EFFECT

It is true that in far too many ways, the barriers that girls face in order to know and access their rights are high. The mountains they have to climb in order to gain the all-important education that is rightfully theirs are sometimes insurmountable.

It is my vision that we find every last girl in India and ensure that she is able to access the education that is rightfully hers. If through inclusive enrolment programmes, through the mobilization of local champions to ensure local solution to barriers that keep girls out of school, and through community engagement in the ability of girls to stay in school and complete their 10th Grade, we are able to make school exclusion a thing of the past, I am convinced we will be setting up the next generation to survive and break the cycle of poverty and illiteracy that is holding back our country. And you do not need to take my word for it, as academics and development professionals the world over have evidence on the subject, and are of the belief too that 'Investing in [...] girls' education isn't just the right thing to do; economically, it's one of the smartest things to do.' This was said by World Bank Group President Jim Yong Kim back in 2016[4]. Educated women exhibit enhanced abilities to access life-saving healthcare, resulting in reduced infant and maternal mortality rates.[5] Girls' education strategically influences demographic trends, with educated women having the ability to choose if they want to have fewer children. Investing in education programmes in India is said to have boosted income for female farmers by 61%, demonstrating significant economic benefits for families and communities[6].

Educated women have the potential to reshape society by participating in decision-making. In India's village councils, women leaders increased investments in development, signalling broader socio-political changes[7], and higher education levels,

[4]World Bank Group, Press Release, 'World Bank Invests US$3.2 Billion in Adolescent Girls' Education in 2 Years', 7 March 2018, https://tinyurl.com/yznk8d8m. Accessed on 23 August 2024.
[5]Sperling, G.B., R. Winthrop, with C. Kwauk, *What Works in Girls' Education: Evidence for the World's Best Investment*, Brookings Institution Press, Washington, 2016, p. 18.
[6]Ibid., p. 22.
[7]Ibid., p. 57.

particularly for girls, contribute to increased resilience in the face of natural disasters. This is evident in estimates that deaths due to disasters could be reduced by 60% if a significant section of young women completed lower secondary school[8].

Finally, from a broader economic perspective as well, the potential gains are substantial. If every girl globally received 12 years of quality education, women's lifetime earnings could increase by $15 trillion to $30 trillion, subsequently adding $28 trillion to the global annual GDP[9]. The impact in India, too, would be transformational.

All these strategies I have laid out here make sense for everyone. There is a clear curb-cut effect[10], whereby designing for the most vulnerable, in this case for the girls, the system is augmented for everyone; everyone benefits, including boys! Boys and girls benefit from community engagement that values education, and extends a support network around the identification, enrolment and retention of children in school. Boys and girls benefit from additional learning support in the classroom that has a demonstrated ability to improve learning outcomes in a short period of time. Besides, it also imparts gender-transformative content. And an improved open schooling system will not only support girls and young women who are unable to enrol in the formal school system, but also offer an alternative provision for education in times of crisis and school disruption, whether due to another pandemic or a climate-related extreme weather event. Again, everyone could benefit!

All that said, at a simpler and more individual level, an educated woman is far more likely to educate her own children, and that is what we need if we are to truly bring balance and

---

[8]Ibid., p. 60.
[9]World Bank Group, 'Missed Opportunities, The High Cost of Not Educating Girls', 11 July 2018 https://tinyurl.com/yj69u8m9. Accessed on 23 August 2024.
[10]*Stanford Social Innovation Review*, Winter 2017, https://tinyurl.com/sa7cu8v9. Accessed on 23 August 2024.

participation to India's education. We need girls and boys receiving an equal chance of enrolling in school, no matter where they live, or who they are. We need girls to stay in school beyond adolescence and transition into further education or skilling with the foundation and the right ability to choose.

In 2010, we were running a training programme for village volunteers in Jalore. A strident young lady called Nagini Bano stood up at the back of the room and announced to the audience that had gathered for the programme: 'My education is the only thing that is truly mine. No one can take it, no flood can take it away, no one can steal it, nor beat it out of me. My education is mine.'

6

CLIMATE RESILIENCE THROUGH WOMEN'S KNOWLEDGE: TOWARDS ETHICAL BIO-ENTREPRENEURSHIP PATHWAYS

Anamika R. Dey and Dr Anil K. Gupta

Professors at IIM Ahmedabad &
Members of Honey Bee Network

The discussion around development, women and empowerment stands incomplete without the inclusion of what is the most crucial and yet most ignored relationship—the one between nature and women. The role of women is central to household survival strategies in regions where ecological and climatic stress is high, male emigration is a dominant coping strategy due to lack of enough local employment opportunities, and the portfolio of economic and socio-cultural activities is guided by constrained access to factor and product markets[1]. Women-led or managed households are often predominant in such high-risk regions. Their intimate knowledge of biodiversity comes in handy in meeting nutritional and medicinal deficits

---

[1]Dey, Anamika, Gurdeep Singh & Anil K. Gupta, 'Women and Climate Stress: Role Reversal from Beneficiaries to Expert Participants', *World Development*, Vol. 103, 336-359, March 2018, https://tinyurl.com/yewbkf9b. Accessed on 27 August 2024.

in their households. Women, especially from rural and tribal regions, have over centuries always worked in strong and close correlation with the environment. They have devised and curated their own knowledge systems to cope with the surprises that come with nature. As we have seen in the past decade, the rising intensity of climatic fluctuations have now left us with no option but to adopt a deeper understanding of biodiversity resources which are impacted by these changes. Women are our best bet, moving forward.

The role of women in mitigating risks in other high-risk environments such as rainfed dry regions, flood-prone regions, mountains, etc., is significant[2]. The vulnerability of women in formal and informal scientific systems also warrants attention to their empowerment[3]. Among various empowerment strategies for overcoming their vulnerabilities, in this essay, we share entrepreneurial opportunities-based biodiversity and associated knowledge systems in the specific context of mountain regions. Some of these strategies might work equally well in other regions too. Insights from the field in the Global Initiative of Academic Network's (GIAN) project supported by the Department of Biotechnology (DBT), Government of India, in three mountainous regions of the Union Territory of Jammu and Kashmir, Sikkim and Nagaland, provide the empirical context for this essay.

Livelihood options in the mountains are generally limited to tourism, agriculture and horticulture, and other restricted

---

[2]Ibid.; Gupta, Anil K., Yugandhar Mandavkar, Amin Surekha & Shah Rekha N., 'Role of Women in Risk Adjustment in Drought Prone Regions', IIMA Working Paper No. 704, 1 October 1987, https://tinyurl.com/h894nac4. Accessed on 27 August 2024.

[3]Gupta, Anil K., & R.A. Mashelkar, 'Women and Formal and Informal Science', IIMA Working Paper No. 2005-05-02, May 2005, in *History of Science, Philosophy and Culture in Indian Civilisation* (Gen. Ed. D.P. Chattopadhyaya), Volume IX, Part 3, *Women of India: Colonial and Post-Colonial Periods* (Ed. Bharati Ray), New Delhi, Sage Publications India Pvt. Ltd, Chapter 10, pp. 208-235, https://tinyurl.com/mtpju73f. Accessed on 27 August 2024.

bioresource-based options like herbal products, crafts, etc. In the wake of male emigration, women, children and the elderly are left behind to take care of households, agriculture and animal husbandry, and also often work as farm labourers[4]. Diversification of the household portfolio is inevitable in the risky environment since no one livelihood strategy would be viable all through the year and in all sub-regions[5].

Climatic fluctuations lead to occasional forest fires, early or delayed flowering, or seed setting of herbs, shrubs, trees, or rejuvenation of pastures and other fragile landscapes. Excessive selective extraction of certain species may disturb the ecological diversity, succession, resilience and regeneration of the desired herbs. Livestock grazing influences the landscape quality, diversity, and density distribution of different edible and non-edible species. A sustainable supply of raw materials for formal or informal bio-enterprises may thus be affected by many of these factors if not attended to carefully through community leadership, not just participation.

Women develop deep local or indigenous knowledge while dealing with nature and figuring out various uses of the local biodiversity for health, nutrition, food, fuel, furniture, dyes, handloom, and numerous other purposes. It is this knowledge richness, among other sources of grassroots innovations, which Honey Bee Network volunteers have tried to leverage over the last 35 years to expand livelihood choices of communities and

---

[4]Goodrich, Chanda Gurung, Pranita Bhushan Udas & Harriet Larrington-Spencer, 'Conceptualizing gendered vulnerability to climate change in the Hindu Kush Himalaya: Contextual conditions and drivers of change', *Environmental Development*, Vol. 31, pp. 9-18, September 2019, https://tinyurl.com/22ma5ap4. Accessed on 27 August 2024.

[5]Gupta, Anil K., 'Ecology, Market Forces and Design of Resource Delivery Organizations', in *International Studies of Management and Organization*, 18 (4) 64-82, 1986; Gupta, Anil K., 'Socio-Ecological Paradigm for Analyzing Problems of Poor in Dry Regions', *Ecodevelopment News*, (Paris) No. 32-33, March 1985, pp. 68-74.

individuals[6]. In this essay, we describe a bio-entrepreneurial strategy for leveraging women's knowledge in the Himalayan region of Jammu and Kashmir, Sikkim and Nagaland as a part of the DBT-supported project. It may also have implications for various action research studies in high-risk environments and not just the mountains. There are lessons for policymakers too who often find that strategies that work in well-endowed socio-ecological regions[7] do not seem to work in high-risk regions. For instance, the design of stationary organizations in regions where people are mobile, such as pastoralists, is unlikely to work[8].

The essay is divided into three parts. Part I presents a brief review of various strategies of coping with climatic risk in the Himalayan region. The concept of bio-entrepreneurship is elaborated in Part II. Finally, Part III has lessons for learners which may help all those who wish to leverage women's knowledge for alleviating poverty and conserving biodiversity through ethical entrepreneurship pathways.

PART I
COPING WITH CLIMATIC COMPLEXITY AND FLUCTUATIONS

With extreme climatic events, fluctuations and changes, agriculture and allied sectors in the Himalayas are already vulnerable due to their topographical and ecological characteristics. Changes

[6]Gupta, Anil K., & R.A. Mashelkar, 'Women and Formal and Informal Science', IIMA Working Paper No. 2005-05-02, May 2005, in *History of Science, Philosophy and Culture in Indian Civilisation* (Gen. Ed. D.P. Chattopadhyaya), Volume IX, Part 3, *Women of India: Colonial and Post-Colonial Periods* (Ed. Bharati Ray), New Delhi, Sage Publications India Pvt. Ltd, Chapter 10, pp. 208-235, https://tinyurl.com/mtpju73f. Accessed on 27 August 2024.

[7]Gupta, Anil K., 'Socio-Ecological Paradigm for Analyzing Problems of Poor in Dry Regions', *Ecodevelopment News*, (Paris) No. 32-33, March 1985, pp. 68-74.

[8]Gupta, Anil K., 'Ecology, Market Forces and Design of Resource Delivery Organizations', in *International Studies of Management and Organization*, 18(4) 64-82, 1989.

are indicated in the seasonal patterns such as overall decreasing monsoons and rainfall, increase in winter and monsoon temperatures as well as decreasing winter snowfall[9]. Melting glaciers pose another problem for irrigation and livestock water supply as it increases short-term water availability but may cause scarcity over the long term. Hence, the whole cropping pattern and cycle is affected.

With increasing temperatures, agro-climatic zones in the Himalayan region are shifting, impacting the suitability of certain crops for specific areas. Traditional crop patterns may need to be adapted, and new challenges may arise in pest and disease management[10]. Reduced crop productivity can lead to food insecurity and economic losses for farmers. It can affect the well-being of livestock, leading to heat stress and increased vulnerability to diseases. Changes in vegetation patterns can also affect the availability and quality of forage for grazing animals, affecting traditional practices like transhumance (seasonal movement of livestock) and pastoralism.

Climate change-induced disruptions in agriculture and animal husbandry lead to economic hardship for communities dependent on these activities. These disruptions also contribute to emigration and changes in local cultures and traditions. Due to rising temperature, many plant species are moving upwards, which may increase the workload and time required to collect them. To avoid excessive extraction of medicinal plants and ensure their regeneration, development of sustainable extraction protocol is required though this is a rather neglected area of current

---

[9]Bhutiyani, M.R., V.S Kale & N.J. Pawar, 'Change and the precipitation variations in the northwestern Himalaya: 1866–2006', *International Journal of Climatology*, 9 April 2009, https://tinyurl.com/2w5tvvkm. Accessed on 27 August 2024.
[10]Vedwan, Neeraj, & Robert E. Rhoades, 'Climate change in the Western Himalayas of India: A study of local perceptions and response', *Climate Research*, 19 (2), pp. 109–17, 2001, https://tinyurl.com/yka6xmb2. Accessed on 27 August 2024.

research in the region. Women's knowledge is being harnessed for the purpose of minimizing the effect of climatic fluctuation and consequent disturbance in the community ecology of plants.

We need to build resilience in these communities to address their needs. Adaptive measures like diversification of the portfolio of sustainable livelihood options along with diversification of food and nutritional choices for humans and livestock may help. Another strategy may be to characterize the nutritional richness of different varieties of cultivated and uncultivated foods.

The socio-economic and ecological resilience of communities depends largely on available policy, institutional and market-based options. These may help in tiding over lean periods exacerbated by climatic fluctuations. The extent to which biomaterials can be stored during the winter period when much of the higher altitude villages are covered in snow, also influences the way communities use their idle time for crafts, household necessities, weaving, and processing of stored herbs for food, medicines, aromatic oils and powders, dyes, other colours, beverages, etc.

PART II
BIO-ENTREPRENEURSHIP: LEVERAGING STRATEGY FOR BIODIVERSITY AND ASSOCIATED KNOWLEDGE

The term 'bioresource-based entrepreneurship' refers to businesses that use renewable biological resources as inputs or raw materials to create new products and/or services. Numerous natural resources including plants, animals, microbes, and agricultural waste are included in these bioresources. These bio-enterprises or green businesses frequently have a lesser carbon impact, attracting environmentally-conscious customers. These come in a variety of forms, including a) enterprises that create new goods using biological creatures or processes such as biofuels, medicines and biodegradable plastics; b) agricultural enterprises that concentrate on sustainable farming methods, organic products, or recycling agricultural waste for a variety of uses like composting, biogas production, or creating biodegradable packaging; c) start-ups and farmer producer organizations (FPOs) or companies engaged in the manufacture of products such as biofuels made from renewable plant sources, such as biodiesel and bioethanol, food products and beverages, etc.; and d) businesses that make organic food and drinks, processed foods, herbal oils, drugs, aromatic substances, etc., from sustainable harvesting methods[11].

Local markets are not much developed in most remote areas, particularly in the mountains, because of low population density and rough terrain. But a few women try to access weekly markets for selling some of the bioresources, pickles and a few other products. There is no certainty of demand and also, they lack too many opportunities for value addition. Under state livelihood missions, self-help groups of women have been provided some resources for making progress, but with mixed results.

Women face several challenges while delving into this field: they lack access to financial, technological and various other institutional resources. While shouldering the greater burden of managing households, taking care of children and the elderly in the families due to frequent emigration of males from the mountains, they also have to contend with various other vulnerabilities. But given their deep knowledge about local biodiversity resources and rich experience of food processing, local health traditions and crafts, women can amplify their skills and aspirations if they can get sufficient support. Several dilemmas arise in sustaining community-based bio-enterprises run by women:

a) **Sustainability of extraction:** When it comes to collection of biomasses of medicinal or other plants, studies have shown that pregnant women or mothers carrying young

---

[11]Biotech Consortium India Limited (BCIL), '28th Annual Report 2017-2018', 2018, https://tinyurl.com/bdf93wyv. Accessed on 27 August 2024.

child cannot go very far. This causes concern when the plants are collected from the roadside and if these roads have traffic, then effluents of these vehicles may affect the quality of the plants. During a visit to Trinity County, California, local communities allocated other tasks to such women such as drying the plants, sorting them or making bundles of them, etc. Groups of women need to pay attention that both the quantity and the quality of the extracted biomass do not impair the quality of the outputs as well as sustainability of the landscape.

b) **Renewability of biodiversity:** This requires extraction to be pursued within sustainable limits. But when contractors compete with local community bio-enterprises, the prisoner's dilemma-like situation arises. In such situations, collective assurances and regulation of contractors' behaviour by the village council and the forest department can help sustain local control over excessive extraction. The weak position of women in village councils and forest bureaucracies exacerbates the tension.

c) **Knowledge and practice differentiation:** Not all who know the uses of bioresources have the capacity and competence of using them, or practising the knowledge adequately or effectively. While creating a portfolio of incentives for local communities, some differentiation is needed among people having general information vis-à-vis those who have expert knowledge. Once during a *shodhyatra* (journey for the search of knowledge, creativity, and innovations at the grassroots) in Malnad region, Karnataka, a young person was upset that all *yatri*s (travellers) were paying a lot of attention to an elderly knowledge expert. The young person also knew the specific uses of the plants the expert was talking about. Then a question was asked: When the need arose, whom did the community consult? The young person who knew the uses of the same plant or the expert who knew how to dose it, relate it to the conditions of the patient? The answer became obvious from the laughter of the group.

d) **Benefit sharing:** There are several exchanges through which local community members and an enterprise, whether local or external, can share benefits: procurement price of raw biomaterials; opportunity for local women groups or individuals to sell final products at discounted price in local markets; share in profits; investment in conservation of landscapes; investment in capacity building, etc. Under no circumstances should the local biodiversity resources become extinct or out of reach of local communities because of external demand. In the first issue of the *Honey Bee Newsletter* (HBN), we had shared the dilemma expressed by a young friend; whether the HBN strategy of conservation, characterization and commercialization will make local resource so costly that they go out of reach of the local people who have conserved them so long. The example of tea was given in which the best tea is sold at London and cannot be afforded by the poor tea garden workers. This should serve as a constant reminder in every entrepreneurial venture that local access to raw materials to meet their basic needs is not hampered by the improvement in market access—certainly not an easy goal.

There are several other dilemmas such as dealing with trade-offs between managing family duties and balancing these with entrepreneurial duties; tensions between the role of daughters versus daughters-in-law; gender discrimination in risk-taking allowances; freedom to deal with market and external customers; balancing economic interests of biomaterial collectors and customers, etc.

PART III
LESSONS FOR LEARNERS—MANAGING TENSIONS

Here are a few lessons we have learned while working with communities in the Himalayas in Jammu and Kashmir, Sikkim and Nagaland as part of the project sponsored by the DBT, Government of India. Given the ability of women to handle multiple tasks, and balance domestic and external duties, responsibilities and opportunities, their strengths can be leveraged through micro- and macro-entrepreneurial support systems.

a) **Respect for local norms:** Respecting the norms and traditions of the community is of utmost importance. This does not mean that we need to endorse some of the superstitions that are still followed in many communities. Disrespect to their customs and traditions is often not well taken. For example, in one of our meetings with community members, the members offered us some biscuits with eggs. One of our colleagues is vegetarian and declined this. When the community insisted, he grew increasingly impatient, which would eventually have upset them. Hence, we informed them about his religious beliefs, which they understood. In Assam, local communities would offer *tamul* (betel nut) and betel leaves served in a special utensil called *bota* to guests, which some do not consume due to health reasons. Hence, we have to communicate to the community our diffidence in certain matters without being disrespectful. There are sacred groves in the North-Eastern Himalayas and rituals surrounding them. We need to be aware not to step into such areas without the permission of the locals. Protected herbs cannot be collected from these areas unless under specific conditions that have been laid down by the communities[12].

---

[12]Kandari, L.S., V.K. Bisht, M. Bhardwaj & A.K. Thakur, 'Conservation and management of sacred groves, myths and beliefs of tribal communities: A case

Such care will ensure respect for new norms being evolved among communities.

b) **Initial disclosure of purpose:** Telling people about the intention, aim and objective of the project, or simply put, 'Why are we doing this?', is very important[13]. At times, intermediary organizations do not share the bigger picture with the communities, doubting the ability of the communities to understand or know about such scientifically written proposals. However, if we make our intentions clear, it is possible that the village community will not only trust us, but also suggest to us better ways of achieving our goals. Our intentions need to be communicated in the local language to the extent possible. In the absence of such a practice, the communities' trust of outside agencies may become shaky and impair long-term prospects of viable outcomes.

c) **Legitimizing entrepreneurial interventions:** Meeting the gram pradhan or village head/gram budha or village elder is of utmost importance in situating entrepreneurial plans focused on women. These leaders, often conservative men, know the customs, traditions and limitations of the community and its resources. People listen to them, helping us gain their confidence. It should be recognized that most communities are factionalized. Thus, contending parties may need to be kept in the loop. One should also meet innovative farmers, teachers, healers, and others who are generally respected in society. This has to be done knowing fully well that many local community leaders do not like women being empowered or given independence to make autonomous market-linked decisions. There is a risk that involving local leaders may

---

study from north-India', *Environmental Systems Research*, 16 (2014), https://tinyurl.com/2hrdw3pt. Accessed on 27 August 2024.

[13]Pew Research Centre, 'Energized Democrats Backing Clinton: The Buck Doesn't Stop Here...', 14 November 1995, https://tinyurl.com/bdd7crsr. Accessed on 27 August 2024.

make our selection of participants/suppliers/entrepreneurs biased in favour of those closer to the leaders. To ensure that real creative and knowledgeable people are not ignored, one needs to balance conflicting interests through prudent participatory processes.

Transforming Knowledge for Markets

1. **Leveraging grassroots innovations ethically:** Meeting innovative farmers, traditional knowledge holders, healers, centenarians, existing entrepreneurs, knowledge holders, artisans, craftsmen, etc., helps discover local problem-solving potential. When the aim is to get value from bioresource-based products, interaction with some herbal healers and other knowledge experts would make sense. Much of the oral knowledge of the healer is generally passed down inter-generationally. But due to changes in biodiversity and climate fluctuation levels, contemporary knowledge is also produced through diverse experiments. Much of this knowledge is buried or cremated with the passing away of the elders since hardly anything is documented. More knowledge is being lost in the current generation than in the entire history of humanity. Local experts may not trust us in the beginning. It is advised not to pester them into saying something they are not yet ready to share, like a complete list of ingredients and dosage in case of herbal practices. Once we have the Prior Informed Consent (PIC) in place and we have built a rapport, they may wish to share more details. If the person is willing, we go to different parts of the villages from where they collect plant materials and samples for the herbarium, and see the habitat as well.

It is important to declare the following that as per the HBN philosophy: a) Their name will be acknowledged in all products/publications; they will not be made anonymous; their contribution will be identified on the labels of the products; their Intellectual Property Rights (IPRs) will be protected if their knowledge is found to be unique. b) They will receive a copy of the knowledge collected from other communities as a part of the cross-pollination. c) They will also receive a summary of the findings of the research in the local language besides products at discounted price to sell locally. d) They will get a share of the profits made through the commercial utilization of their knowledge, besides other intangible benefits, including capacity-building and free access to databases.

It is very important that acknowledgement, attribution, appropriation and benefit-sharing norms are spelt out in the beginning for total clarity on mutual expectations and obligations.

Mapping Aspirations, Expectations, and Collective Understanding

2. **Rise in mutual expectations and community aspirations as interactions progress:** Sustained augmentation of livelihoods through continuous experimentation requires constant upgradation of competencies on both sides. Also, the calibration of expectations and aspirations is needed so that market realities and risks and chances in the value chain are properly understood and appreciated. Mapping out the dreams and aspirations of the communities may help them cooperate to realize a bigger common goal. Connecting their aspiration with a proposed action plan will bring clarity and also avoid the pessimism of members when unavoidable delays happen.

At times, the aspiration may be low while the natural resource base may be high. People collectively may not extract the best potential out of the local resources while a few might be able to extract rent from them. This has happened in several regions. When women are conditioned to have low aspirations, their self-esteem suffers and their resilience also goes down. Their aspirations can be raised by providing wider exposure and opportunities for market encounters to learn and grow. Failures in the marketplace is a part of life and the less the experience, the higher are the chances of being taken advantage of. Investment in failures is an important part of developing entrepreneurial abilities.

When aspirations are high and natural resources are limited, the community can sometimes become very entrepreneurial. When both are low, there is widespread inertia. Often, resources are high, but aspirations are low, or maybe the manifestation of aspirations is low, as in many cases. Women fall into this category due to various social and cultural limitations, like in Kashmir, or the aspirations as a community can be hindered due to low accessibility to technologies or infrastructure, like in Nagaland. The ideal case is when aspirations and natural resources are available aplenty, but that may not always be the case.

Collective aspirations may pave the way for collective action along with individual enterprises. High aspiration and low resources may pose problems for peace and security if community order and stability are destabilized. This is a delicate issue and must be handled with care, responsibility and clarity.

Taming Young and Diverse Talent

3. **Harnessing young bio-geniuses:** Organizing biodiversity competitions has been a very useful means of discovering young talent during *shodhyatra*s, and otherwise. Children are asked to bring samples of plants they know, and list their uses. They are allowed to seek the help of elders if they wish, but time is limited. Sometimes, children are able to discover by the age of 10–12 years almost half the number of diverse plants the elders knew. But there is no career

path for such bio-geniuses. They are not given a chance to become bio-entrepreneurs or foresters. Sometimes, girls have less knowledge than boys because they are not allowed to roam as far as the boys. Constrained opportunities, however, do not always imply lifelong lesser learning. Paradoxically, among adults, many women know much more compared to men about nutritious weeds, uncultivated plants products for pickles, medicines, dyes and aromatic purposes. Recipe or food formulation competition among women helps uncover very useful insights about how they manage the nutritional needs of the family by tapping into wild biodiversity and weeds. Discovering young talent can be harnessed for grooming future conservators and bio-entrepreneurs. Socially constrained opportunities among young girls may distract attention from their higher potential at the adult stage. Thus, there is a need to build the capacity of girls along with other deserving children through forest and pasture walks, advising them to seek the guidance of elders and bridge the gender gap if any.

Seeking Consent of Knowledge Providers

4. **Ethical exchange of knowledge and resources through prior informed consent:** Prior Informed Consent (PIC) is an important tool for ensuring that the rights of the knowledge provider(s) are protected under relevant provisions at different stages of knowledge collection and sharing. If the knowledge is relatively novel, one can also file a patent/intellectual property (IP) in their name. While the process is lengthy and time-consuming, the knowledge provider(s) may give permission to share the formulation for validation and value addition. While exploring commercial returns on the knowledge, it is imperative to seek permission from the knowledge holder(s). One has to specify under which conditions the formulation can be shared and how the knowledge provider(s) will be

compensated in case monetary value is generated from the IP. Way back in 1989–90, a letter was given to every knowledge provider while seeking their knowledge, assuring them of their rights and seeking their permission to publish it in the *Honey Bee Newsletter.* This was the seed which was elaborated in detailed PIC guidelines in SRISTI[14], NIF[15] and GIAN.

It helps to build trust with the community as they are now assured that one is not trying to steal their knowledge. Their knowledge will be shared with third parties as per their preferred conditions. This can be recorded if signing forms is not possible.

By implementing these adaptive measures and fostering sustainable social and bio-entrepreneurial practices, the Himalayan region can enhance its resilience to climate change impacts and support the portfolio of livelihoods mediated by women in high-risk environments.

---

[14]Society for Research and Initiatives for Sustainable Technologies and Institutions.
[15]National Innovation Foundation.

7

SMEs AND WOMEN'S ENTREPRENEURSHIP

Prashant Girbane
Director General, Mahratta Chamber of Commerce,
Industries and Agriculture (MCCIA)
Gunjan Bhojwani
Youth Fellow, MCCIA

It has long been understood that entrepreneurship plays a leading role in the economic development of any nation. But only in recent years has the idea of economic development and entrepreneurship drawn increasing attention. There is a body of great literature in the hands of researchers on these two notions. On the one hand, economic development can be regarded as the general theory of entrepreneurship, which encompasses a variety of development outcomes. On the other hand, the government and policymakers have been giving greater importance to entrepreneurship as a means of economic development.

Entrepreneurship influences the growth process of any economy. It gives rise to structural transformations, technological upgradations and innovations at a macro level on varied scales in different countries. The result is that every nation varies in its level of entrepreneurial activities. Thus, the degree of economic disparity also differs greatly among nations. Studies have shown that nations with high level of economic inequality tend to have high rates of entrepreneurial activity. Developing countries like India support this hypothesis.

Most of India's enterprises are entrepreneurial, and stunted at small and medium enterprises (SMEs) level. Globally, women own 34%[1] of SMEs, which is significantly less than their proportional share of 50%. In India, the number is far lower at 20.5%[2], almost half of countries like the USA that has 39.1%[3].

In general, inequality in ownership of enterprises has deep roots in gender inequality. Despite significant economic advances, inequality is deeply rooted in the Indian economy. On the Gender Inequality Index (GII), India ranks 108 out of 193 countries. The desired per capita growth to the levels of countries with upper middle income is impossible to achieve with the current state of affairs where one engine, male entrepreneurship, is fuelling 79.5% of the growth while the other engine, female entrepreneurship, is fuelling only 20.5%[4].

When both engines of growth fire well, India would move far beyond the current 7%[5] of the world's output, more in tune with its percentage of the world's population—16%. If the importance of female entrepreneurs is overlooked, the conversation about the importance of entrepreneurship will be incomplete.

The benefits of women entrepreneurship[6] go beyond

[1]World Bank Blogs, Halim, Daniel, 'Women entrepreneurs needed—stat!', 5 March 2020. https://tinyurl.com/2ehdbz2z. Accessed on 9 September 2024.

[2]Press Information Bureau, Government of India, Ministry of Micro, Small & Medium Enterprises, 'Women Entrepreneurs in MSMEs', 5 February 2024, https://tinyurl.com/2h44yftz. Accessed on 9 September 2024.

[3]Wells Fargo, *The 2024 Impact of Women-Owned Businesses*, https://tinyurl.com/mrxufavj. Accessed on 9 September 2024.

[4]Press Information Bureau, Government of India, Ministry of Micro, Small & Medium Enterprises, 'Women Entrepreneurs in MSMEs', 5 February 2024, https://tinyurl.com/2h44yftz. Accessed on 9 September 2024.

[5]Varghese, P.N., AO., *AN INDIAN ECONOMIC STRATEGY TO 2035: NAVIGATING FROM POTENTIAL TO DELIVERY*, A report to the Australian Government, 27 April 2018.

[6]The Government of India defines 'women entrepreneurship' as an enterprise owned and controlled by a woman having a minimum financial interest of 51 per cent of the capital and giving at least 51 per cent of the employment generated by the enterprise to women. https://tinyurl.com/evwzbkv6. Accessed on 9 September 2024.

numbers in terms of percentage share. Breaking down barriers, challenging norms, and fostering an inclusive environment for women entrepreneurs drives transformative shifts that extend far beyond the realm of commerce. Empowerment of women can serve as a powerful driver of social change, shift in attitudes, and opportunities in societies worldwide.

Women entrepreneurs' decision on whether or not to enter the entrepreneurial landscape is influenced by various factors. One of the primary motivations for women to pursue entrepreneurship is the desire for financial independence and autonomy. Especially for those women who seek greater flexibility of balancing work and family responsibility, entrepreneurship offers a compelling alternative. By building successful businesses, women can unlock new sources of income, build assets and secure their financial future.

Given the obvious gaps in the percentage share of women entrepreneurship in India, their comparison with women entrepreneurship, in more developed economies, and the benefits of women entrepreneurship in terms of positive social externalities, there is an urgent need to focus on increasing female (women) entrepreneurship so that their contribution to the economy is at least double the current 20.5%.

This essay covers various aspects of women entrepreneurship, including its definition, current status, key challenges, extant policies of the Government of India aimed at boosting women entrepreneurship, and what more is required from the policy to further empower women entrepreneurs.

WOMEN ENTREPRENEURS: BIG FIRMS & MSMEs

Women are increasingly taking on key leadership roles in large corporations and transforming the business landscape. This is now visible in India, where female entrepreneurs and executives are making some progress in previously male-dominated industries.

A noteworthy example is Vandana Luthra, Founder of VLCC, the renowned wellness and beauty company. A trailblazer, she is one of the few successful first-generation Indian women entrepreneurs. Under Luthra's leadership, VLCC grew exponentially. From a single centre in New Delhi, it expanded to over 310 locations and 11 countries. She has received numerous awards, including the Padma Shri, one of India's highest civilian honours. Luthra's journey from a young woman with a vision to becoming the founder of a global wellness empire is truly inspiring. Her story is a beacon of hope and motivation for women entrepreneurs everywhere.

Another noteworthy example is Kiran Mazumdar-Shaw, Founder and Chairman of Biocon Limited, one of India's leading biotechnology corporations. Due to Mazumdar-Shaw's innovative leadership, Biocon has gained international prominence, and her ground-breaking work in biopharmaceuticals has earned her multiple honours, including the Padma Shri and Padma Bhushan.

Furthermore, in the world of e-commerce, women like Falguni Nayar have emerged as trailblazers, defying conventional wisdom and propelling innovation. Nayar, the creator and CEO of Nykaa, India's leading online cosmetics retailer, is transforming the beauty sector with her e-commerce platform.

A handful of such names demonstrate 'some' progress has been made by women entrepreneurship, and that is indeed encouraging. However, these names constitute only the tip of the iceberg. The larger chunk of the iceberg under water is constituted by not well-known corporations like Biocon and Nykaa, but by millions of micro and small-size businesses owned, promoted, and run by women entrepreneurs.

In their report, Bain and Co. estimate that there are roughly 15.7 million women-owned businesses in India, making up 22% of the country's total entrepreneurial landscape.[7]

---

[7]Google | Bain & Company, *Powering the Economy with Her: Women*

Barring a handful, all these businesses are micro, small and medium enterprises (MSMEs) where micro-sized businesses have annual turnover less than ₹5 crore, small businesses have a turnover of ₹5–₹50 crore, and medium business have a turnover of ₹50–₹250 crore. Majorly, women-owned businesses are concentrated in the micro segment (228,450 MSMEs)[8].

In India, the MSME sector contributes to 30% of the GDP and to around 43% of total exports[9]. Yet MSMEs run by women entrepreneurs represent only 20.5%[10] of the total MSME landscape in India.

Apart from large corporations and MSMEs, new-age tech start-ups are another domain to explore for the current status of women entrepreneurship. The trend there is very encouraging—in the last five years, the share of women founders (owner-promoters) has almost doubled from 10% to 18%[11]. However, this 18% is not remarkably more than the 20.5% of women entrepreneurs in MSMEs.

Entry of women in business is usually seen in smaller, younger and less profitable sectors. According to the 73rd survey of the National Sample Survey Office (NSSO), women-owned enterprises are concentrated in sectors like manufacturing of wearing apparels (26.4%), tobacco products (22.6%), textiles

Entrepreneurship in India, 2019, https://tinyurl.com/mrxh24d4. Accessed on 9 September 2024.

[8]Press Information Bureau, Government of India, Ministry of Micro, Small & Medium Enterprises, 'Women Entrepreneurs in MSMEs', 5 February 2024, https://tinyurl.com/2h44yftz. Accessed on 9 September 2024.

[9]Press Information Bureau, Government of India, Ministry of Micro, Small & Medium Enterprises, 'Role of MSME Sector in the Country', 7 August 2023, https://tinyurl.com/3duw2yx2. Accessed on 9 September 2024.

[10]Press Information Bureau, Government of India, Ministry of Micro, Small & Medium Enterprises, op. cit.

[11]Gupta, S. N., and A. Ghosh, 'Rising Above Uncertainty: The 2022 Saga of Indian Tech Start-Ups', in *India Tech Start-Up Landscape Report 2022 Edition*, NASSCOM, & Zinnov, https://tinyurl.com/2s3r2ahd. Accessed on 9 September 2024.

(10.8%) or in retail trade (15.7%)[12]. Women entrepreneurship needs to expand beyond these select few sectors. Majority of women entrepreneurs working in these sectors are from rural areas. Less supported and empowered, they operate in more informal, unregistered and disorganized ways. India has a total of 1.29 crore informal micro enterprises (IMEs); 70.49% of these are owned by women[13].

This clearly depicts the underrepresentation of women in entrepreneurship, and underscores the need to cultivate a supportive ecosystem that encourages and enables more women to enter businesses. The supportive system needs to be built to address current challenges faced by women entrepreneurs. Let us look at some of the main challenges faced by women entrepreneurs.

CHALLENGES

Among the myriad reasons for the gap in share of women entrepreneurship, this section groups the challenges along a few critical dimensions. The Weiss (2015:23), UNCTAD framework on Structural Transformation and Industrial Policy[14] identifies five key categories that group challenges in any economy, and give a structure for public policy intervention. These categories include Land, Labour, Capital, Product and Technology, collectively constituting the fundamental elements or building blocks of any economy, often referred to as 'factors of production'.

According to the World Bank Atlas, with a GNI per capita of $2390 (2022), India is a lower middle-income economy that has

---

[12]Ibid.

[13]Press Information Bureau, Government of India, Ministry of Micro, Small & Medium Enterprises, op. cit.

[14]Guadagno, Francesca, M. Bateman, C. Rada, & K. Vrolijk, *Virtual Institute Teaching Material on Structural Transformation and Industrial Policy* (Fortunato, P., R. Kozul-Wright, & D. Einhorn, Eds.), United Nations Conference on Trade and Development (UNCTAD), 2016, https://tinyurl.com/4mnh9t3s. Accessed on 9 September 2024.

a range of GNI per capita between $1136 and $4465. However, since India aspires to be an upper middle-income country, this chapter uses the framework relevant for middle-income countries.

Table 1
Industrial Policies in Middle-Income Countries

Policy Domain	Instruments	
	Market-Based	**Public Good**
Product Market	Import tariffs, duty drawbacks, tax credits, investment/FDI incentives	Procurement policy, export market information/trade fairs, linkage programmes, FDI country marketing, one-stop shops, investment promotion agencies
Labour Market	Wage tax credits/ subsidies, training grants	Training institutes, skills, councils
Capital Market	Interest rate subsidies, loan guarantees	Financial regulation, development bank (first/second tier) lending, venture capital
Land Market	Subsidized rental	Export processing zones (EPZs)/ special economic zones (SEZs), factory shells, infrastructure, legislative change, incubator programmes
Technology	R&D subsidies, grants	Public-private research consortia, public research institutes, technology transfer support, technology extension programmes

Source: Weiss (2015:23), UNCTAD—Structural Transformation and Industrial Policy

The challenges and opportunities in each of the 5 policy domains enumerated in Table 1 are as follows:

Women often lack access to resources needed for land acquisition and infrastructure development. In India, only 9.5% of women (aged 15-49) own land alone.[15] Prevalent social norms of treating only men as heirs to land and property certainly contributes to this problem.

Many people assume that public investment in infrastructure initiatives serve both men and women equally, without considering their unique implications. Women and men experience different issues with infrastructure.

Furthermore, remote areas where women may own a little larger share of enterprises sometimes lack basic social infrastructure such as roads and electricity, which impedes business operations. An estimated 22.24%[16] women-owned enterprises are from rural areas, and even though India has the second largest road network in the world, Road Transport Performance[17] for the country is only 27.5% in the urban sector, and even lesser—18.2%—in rural areas[18] where women entrepreneurs own a little larger share of enterprises. This means commuting to workplaces is difficult due to inadequate transportation infrastructure. Improved infrastructure facilities especially oriented towards women entrepreneurs will have a positive impact on the increase in entrepreneurial activities, as improved transportation networks can help women, particularly in rural areas, access markets, suppliers, and customers more efficiently.

[15]World Bank Group, Gender Data Portal (n.d.), 'Ownership of land (%)', https://tinyurl.com/98p5h53n. Accessed on 9 September 2024.
[16]Jaitly, S., L.S. Thangallapally & MicroSave, *Decoding government support to women entrepreneurs in India: The anatomy of entrepreneurship support schemes*, in NITI Aayog, Government of India, www.microsave.net [Report], October 2022, https://tinyurl.com/33khkdmc. Accessed on 09 September 2024.
[17]Kompil, M., J. Gao, Y. Li, A. Narayanan, J. Su, & Asian Infrastructure Investment Bank (2023), 'ROAD TRANSPORT PERFORMANCE IN INDIA', in AIIB WORKING PAPER [Report], https://tinyurl.com/2s42d9mh. Accessed on 9 September 2024.
[18]Ibid.

Labour and Product

Compared to men, most women entrepreneurs are not full-time entrepreneurs as, at least in the most crucial early days of an enterprise, they are doing a fine balancing act between their domestic chores and building a new business. The literacy rate for Indian women is 69%[19], while for men it is 83%[20]. Given the lower literacy rate and less amount of time allocated to enterprise building, the opportunities to hone their skills in growing their enterprises are limited.

The lower labour force participation rate (LFPR) among women is also a significant challenge as many small entrepreneurs start their business after a few years of work experience. With a far lower number of women in the workforce, the non-availability of that base pool for women who aspire to start their business, negatively impacts the number of women entrepreneurs. As per the International Labour Organization (ILO)[21], in 2023 the male LFPR was at 78.5% while the women LFPR was a mere 37%, which is far lower than the world women LFPR at 49%.[22]

Impact on product choices: In India, women often run micro-businesses from home due to domestic responsibilities. As a result, they prefer flexible roles that allow them to devote time to the business and home. So, mostly women-owned business are concentrated around sectors like textile, wearing apparels, food and allied activities. No wonder that in India, women are

---

[19]World Bank Group I Data, 'Literacy rate, adult female (% of females aged 15 and above)—India', https://tinyurl.com/4m6ktjt6. Accessed on 9 September 2024.
[20]'Literacy rate, adult male (% of males aged 15 and above)—India', World Bank Group I Data, https://tinyurl.com/mrany7x7. Accessed on 9 September 2024.
[21]International Labour Organization, Ghose, A.K., M. Miyamoto & A. Sharma, 'India Employment Report 2024: Youth employment, education and skills', in *India Employment Report 2024*, https://tinyurl.com/3sejzy6j. Accessed on 9 September 2024.
[22]International Labour Organization, *World Employment Social Outlook: Trends for Women 2017*, https://tinyurl.com/bwcj24ck. Accessed on 9 September 2024.

underrepresented in manufacturing activities. According to the Global Entrepreneurship Monitor (GEM) report, 51.7%[23] women-owned, early-stage start-ups are largely in wholesale or retail, compared to only 3.3% in manufacturing and transportation.

Additionally, given the balancing act women entrepreneurs have to do between work and domestic responsibilities, accessing markets for selling goods and services can be challenging in India.

As per a report published by the International Finance Corporation (IFC) in 2022, around 90% of women entrepreneurs do not borrow from formal sources of finance. An estimated 70% of credit demand by women-owned very small enterprises goes largely unmet by formal financial institutions[24].

In India, credit for women is equal to 27% of the deposits they make, while credit for men is equal to 52% of their deposits[25]. During the Covid-19 lockdown, women were impacted more than men. According to surveys conducted by SEWA Bharat, almost 78% of women entrepreneurs lacked financial reserves versus 53% of men.[26]

[23]Kühn, S., R. Horne, S. Yoon, J. Rafferty & S. Kapsos, *World Employment and Social Outlook: Trends for Women 2017* (Tobin S., S. Lee, L. J. Johnson, D. Greenfield, J. Howard, L. Addati, A. Asenjo, F. Bonnet, M. Corley-Coulibaly, F. Dutra, E. E. Manrique, S. Elder, E. Ernst, M. Esposito, V. Esquivel, A. `Gama, C. Henry, P. Huynh, T. Kizu...Z. Wang, Eds.), 2021–2022, p. 95, https://www. gemconsortium.org/file/open?fileId=51352).

[24]Garg, Amit, 'Improved credit access to women entrepreneurs is good news for the Indian economy!', *The Times of India*, 28 February 2024, https://tinyurl.com/ yc29e9ny. Accessed on 9 September 2024. International Finance Corporation (IFC), 'Opportunities and Constraints of Women Owned Very Small Enterprises in India', in Bali, V., M. Prasad, A. Gokhale, A. Gupta, & N. Kumar (Eds.), 2022, https://tinyurl.com/3ac7r2ka. Accessed on 22 October 2024.

[25]Chavan, Pallavi, 'Women's Access to Banking in India: Policy Context, Trends, and Predictors', *Review of Agrarian Studies*, Vol. 10, No. 1, January–June 2020, https://tinyurl.com/4bpvj499. Accessed on 9 September 2024.

[26]International Finance Corporation (IFC), World Bank Group, Bhattacharjee, P., S. Kaushik, A. Birla, & N.K. Bhatia, 'Opportunities and Constraints of Women Owned Very Small Enterprises in India', in Bali, V., M. Prasad, A. Gokhale, A. Gupta, & N. Kumar (Eds.), 2022, https://tinyurl.com/yrnkeecz. Accessed on 9 September 2024.

Technology

Adoption of technology has emerged as a transformative force in business, particularly for women entrepreneurs, providing new chances for growth and success. Despite tremendous developments in the digital sector, women entrepreneurs continue to confront considerable barriers to accessing and realizing the full potential of technology for their businesses. One of the most significant hurdles is the digital gender gap, which manifests itself in unequal access to and usage of technology between men and women. Use of telecommunications is one of the most basic technology uses these days. In India, only 31% of women use the internet compared to 67% of men, and only 29% of women own a smartphone versus 48% of men.[27] Also, many Indian women, particularly in rural areas, are not yet fully exposed to the benefits of digital literacy and technology adoption.

Science, Technology, Engineering, and Mathematics (STEM) fields represent hubs of innovation and technological advancement. However, despite the increasing prominence of STEM-driven industries, women entrepreneurs remain significantly underrepresented in these domains. India has more women enrolled in STEM than some developed countries, with 43% female graduates at the tertiary level. It is ironical that in a country which has recently claimed being the first Asian country to accomplish its Mars mission in its maiden attempt, out of 43% women graduates in STEM at the tertiary level, only 29% actually joined the STEM workforce, and only 3% of women hold CEO posts in the STEM industry.[28]

---

[27]Global System for Mobile Communications (GSMC), Jeffrie, Nadia, Kalvin Bahia, Isabelle Carboni, Dominica Lindsey, Claire Sibthorpe, & Jakub Zagdanski, *The Mobile Gender Gap Report 2023*, May 2003, https://tinyurl.com/267c58e3. Accessed on 9 September 2024.

[28]National Center for Science and Engineering Statistics | NSF 23-315, in *National Center for Science and Engineering Statistics* (NSF 23-315; p. Table of Contents), 2021, https://tinyurl.com/yjks9bhx. Accessed on 22 October 2024.

This underrepresentation not only limits the diversity of perspectives and ideas in the entrepreneurial ecosystem but also perpetuates systemic inequalities and hampers the full realization of women's potential as leaders and innovators in STEM-related ventures.

Beyond leaders, given the disparity in access to technology, women face more hurdles in dealing with economic and social challenges.

SUPPORTING WOMEN ENTREPRENEURS: EXTANT POLICIES

Modern economics supports the notion that markets are competitive, leading to efficient allocation of resources. The market's competitive forces contribute to high levels of efficiency, competition being an essential motivator for innovation. But practically, markets do not perform efficiently, and markets fail, which gives rise to inequality, unemployment and inflation. Compared to men, women are faced with specific obstacles that have to be overcome to give them access to the same opportunities as men. Ongoing constraints faced by women along multiple dimensions demonstrate the market failures that demand further government interventions through effective design and implementation of policies.

There are many examples of how public policy interventions have worked in India both for economic and social development. The 73rd and 74th Amendments to the Constitution are among such reforms. These reforms allocated one-third of the Panchayati Raj seats to women, ensuring their representation and participation

---

Swarup, Renu, and Shagun Sabarwal, 'More Indian women in STEM but few are becoming leaders. Hard to retain them in workforce', *ThePrint*, 23 March 2023, https://tinyurl.com/mtum5cma. Accessed on 22 October 2024. Kalra, Mugdha, 'Dear India Inc., Let's Talk About The Missing Women In STEM', *NDTV Profit*, 13 January 2023, https://tinyurl.com/5n8byk6r. Accessed on 22 October 2024.

in grassroots decision-making processes. These modifications have helped create inclusive and equitable development in India by giving women a forum to express their concerns and advocate for the interests of their communities. While the implementation of these reforms has left a lot to be desired, there are some positives to take away from them. Success stories of women leaders at the municipal level, made possible by these constitutional provisions, serve as beacons of hope and inspiration for aspiring women across the country. This demonstrates how public policy interventions deliver over time.

To boost women entrepreneurship, government intervention can address market failures and provide women entrepreneurs with the resources, networks, and mentorship they need to succeed, through targeted support programmes and incentives.

The Government of India is currently implementing several central schemes aimed at promoting women entrepreneurs. Through comprehensive analysis, we have identified a total of 19 such schemes administered by various government ministries. While there are other schemes as well run by various ministries, since there was no data available on the share of women beneficiaries in these, they have not been included here.

Out of these 19 schemes, six schemes are run by the Ministry of Micro, Small & Medium Enterprises (MoMSME), four by the Ministry of Science and Technology (MoST), three by the Ministry of Women and Child Development (MoWCD), and two each by the Ministry of Commerce and Industries (MoCI), Ministry of Finance (MoF), and Ministry of Social Justice and Empowerment (MoSJE).

Tabulated below is the list of schemes, which can be broadly grouped into three of the five domains, as outlined in our framework earlier in Table 1.

Table 2
List of Schemes by Government of India

1	Labour Policies	2	Capital Policies	3	Product Policies
1.1	Skill Upgradation and Mahila Coir Yojna	2.1	Mudra Yojna for Women	3.1	Government E-Marketplace (GeM)
1.2	Nari Shakti Puraskar	2.2	Credit Guarantee Scheme for MSME	3.2	International Cooperation Scheme
1.3	National Startup Awards	2.3	Stand-Up India	3.3	Zero Defect Zero Effect (ZED)
1.4	Support to Training and Employment Program for Women	2.4	Mahila Samridhi Yojna		
1.5	Mahila Shakti Kendra	2.5	Women Scientist Scheme		
1.6	PM Vishwakarma Scheme	2.6	Mahila Adhikarita Yojna		
1.7	Entrepreneurship Skill Development Programme (ESDP)				
a	NIDHI—National Initiative for Developing and Harnessing Innovations				
b	BIRAC Regional Techno Entrepreneurship Centre				
c	BIRAC TiE WInER Awards				

These policies have had a mixed impact. Some have had a large impact while many have had a far lesser impact. One key measure to assess impact is coverage (in terms of number of beneficiaries) of the policy. In a country with the world's largest population of 140 crore individuals, and crores of MSMEs, any meaningful impact of policies would require coverage of lakhs, if not crores, of MSMEs.

Based on data on the impact of these schemes, this essay attempts to delve into eight of the 19 schemes to highlight which ones have worked better than the others. Five of the policies with meaningful impact are listed below.

Pradhan Mantri Mudra Yojna is a good example of a policy intervention with broad coverage. The cumulative outreach of 2022–23 through the Mudra Yojna was 41.16 crore MSE borrower accounts, with credit support of 22.89 lakh crore, of which 68.62% loan accounts belonged to women beneficiaries.[29] Such schemes have confronted the issue of financial capital head-on, and have delivered direct benefit on a widespread scale.

Another scheme with sizeable impact is the Credit Guarantee Fund Trust for Micro and Small Enterprises (CGTMSEs). It facilitates access to finance for women entrepreneurs, enabling them to invest in their businesses. It enhances women's access to formal credit by reducing collateral requirement and incentivizing banks to lend to women entrepreneurs. The scheme guarantees 85% credit guarantee for women entrepreneurs as against 75% for men. Also, it gives 10% concession on standard rate of fees. Under the CGTMSE scheme, 1,691,958 guarantees have been approved for women-owned MSMEs amounting to ₹83,222 crore since the inception of the scheme,[30] which is 38.64% of the total guarantees approved under the scheme.

The third impactful scheme is Stand-up India. Since the launch of the initiative in 2016 by the government, 55,816 start-ups

---

[29]Mudra (n.d.), 'Eight years of Pradhan Mantri Mudra Yojana', Annual Report 2022–23, https://tinyurl.com/5n9bec6d. Accessed on 22 October 2024.
[30]Press Information Bureau, Government of India, Ministry of Micro, Small & Medium Enterprises, 'MSMEs Run by Women', 8 February 2023, https://tinyurl.com/25j45256. Accessed on 9 September 2024.

recognized by the Department of Promotion of Industry and Internal Trade (DPIIT)[31] have at least one woman director, and approximately 80.1% (144,787) of the total accounts opened under the scheme belong to women. Moreover, an impressive 81.4% of the total amount sanctioned, amounting to ₹33,152.43 crore, has been allocated to women entrepreneurs.[32]

While each of these three examples relates to 'capital', the fourth example of good coverage of a scheme relates to the dimension of 'product-market'. The Public Procurement Policy for Micro and Small Enterprises (MSEs) Order, 2012, mandates that Central Ministries/Departments/PSUs must aim to procure at least 25% of their total annual purchases from MSEs through the GeM Portal[33]. Within this target, 3% is reserved for those owned by women entrepreneurs. In 2019, GeM launched an initiative called 'Womaniya on GeM' to enable women entrepreneurs and self-help groups (SHGs) to market their products directly to various government ministries, departments and institutions. Currently, 1.44 lakh+ Udyam-verified women-owned micro and small enterprises (MSE) are registered as vendors and service providers on the GeM platform, fulfilling 14.76 lakh+ orders worth ₹21,265 crore in gross merchandise value (GMV).[34]

---

[31]Press Information Bureau, Government of India, Ministry of Commerce & Industry, 'DPIIT recognises 1,17,254 startups as on 31 Dec 2023: Startups create over 12.42 lakh direct jobs: At least one recognised startup in every State and UT; spread across over 80% of districts', 2 February 2024, 'https://tinyurl.com/62z838m5. Accessed on 9 September 2024.

[32]Press Information Bureau, Government of India, Ministry of Finance, 'More than Rs. 40,700 crore sanctioned to over 1,80,630 accounts under Stand-Up India Scheme in 7 years', 5 April 2023, https://tinyurl.com/4de7y8va. Accessed on 9 September 2024.

[33]MSME SAMBANDH, Government of India, 'Welcome to Public Procurement Policy', https://tinyurl.com/4e8hny4b. Accessed on 9 September 2024.

[34]Press Information Bureau, Government of India, Ministry of Commerce and Industry, 'GeM holds event to commemorate success of Women entrepreneurs on GeM', 14 January 2023, https://tinyurl.com/4ndkfzb6. Accessed on 9 September 2024.

The fifth scheme that has had impactful coverage is the PM Vishwakarma Scheme, aimed at supporting and uplifting artisans and craftsmen from the Vishwakarma community. The scheme provides financial aid, skill development and marketing support to traditional craftsmen engaged in professions like carpentry, blacksmithing and metalworking. To date, the project has trained 400,363 people; 68.76% (261,049) are women, and 31.3% (139,315) are men. Out of these 247,895 women participants learned tailoring skills.[35] This scheme goes beyond capital intervention to build the skills of the smallest existing and aspiring micro women entrepreneurs, also called 'nano entrepreneurs' by some scholars.

The objective of presenting the above-mentioned five relatively impactful schemes is to advise the government to continue expanding the coverage of these schemes.

A closer look at eight of these 19 schemes, or for that matter any other portfolio of the scheme (ex post facto), would highlight that these are a mixed bag in terms of success measured in coverage of beneficiaries. Schemes like the above-mentioned five have delivered acceptable impact (e.g. lakhs of beneficiaries). However, others have delivered far lesser impact (e.g. hundreds of beneficiaries). Hence, these need an evaluation, and may necessitate possible amendments to the existing policy. In some cases, it may be prudent to discard the scheme altogether.

Here are three schemes that have delivered far lesser coverage/impact as per the data. The International Cooperation (IC) scheme facilitates MSMEs' entry into export markets through participation in international events, market intelligence, and cost reimbursements. Under this scheme, priority is given to women entrepreneurs, along with SC/ST entrepreneurs and start-ups. In 2022–23, 10,058 MSMEs received financial incentives through the International Cooperation scheme. Of 10,058 MSMEs, only

---

[35]Ministry of Skill Development & Entrepreneurship, Government of India, Power BI Report (n.d.), https://tinyurl.com/ykcwcbw5. Accessed on 9 September 2024.

57 were owned by women entrepreneurs.[36]

The second scheme on women empowerment, titled 'Mahila Adhikarita Yojna', provides loans to women for small income-generating activities for projects costing up to ₹500,000. Under this scheme, only 187 women have benefitted during year 2022–23.[37]

The third scheme under discussion here is the National Initiative for Developing and Harnessing Innovations (NIDHI), an umbrella scheme for nurturing ideas and innovations (knowledge-based and technology-driven) into successful start-ups. The programme works in line with national priorities and goals and its focus is to build an innovation-driven entrepreneurial ecosystem with the objective of socio-economic development through wealth and job creation. The scheme has various sub-components.

Under the scheme, 105 Women Entrepreneurship Development Programmes were conducted in which 2,625 women were trained.[38]

The IC, Mahila Adhikrita and NIDHI schemes are examples where despite the focus being on women entrepreneurs, the real beneficiaries number only in tens, hundreds or thousands. Compared to the size of the target segment (existing and potential women entrepreneurs) which runs in crores, these numbers look insignificant.

One case for justifying the low number of beneficiaries is when the scheme has a demonstration effect. Schemes like Women in Science and Engineering-KIRAN (WISE-KIRAN) that has encouraged about 2,000 scientists over the past few years

---

[36]Press Information Bureau, Government of India, Ministry of Micro, Small & Medium Enterprises, 'WOMEN-OWNED ENTERPRISES', 16 March 2023, https://tinyurl.com/bdfsnr6k. Accessed on 9 September 2024.

[37]National Scheduled Castes Finance and Development Corporation (NSFDC), *Annual Report 2022–23*, 2023, https://tinyurl.com/bddeb4ka. Accessed on 9 September 2024.

[38]Government of India, Ministry of Science and Technology, Department of Science & Technology, *Brief Statement of Activities 2023–24*, https://tinyurl.com/27923jpw. Accessed on 9 September 2024.

can be considered schemes with a demonstration effect as 2,000 is a sizeable number compared to the base number of women scientists. Even some of the awards mentioned in Table 2 aim to have a demonstration effect to encourage women entrepreneurs, with negligible cost associated with such schemes.

However, in case of the IC, Mahila Adhikrita and NIDHI schemes, the numbers are too small (compared to the lakhs of women who could aspire to benefit from them) to have any demonstration effect. Also, schemes like the IC have been running for many years to not have progressed beyond the demonstration-effect stage.

These and more such schemes either lack awareness generation among the target segment (existing and aspiring women entrepreneurs) or a more enabling environment. A thorough evaluation of every scheme that aims to benefit women entrepreneurs needs to go through periodic robust evaluation so that it is appropriately amended or even closed in some cases.

RECOMMENDATIONS

The government has made some policies and undertaken various initiatives to encourage women entrepreneurship, but the fact that women entrepreneurs represent only 20%–22% of formal enterprises—almost half of the global levels—demonstrates a big gap that is yet to be bridged. Current policies in their existing shape and form have proved insufficient to bridge the gap. Hence, here are some recommendations on the five dimensions of Land, Labour, Capital, Product and Technology as articulated in the framework by Weiss (2015:23), UNCTAD—Structural Transformation and Industrial Policy (Table 1).

Public policy interventions undertaken in the past and including the extant ones have very few initiatives that are meant only for women entrepreneurs. Mostly, women entrepreneurs are covered under various ongoing policies by giving additional weightage to the benefits announced. This would be fine as long as there is periodic monitoring and evaluation of ongoing schemes so that they can be tweaked to make them 'fit for purpose.' In some areas like Land, ongoing interventions are negligible. Hence, completely new interventions need to be introduced.

Land

Lack of land ownership by women is a major impediment to their entrepreneurial ventures. A look at industrial zones in any district would suggest that there is a lack of land ownership by women entrepreneurs in these zones. States like Maharashtra have taken initiatives wherein the Maharashtra Industrial Development Corporation (MIDC) has reserved 20% of plots for SMEs, and within that, 5% of plots are reserved for SC, ST and women entrepreneurs. This is laudable as it is far better than nothing at all, but it is still clearly insufficient.

There is a need for dedicated zones for women entrepreneurs that can take into account various needs of women, including, dedicated transport from city centres to the industrial area, common facility centres focused on women-run enterprises, common facilities like toilets and changing rooms, healthcare centres and childcare centres.

A series of discussions by the Mahratta Chamber of Commerce, Industries and Agriculture (MCCIA), an industry association, with its women entrepreneur members highlights the need and demand for such clusters. Each manufacturing cluster could be set up with a budget of ₹50 crore on an average. Hundred such manufacturing clusters across the country with a total budget of ₹5,000 crores will go beyond demonstrative purpose, and bring about the desired societal change by encouraging more women to participate in entrepreneurial activities.

Beyond manufacturing, there is also a need for such clusters for services-based organizations of women entrepreneurs. The MCCIA has set up a model cluster in Pune where women entrepreneurs get not only a neat, clean and safe co-working space but also 20 common services under one roof. These services range from the establishment of an organization, business development, branding and marketing to benefitting from government services and shutting down a unit if required.

The MCCIA has invested ₹1 crore in setting up and running this cluster. The government can run 100 such clusters in the first phase with a budget of ₹100 crore, in partnership with industry associations or the private sector with Viability Gap Funding[39].

Together, the manufacturing and services-based zones for women entrepreneurs would enhance their access to land and infrastructure.

Labour

This dimension of public policy understandably focuses on improving the productivity of employees as against that only of entrepreneurs. However, there are many examples of soft and hard skills training that have helped create micro and nano enterprises. The skills component of the Vishwakarma Scheme is helping women entrepreneurs in the tailoring sector. Similar success needs to be achieved in other skill-based solo or nano entrepreneurship sectors.

Designing specific courses focused on building organization management skills of budding and aspiring women entrepreneurs is equally important. The ESDP (Entrepreneurship Skill Development Programme) that is conducted with premier institutes in India is a very good beginning as it has already

---

[39]Viability Gap Funding is a financial mechanism used by governments to bridge the gap between the cost of infrastructure projects and their economic viability. It is typically employed in projects that are considered economically unviable or financially unattractive for private investors due to various reasons, such as high capital costs, low revenue potential, or long gestation periods.

received about 900,000 aspiring entrepreneurs as of May 2024. However, the ESDP must engage other channel partners like industry associations spread across more than 800 districts in India to ensure that the programme is even more accessible, especially for women entrepreneurs. While the dashboard of the ESDP highlights the number of programmes conducted, and the number of aspiring entrants in the programme, it would do even better by highlighting the share of women entrepreneurs among the aspirants, especially as it mandates 40% of targeted beneficiaries from SC/ST/Women/Physically Handicapped categories and offers them free training.

Capital

Schemes like Mudra and CGTMSE have shown significant success in making capital accessible and affordable for women entrepreneurs. However, to bridge the gap of ₹83,600 crore of unmet credit demand by women entrepreneurs, there is a need for more schemes to facilitate credit. In design, the schemes must allocate higher weightage for women entrepreneurs, and in implementation, each scheme should ensure wider awareness generation and hand-holding documentation support.

Product

Under the dimension of Product-Market, among the extant schemes, the GeM (Government E-Marketplace) platform has proved to be a boon for women entrepreneurs.

On the trade fair front, the IC scheme has been far less effective as detailed earlier in this essay. It is necessary to tweak the scheme with innovative approaches like 'reverse buyer-seller meets' wherein potential verified buyers are attracted and facilitated to visit a cluster of women entrepreneurs, in India.

On the schemes from the Ministry of Commerce and

Industries, there is scope for special emphasis on women entrepreneurs on duty drawbacks, as is done in some other schemes (e.g. GeM, ZED) of the government.

Technology

Currently, there are no schemes dedicated to supporting technology enhancements in enterprises run by women. Even in general (for women and men), there is a dearth of schemes focused on technology enhancement.

Schemes like 'MSME Technology Centres' and 'Digital MSME' can shape up better with certain components of the schemes giving higher weightage to benefits for women entrepreneurs. To begin with, this will serve a significant demonstration purpose across the country.

Ramp Impact

The Raising & Accelerating MSME Performance (RAMP) scheme is a World Bank-assisted Government of India programme that aims to improve the performance of MSMEs in India. This programme aims to support awareness generation and capability building, and hence is very useful for all MSMEs, especially women-owned ones that need even more of both interventions. The central RAMP committee should incentivize states that present proposals with higher allocations for women entrepreneurship.

For a public policy to be successful in any domain, including those directly or indirectly meant to boost women entrepreneurship, it must follow certain frameworks to increase the chances of its success in terms of larger number of beneficiaries among the target segment.

According to Prof. Dani Rodrik, Turkish economist and Ford Foundation Professor of International Political Economy at the John F. Kennedy School of Government of Harvard University, there are three key principles that every public policy should possess:

- Embeddedness
- Carrots & Sticks
- Accountability

Embeddedness

Governments often design a policy assuming they have complete information, but in reality, governments do not have complete information, and they design the policy based on the typical model of principal-agent problem. However, this approach takes information externality as it is. So, to tackle this problem, Rodrik proposes the principle of embeddedness, which concerns how close state-business relations should be with the private sector.

So, while designing policies for women entrepreneurs, women should play a key role and should be consulted in the policy formulation. Many rounds of discussion should be held with relevant stakeholders to avoid the problem of information externality. Though the private sector—women entrepreneurs in this case—can play a crucial role during the process, they should not be given complete autonomy. To ensure that the goals of society as a whole are met rather than those of 'involved' private entities, 'embedded autonomy' should be maintained, which affirms that the state should proactively collaborate with the private sector and non-governmental organizations. Simultaneously, however, it should resist being captured by such interests. Such embedded autonomy could be achieved by engaging with 'industry associations' as against individual enterprises.

A periodic, say quarterly, review of all extant policies and gaps therein can be discussed at a forum chaired by the Minister of Mico, Small & Medium Enterprises. Representatives from other relevant ministries like the Ministry of Skill Development and Entrepreneurship, Ministry of Social Justice and Ministry of Finance should also be involved for a 'whole of Government' approach.

Carrots & Sticks

In public policy, the expression 'Carrots & Sticks' refers to the combination of incentives (carrots) and discipline (sticks). This approach can be used to design a policy to influence more women to enter the entrepreneurial landscape by giving them some incentive to achieve the desired outcome. An example of such a strategy can be seen in policies like Zero Defect Zero Effect (ZED); the policy offers incentives in terms of financial assistance, support for hand-holding and consultancy, and achieving certain certification levels, through mandating MSMEs to meet compliance requirements. While there are carrots in terms of incentives, the sticks constitute the suspension of benefits if the certifications are not regularly renewed. In its design and communication, every policy should highlight the incentives and disincentives.

Accountability

The effectiveness of a policy depends not only on the incentives it offers but also on how well it is put into action. To gauge its success, systems need to be put in place for assessing how the policy implementation is carried out.

The government should predefine the mechanism to capture the impact in terms of the share of women beneficiaries. This can be captured through dashboards, like the CO-Win platform was designed to capture the count of the vaccinated population during the pandemic. If not on real-time basis, such dashboards should be updated at a daily, weekly or monthly frequency.

India should evaluate programmes from other countries for possible lessons. For example, Canada's 'Women Entrepreneurship Strategy Program' uses the 'whole of government' approach where 20 government departments have come together to support women entrepreneurs through one programme. Even in India, more than six ministries run parallel schemes where overlaps are studied for potential convergence, and monitoring mechanisms can be predefined and captured through a single dashboard which will stay constant throughout.

The NITI Aayog has put in effort to build a 'Women Entrepreneurship Platform' which has information about various government support schemes for women entrepreneurs, but it lacks updates on the impact of the schemes on a periodic basis.

CONCLUSION

This chapter records the significant gaps between women and men on dimensions of entrepreneurial activities. It highlights the key challenges faced by women using the 'Weiss (2015: 23), UNCTAD-Structural Transformation and Industrial Policy' framework on dimensions of Land, Labour, Capital, Product and Technology. It uses the same framework to take note of existing schemes and the need for either tweaking some of these schemes or introducing some new schemes on the dimensions of Land, Labour, Capital, Product and Technology.

The following facts and projections highlight that consideration of the recommendations in promoting women entrepreneurship needs to be a high priority as women entrepreneurship is a growth sector and it holds the potential to make pole-vaulting contributions to India's GDP.

- While women entrepreneurs represent less than 22% of total MSMEs registered, they have experienced a massive 75% growth in FY 21–22, as highlighted by the Minister of State for MSME in his address in the Parliament of India on 31 March 2022.
- Women-owned MSMEs have a lower base. However, it is set to grow 90% over the next five years.
- According to consulting firm BCG, women-founded

companies perform better. They can generate 10%[40] higher returns cumulatively over five years. Women-led enterprises employ three times more women and hence demonstrate more inclusivity.

- More women employment would contribute to more growth. India can potentially add $700 billion[41] to the GDP by 2025, as per a report by consulting firm McKinsey and Company.

---

[40]Abouzahr, K., Brooks Taplett, F., Krentz, M., & Harthorne, J. (n.d.), 'WHY WOMEN-OWNED STARTUPS ARE A BETTER BET', The Boston Consulting Group, 2018, https://tinyurl.com/mkn52jye. Accessed on 22 October 2024.

[41]Woetzel, J., A. Madgavkar, R. Gupta, J. Manyika, K. Ellingrud, & McKinsey & Company, 'THE POWER OF PARITY: ADVANCING WOMEN'S EQUALITY IN INDIA', November 2015, https://tinyurl.com/4yr3bmd8. Accessed on 22 October 2024.

8

WOMEN FOR EXCELLENCE: GREAT ENGAGEMENT IDEAS FROM CORPORATE WORKPLACES

Sushma Rajagopalan

Corporate veteran, entrepreneur and venture capitalist

On a cold wintry night in late November 2023, in Philadelphia, I attended a dinner hosted by a recruiting firm for about 12 very accomplished women. To begin with, I was apprehensive about attending it. But the evening turned out to be one of shared learnings, unprecedented openness and plain camaraderie. In short, fabulous, and I left looking forward to the next one in February 2024. There were CEOs, presidents, board members, CHROs, legal heads of some corporates that were household names in the United States. After nearly 30 years in leadership roles in global technology companies, if I could still feel exhilarated at spending a delightful evening in such stimulating company, and come away feeling enriched, I am certain that orchestrated efforts to provide such opportunities to engage women would help unlock their true potential.

Women need to engage with each other to ensure there is peer recognition and learning. Such engagements can happen over a lunch or a dinner, where emerging leaders are happy to share, learn and cheer. As Serena Williams rightly said, 'Every woman's success should be an inspiration to another. We're strongest when we cheer each other on.' While in my long career

I have had the opportunity to meet several highly accomplished women, the frequency of such meetings and the ability to form a bond with a few could be critical to another woman's quest for excellence. Mentorship is a conscious choice and must be woven into the DNA of a leader; it cannot be relegated to a casual 'it would be nice to do' or 'I'll do it when I have the time!'

For a leader, one of the most daunting tasks is spotting talent. Having done so, how do you help that talent grow? Various questions come to your mind: What is excellence? Is it consistence? Is it the ability to think ahead? Is it doing whatever is assigned to you to the best of your ability? Is it wanting more? Possibly all of the above, and more. When it comes to spotting talent in women, most leaders tend to ask themselves some of these rather stereotypical questions: Can they outperform men? Can they juggle their multiple roles efficiently? Do they feel the need to achieve? Leaders have to accept that most women have excellence in them, but the desire to achieve is hemmed in by many constraints and an excess of self-doubt: Will I be able to do more? What are the pitfalls of aiming high? Will aiming high professionally prevent me from being a wife, a mother, a daughter...the various roles I am expected to perform to perfection? By helping answer such questions, a leader can play a crucial role in promoting excellence. Mentoring women to overcome self-doubt is pivotal to their quest for self-realization and excellence.

To me, the ability to do whatever you do better than others, most of the time, is what qualifies as excellence. Knowing and honing your skills and expertise are key to success. The need to achieve higher standards must be complemented with eagerness and determination. This is where the trained eye of a leader helps. By knowing the difference between mere enthusiasm and well-channelled eagerness, combined with the requisite capability, a leader can help hone both the capability and the aspiration.

LESSONS IN SHAPING WOMEN'S CAREERS

I will share examples from my life to expand on the thoughts expressed thus far; I will also share some engagement models I have been a part of or have created. In some cases, for the sake of confidentiality, I will neither name the individual nor the organization.

One of my earliest experiences in helping shape a woman's career and bring excellence to the fore was decades ago. As part of the senior executive team of a fast-growing company, I was handling a global portfolio at a time when we used faxes and made telephone calls to communicate globally. Back then, there was no internet, no email. One had to physically visit countries and put in place business partnerships for sales and recruitment.

My executive assistant was an extremely capable woman with impeccable work ethic. A superfast learner, with attention to detail, she had a very pleasant way with people, even when she had to say no. She was clear she did not want to remain an executive assistant (so was I), but was not sure what else she could do. I was known for my unorthodox hiring methods, especially in finding ideal recruiters and people in sales roles. I turned technical people into very successful recruiters, and made people with HR credentials get into sales, and more. Instinctively, I knew she would make either a great global recruiter or a programme manager. When I broached her new role with her, of being part of the global recruiting team, and asked if she could go on a recruiting trip to the Philippines (or was it South Africa? I forget), her first reaction was, 'What?!! I have never travelled by plane to any city in the US, let alone to a new country.' This was quickly followed by, 'Will you be hiring someone else to do my job of supporting you, or can I do both?' I was expecting her to tell me she did not have the requisite 'technical know-how', and I was prepared to tell her how she could come up to speed on technology and that the company would put her through some training programmes. What I sensed instead was curiosity and excitement at the prospect of global travel and learning, coupled with a very high degree of fear. This is the first lesson I learnt while scouting for excellence.

Excellence in women is often latent and comes with a level of trepidation and fear of failure. As leaders, we need to understand that and provide some safety nets. I had no hesitation in committing that she could do both for a year before she decided. Since then, she made several trips overseas, including a few to Brazil. About five or six years ago, she was part of the hiring team of a very large company. I connected with her on this piece that I was writing and she wanted me to add the following: 'Your identification of my abilities and strengths enabled me to move forward confidently on a career path I had originally never imagined for myself. There's much to be said about having a job in which the strength of one's skill sets enables a fulfilling career where you feel you are making a positive impact. Through your confidence in me, and my own that I developed later in life, I felt empowered to create my own opportunities that aligned with my lifestyle. I think it's very important that people understand how confidence and feeling empowered unlock out-of-the-box opportunities for oneself. You enabled me to do exactly that!' Good leaders find a way to instil confidence in others.

The second biggest lesson I learnt was that excellence once spotted needed nurturing. Nurturing is not making concessions in performance, but enabling the highest level of performance. Engagement is key. Enabling one to perform to their fullest potential is an imperative. Many leaders know this intuitively, but few act on it due to the pressure of meeting financial targets and fulfilling other professional responsibilities.

I owe the third realization to a senior colleague, who had far more years of experience than me. He asked how I would unearth excellence in a systemic manner? My immediate response was, 'Excellence has to be in the organizational culture; it all starts with engagement.' Easier said than done but organizational culture was the only sustainable way to nurture excellence. I decided to focus on engaging with capable women, one or two people at a time, till such time I could shape the organizational culture.

REDEFINING ORGANIZATIONAL CULTURE

Much later in life, I did get a chance to shape an organization. I was transforming a traditional company into a digital company. As part of the transformation, I was keen on four initiatives: a) institutionalizing and building a culture of excellence and innovation, b) diversifying the management team—not just the executive team but the entire leadership team, c) increasing relevance and the competitive quotient, and lastly, d) growing and scaling the company to be a dominant player in the industry.

While I was deeply aware that implementing all four initiatives would be time-consuming, and that the first three would have a great bearing on the fourth, it was imperative to set the ball rolling. Balancing these initiatives while producing financial results is the challenge most leaders face, as I have mentioned earlier.

As a leader, we have to examine how to achieve growth and financial targets. Many leaders may argue over whether a culture of performance is synonymous with a culture of excellence. Unfortunately, that is not always the case. Initiating change is easier than sustaining it. Many a times, ambitious projects are launched but die a natural death before they are institutionalized. I wanted all my initiatives to survive me.

Innovation was easiest to set in motion through the creation of a digital lab that would experiment with new maturing technologies. The lab generated a lot of excitement; in the initial batch, no women volunteered. Again, the fear of raising their hand to be part of something experimental had to be acknowledged and changed. The need to nurture excellence (not just in women, but across the board) needs to start from the youngest echelons of an organization. The management team comprised mostly men, which was hardly unusual. I began scouring the organization for capable women. I shortlisted three: one was naturally very talented in technology and in a project delivery role (let us call her Ms T.); the other had a great flair for sales and was known for building great trust and rapport with clients in a sales support role (let us call her Ms S.); and the third was in strategic marketing (let us call her Ms M.). Ms S. had settled very comfortably into a sales support role. All three were ambitious and wanted to do more, but were very hesitant to take on profit and loss (P&L) responsibilities or sales targets. They had to get out of their comfort zones to let their capabilities and potential shine, and I had to help them do just that. I was determined to build excellent women leaders who could manage a P&L and enable them to aspire for the role of CEO or similar roles at the topmost level.

Sometimes, this took much convincing and yes, the assurance that they could have their earlier jobs back in case things did not work out in the new profile. At times, I did not promise the old job but promised something equivalent. Ms T. took on a practice head role with growth targets, and Ms S. moved to a global sales role. Initially, a large part of the management team was sceptical. But soon, a few of them (men) understood the need to promote more capable women and became their champions and started mentoring them.

Taking everyone (men and women) along in the journey of excellence is very important. Ms T. went on to become a successful business leader and Ms S. is a partner in one of the leading global consulting firms. Here are Ms T.'s words on her journey: 'Sushma, thank you for giving me an opportunity to reflect on my journey. Diversity and inclusion despite being much talked about, tend to remain more on paper. I am extremely glad to have witnessed the transformation you brought about in adopting diversity and inclusion. You walked the talk by implementing

"Systemic Processes" and by "Leading by Example". You paved the way for seven women to rise to influential roles. I must admit that it was both exhilarating and daunting to be picked to lead a significant portfolio. Fear of failure loomed large, but your guidance and support gave the required confidence and self-assurance. You did NOT throw us into the deep end. You created an environment where women could voice their opinions, share their perspectives and up their performance to outstanding levels. You had our backs, celebrating successes and offering mentorship when we needed it.

'One striking observation is the difference in how men and women approach leadership roles. Men dive into roles even when they are only 50% ready, whereas women hesitate! Under your leadership, we learned that true empowerment comes from support, encouragement, and the freedom to take risks and learn from them. You set a precedence for inclusive leadership that inspired many women throughout the organization to aim higher and achieve more.'

Ms M. was extremely competent and understood the business very well. She needed more visibility in the world outside, in the industry, to rise to the level of Chief Marketing Officer. I had to get her involved in trade bodies and industry bodies to represent the organization. I had to work very closely with her and accompany her to some of the meetings and make the connections for her. And in a few months, she was championing the organization with external stakeholders in an extremely responsible manner. Today she is Chief Marketing Officer of a growing technology company. 'Your belief that I could connect with industry leaders and represent the company well, helped me build a very good set of friends in the industry, that I am in touch with even today.'

Looking back, it took a lot of engagement to understand them as individuals, and not just the roles they performed professionally. My learning in this case was, 'Engagement is key.' Providing ongoing formal and informal coaching and feedback is vital. I formalized my engagement mechanism as 'Coffee & Conversations'. We had coffee and we chatted. I held at least two hour-long 'C&C' sessions each week, sometimes with just women and sometimes with teams across the globe. The rules of engagement were: a) They could ask me questions on any issue other than their salary, progression, promotion or politics! b) I could pose questions and sometimes initiate a discussion on an industry-relevant topic: Will AI replace your job? c) They could share interesting industry developments, especially in digital adoption. d) Everyone had to speak. The last was the toughest to do since most women preferred to listen than to speak.

After I had done about 25 of these sessions across the organization, C&Cs became very interesting. I then started inviting one of my senior leaders at every session, with the hope that they would incorporate C&C in their daily routine; most of my leaders did. C&C was on its way to being institutionalized. Institutionalizing such engagement mechanisms is key to building and sustaining a culture.

While the examples are anecdotal and perhaps even indicative of excellence being brought to the fore, and establishes that excellence does not always have to lead to a CEO's position, they do *not* talk about institutionalizing excellence or building a culture of excellence. More often than not, most leaders, even enlightened ones, do not build systemic processes to source and build excellence. Here are three things I would do to institutionalize excellence: a) At least once a week, meet a team of 20 people across the organization for an hour over a cup of coffee and discuss innovations in the industry. My secret mission was to scout for excellence, particularly excellence in women. b) Provide such individuals with the ability, the opportunity to experience various roles. c) Create opportunities and place women in leadership roles without being constrained by their years of experience or prior roles. I firmly hold the belief that while you can engage, bring capable women together for them to share and learn—nothing can substitute the actual learning on the job. Therefore, putting women in key positions and enabling them to succeed are paramount in my leadership book.

Many organizations rely on performance assessments to bring top performers to the fore. Is that enough? Why is it that only a few organizations have been able to create a culture of excellence? What does it take to systemically build an organization that believes in excellence and inclusion? Are Diversity, Equity & Inclusion (DEI) programmes effective? And even fewer organizations are able to sustain it over long periods of time and across multiple leaders. GE & Jack Welch's 4 Es of leadership—Energy, Energize, Edge & Execution—hold tremendous significance in the ability to build organizations that sustain over a longer term. The article published by Bloomberg—on 23 February 2024—on management shake-ups at Goldman and Boeing shows that the glass ceiling still exists, even at some of the best organizations. Creating a culture requires extreme clarity on what the fabric of the organization will be, based on what the organization values.

The **first step** in creating a culture is defining a set of shared values. It is interesting to read the values of popular companies. As CEO of a tech company, I used to read the values of every client of ours. Sometimes, values are not that clearly spelt out, but emerge in their strong mission statements. Nike was one of my favourites: 'Bring inspiration and innovation to every athlete* in the world'; the asterisk seems to indicate: 'If you have a body, you are an athlete.' Clearly Nike values and embodies innovation. Values have to align with the mission and vision of the organization.

Once the values are established, the **second step** is communicating these to the team, so everyone understands the values. My C&C sessions did that. A leader has to device ways and means to communicate effectively at various levels, one on one, one to many and many to one! Gamify communications as much as you can. In an earlier role as Chief Strategy Officer of a large technology company in India, I created a Brand Ambassador Program with Brand Champions to communicate the shift in strategy to an organization with over 10,000 employees in more than 10 countries. I picked 11 Brand Champions who in turn had to recruit 11 Brand Ambassadors each, who in turn had to talk to 100 employees each. Then there were Brand Evangelists who pitched in and helped the Brand Champions and the Brand Ambassadors. The Champions, Ambassadors and Evangelists were given prominent badges to arouse curiosity in others.

The **third step** is to ensure everyone has the same understanding of the values. Storytelling helps in this regard. In the Brand Ambassador Program, we held competitions on how to creatively communicate changes to a strategy. Apple does a good job of storytelling. If you look at the Career section on their website, they have quotes from various employees on shared values.

The **fourth step** is to ensure that we monitor and nurture the values and resultant organizational culture and make adjustments as necessary. Explicitly calling out Excellence, Innovation and Women's Empowerment in the rubric of organizational culture could be a fundamental building block for programmes like DEI.

What are the other methods of engagement? I polled several HR groups in the hope of unearthing some novel approaches. However, the most common answers were Executive Inclusion Programmes, Paid Maternity Leave, Career Development & Mentorship Programmes, certifications like Gender Equality European & International Standard (GEEIS). In India, one company—a subsidiary of a global leader in electrical and digital building infrastructure—had an interesting programme. Their core focus was creating awareness among women employees about role models and other senior women in the industry, and across industries, who had succeeded in male-dominated roles. They invited women leaders as speakers in a programmatic fashion, through panel discussions and digital communication.

What I liked even more was the fact that there were two simple objectives for this initiative: a) creating awareness and a network of women that one could reach out to, and b) building the belief that women could aspire to the highest level, and that getting there is possible. This is crucial—building the belief! Interacting with other successful women is a very effective way to overcome apprehensions and instil a sense of 'I can too'.

Nearly 50% of the best 100 companies for women's leadership development offer mentorship programmes. A few companies consider including women in succession planning initiatives. This is noteworthy and can have a positive impact in both assessing and ensuring that women climb the professional ladder too. Some organizations have development programmes like executive inclusion programmes that monitor the growth and inclusion of women, career development and mentorship programmes, and more. And yes, there are organizations that offer flexible benefits and maternity benefits to ensure women are not left behind. Several corporates offer special Employee Resource Groups (ERGs) to empower women. DocuSign is one such organization that has 3 ERGs for women, one for DocuSign Women, one for Solutions Excellence in Women, and another one for advancing women in Product Development. Walt Disney offers over 90 Business Resource Groups (BRGs), with some dedicated to women. What is somewhat disappointing is the number of companies that talk about a high participation of women on their boards but never follow through. Some countries mandate public companies to have women on their Boards, which is laudable in my opinion. While the overall percentage of women on companies' boards has risen and is currently between 25% and 30%, engaging and including women at all levels is an imperative. The story with which I started this piece, where a head-hunting firm is actively building a network of women at the highest levels to interact with, deserves a mention again in this context.

WOMEN ENTREPRENEURS AND WHAT THEY SEEK IN A MENTOR

Let us now look at the world of entrepreneurship, which in my experience is the ultimate leveller! Kindling and nurturing entrepreneurship in women are great ways to showcase excellence. I am absolutely convinced of this and have been committing a lot of time to it over the last five years. Globally, the number of start-ups led by women doubled to 20% from 2009 to 2019[1]. According to the Guidant report, in the US, the reasons and motivations for women to start their own businesses were: 58% wanted to be their own boss, 38% were dissatisfied by Corporate America, 30% were ready to pursue their passion, and 21% did it out of financial insecurity and because they did not want to retire. The reasons for men turning entrepreneurs may not be entirely different. However, women tend to be more solo entrepreneurs than men (82% vs 69%) and seek mentorship more than men[2].

I personally find mentoring selfless and highly enriching, especially mentoring women leaders and entrepreneurs who lead both for-profit and not-for-profit ventures. There was a conspicuous absence of women mentors in my life, but I was lucky to have had a couple of male colleagues/bosses who were fantastic. I firmly believe that women should have both men and women as mentors. I am an active mentor with Harvard i-Labs and Philadelphia Alliance for Capital & Technologies (PACT). While with i-Labs I am a solo mentor to the entrepreneur, at PACT we are a team of mentors, usually no more than three. Usually, I am the only woman in the team of mentors. Co-mentoring with men is extremely rewarding as you gain from their diverse perspectives.

---

[1]STATISTA, Financial Services, 'Proportion of startups worldwide with at least one female founder between 2009 and 2019', https://tinyurl.com/3t79n7e3. Accessed on 27 August 2024.

[2]Guidant Report, '2024 Small Business Trends: A Look at the State of Small Businesses 2024', https://tinyurl.com/286xnc78. Accessed on 27 August 2024.

I am currently mentoring three women-led companies—two in India and one in the US. I started mentoring Where are India's Children (WAIC), an organization in India that helps shed light on children in various adoption centres through technology. Imagine children spending their entire childhood in a shelter, despite having the opportunity to join a loving family, simply because child protection authorities failed to evaluate them for adoption. This heart-breaking scenario prompted the formation of WAIC by three passionate adoptive mothers, who held senior positions in the industry. They gave up those jobs to pursue their mission 'to address the challenge of eligible children living in shelters not entering the legal adoption pool and finding their forever families.'

WAIC devised a technology solution that enabled their social workers to systematically visit every child shelter in a district and digitize every child's data. The solution incorporates a sophisticated rule engine that identifies children suitable for adoption evaluation. Once identified, WAIC's dedicated team collaborates with local authorities to bring these children into the legal adoption pool, maintained by the Central Adoption Resource Authority (CARA), where they can be matched with prospective parents.

Let us meet these extraordinarily capable women driven by a laudable mission, and understand what they seek in a mentor and what they have gained.

Prior to her role in the non-profit sector, Meera Marthi, CEO and Co-founder of WAIC, was in the IT industry, working with corporates such as Oracle Corporation in the US and Apps Associates in India. Drawing from her diverse expertise, Meera is also a coach certified by the International Coach Federation (ICF), specializing in Parenting and Adoption Coaching. Meera resides in Hyderabad, India, with her husband and two children.

Protima Sharma, CHRO and Co-founder of WAIC, is an alumna of the Indian Institute of Science (IISc), Bengaluru, and an expert HR professional. Having worked with corporates like Tata Consultancy Services (TCS) and Thermax, Protima brings her experience on organizational policies, mentorship, and organizational development to WAIC. Protima lives in Pune, India, with her husband and two daughters.

Smriti Gupta, Co-founder of WAIC, is an alumna of Indian School of Business (ISB, Hyderabad) and Carnegie Mellon University. Smriti served as CEO of WAIC for three years. She has worked in corporates like eBay and PayPal and continues to support WAIC in their fundraising and communications strategy. A resident of Pune, India, Smriti presently lives in the US with her husband and two daughters.

This is what they had to say about mentorship in general, and how it helped them think differently: 'One of the main things mentors provide is the feeling that someone cares about our success. Mentors also provide a safe space for us to talk to them about our toughest challenges and vulnerabilities. Even if a mentor cannot solve everything, we know that they will do their best. The knowledge they bring to the table is an invaluable asset.' Specific to my mentorship, this is what they had to say: 'With her extensive corporate background, Sushma provides invaluable insights across various facets, including long-term vision and scale, fundraising strategies, communication tactics, and forming partnerships and alliances. Under her guidance, our organization has begun to reevaluate our approach to corpus funds and our positioning within the government as an integral component of the adoption ecosystem.' One of the cardinal principles of a mentor is to enable mentees to up their game and perform at their highest potential by providing well-researched perspectives, encouragement, and by understanding their needs.

Avishkaar is an organization that makes teaching math and science fun. Started in 2014, Avishkaar is a centre where motivated teachers and young thinkers find a platform to discover the creative, curious and critical thinking side of themselves while exploring the world of math and science. Their goal is to make high-quality STEM education accessible to all. Founder Director & CEO Sandhya Gupta completed her doctorate in Electrical Engineering from Iowa State University, USA, and worked in advanced high-technology research for several years before moving to India and starting Avishkaar.

Prapti Bhasin is COO at Avishkaar. For the last eight years, she has been an educator. In fact, she started her journey as a teacher, and was mentored by Avishkaar.

Here is what Sandhya and Prapti had to say about mentoring: 'Our mentors have believed in us and in our work. That has enabled us to do more. They have been co-walkers in our journey—instead of offering direct solutions, they have always brainstormed with us on challenges, ensuring we expand our thinking. Through constructive feedback and reflective conversations, that are very explicit and not vague at all, they have helped us see things from different angles and pushed us to re-think our approach when necessary. Beyond professional development, mentors have helped us develop self-awareness—very essential for managing the organization. The way they have mentored us has also actually enabled us to mentor our team members further. It is like the butterfly effect.'

I will reproduce the well-known saying by renowned American poet James Russel Lowell, that my mother (my lifelong mentor and champion) often quoted to me: 'As one lamp lights another, nor grows any less, so nobleness enkindleth nobleness.'[3]

My third example is HeyKiddo, a young company in the US. HeyKiddo is a technology company dedicated to reversing childhood mental health crisis by giving parenting adults the tools they need to support their children's mental, social and emotional health at home. Their app, powered by a team of

[3]Laxman, Navaratna, 'As one lamp lights another', *Deccan Herald*, 24 February 2021, https://tinyurl.com/3tuve3y2. Accessed on 27 August 2024.

psychologists in combination with ethical AI, helps parenting adults anticipate, detect, address and prevent emotional health struggles in their children, and helps them understand when to seek professional help.

The founder, Dr Nicole Lipkin, is a clinical and organizational psychologist, with over 20 years of experience in the industry. She founded HeyKiddo because of her firm conviction that we cannot continue to outsource our children's mental, social and emotional health to therapists and schools. We must focus on the third part of the trifecta, which is giving parenting adults the tools and insight they need to help support their children, including recognizing the dynamic that they play in their children's mental well-being. Their technology is designed not to replace therapists at all but rather to build awareness, provide individualized tools that are unique to each family to help create positive and healthy support and communication, and fuel early intervention by helping parenting adults be more in tune with what is going on with their children, and know when to seek help.

Prior to starting HeyKiddo, Nicole had built and scaled service companies, so she figured she knew what she was doing. She realized quickly that she did not, and that founding a technology start-up was a completely different beast. It was, in fact, a truly humbling experience. Says Nicole, 'I knew that I needed to seek out mentors to challenge and guide me in my thinking. My mentors have literally shifted the way I think about business, money, people, and impact. There is no way I would be where I am today without my mentors. The guidance and tough love around navigating equity discussions, business structure, what I should focus on, and more importantly, on what I should not, has been absolutely invaluable. My only hope is that when the time comes, I can help other founders the way my mentors have helped me.'

When I asked her about the tough love comment, she said: 'Sushma, that comment referred to you. I think you have given me the most tough love (and I mean that with love back). You are my only female mentor at this point and you have pushed me in a very different way than my other mentors have. I'm not sure if this makes sense but you haven't accepted my fall-back, typical style of leading with an eye toward empathy for my people. It's not that you haven't supported that but you have pushed me when it was getting in my way or blinding me from making the right decisions for the business. You've stepped in when you have felt I'm getting in my own way or making excuses and really just have directly called me out for it so I can make the change in thinking and make it fast. You've also been the one to coach me/mentor me on not downplaying my talents and my experience and to speak with more confidence (versus always taking the humble approach). That's what I mean about tough love. You haven't let me get away with typical "female founder" stuff. You haven't let me get in my own way.'

The art of mentoring is being able to guide entrepreneurs and leaders through tough decision-making that results in success and excellence, while being supportive. That is what Nicole calls 'tough love'! I am sure the journeys of the various women woven throughout this piece will inspire most of you and help you in your leadership or entrepreneurial journeys.

Through these accounts, an effort has been made to establish how mentorship and other engagement methods are integral to a woman's career; how they boost confidence and help women overcome their apprehensions and level the playing field. In today's collaborative and dynamic world, women have a natural advantage in using their participative and transformative styles of leadership to lead and win. I would like to end with the words of Steven Spielberg: 'The delicate balance of mentoring someone is not creating them in your own image, but giving them the opportunity to create themselves.'[4]

---

[4]Spielberg, Steven, BrainyQuote, https://tinyurl.com/yeuk8nr4. Accessed on 27 August 2024.

9

TRANSLATING GENDER EQUITY FROM POLICY TO ACTION

Pooja Sharma Goyal
Founding CEO, The Udaiti Foundation

One of the great paradoxes in India today is that even as women have become more educated, and metrics like maternal health have improved, their participation in the workforce has plateaued, in spite of the country's rapid economic growth and a lot of noise in the media about the contribution of women. The economic case for women's participation in the workforce has been well established, and there is enough and more evidence pointing to the fact that increasing women's employment rate is the critical missing piece in India's engine of economic growth. Then why, after 76 years of Independence, do we still need to run awareness campaigns about saving daughters and educating them (*Beti bachao, beti padhao*)?

Citizens of the country, regardless of their ideological differences or views about women, want India to become a high-income country with a better quality of life. The Indian government has set a target of achieving developed nation status by 2047, and of becoming a 10 trillion-dollar economy, the 3rd biggest in the world, by 2030[1]. In order to do that, we have to

---

[1] Press Information Bureau, Government of India, Ministry of Commerce and Industry, 'India on track to become $35 trillion, fully developed economy by 2047: Shri Piyush Goyal', 19 February 2024, https://tinyurl.com/mrxae7yc. Accessed on 5 August 2024

grow consistently at 8%–9% annually, at least 1%–2% higher than what we are achieving right now even as we are celebrated as the fastest-growing economy in the world. This projection has been arrived at on the basis of an article published in *Business Today*, January 2024.

How will we get there? There are many schools of thought on how we will make up the difference. Should we focus on manufacturing or services? Should we invest in semiconductors or AI? A lever that has the potential to accelerate this growth regardless of those choices is a resource staring us in the face but one that we are not able to use—471 million working-age women—an estimate arrived at by the author based on Census 2011 data. The global female labour force participation rate (FLFPR) is 53.4% compared to 80% for men. In India, participation rate for men in the economy is almost 80%, but for women it is 37%.[2] Imagine the value we can unleash by taking this 37% to 50% in the next decade. Numerous studies have shown that achieving gender parity can significantly boost the economic growth of a country.[3] In India, we are talking about Nari Shakti, Sashakt Nari, Sashakt Bharat, which are great signalling mechanisms, and the time is ripe for sustained action to systematically dismantle barriers in female labour force participation, and achieve our development goals.

The good news is that India today has all the key elements in place—progressive economic reforms and policies, a large demographic dividend, digital public infrastructure and, more importantly, a talented pool of employable women willing and eager to enter the workforce. The India Skills Report 2023 found

[2]NSSO, Ministry of Statistics and Programme Implementation, Ministry of Statistics and Programme Implementation, 'KEY EMPLOYMENT UNEMPLOYMENT INDICATORS FOR JANUARY 2023-DECEMBER 2023', https://tinyurl.com/2ne6k87y. Accessed on 5 August 2024.
[3]Bertay, A.C., et al., 'Gender Inequality and Economic Growth: Evidence from Industry-Level Data', 3 July 2020, https://tinyurl.com/5hxtfbf2. Accessed on 5 August 2024.

that India has a higher percentage of employable women than men, even as employers struggle to find employable talent.[4] The report, along with the qualitative pulse of women in general, acts as solid evidence that we have been fighting with one hand tied behind our backs all this while.

What explains this apathy to our own best interests? A shallow answer is 'patriarchy.' While that is valid, social norms and roles do not develop in a vacuum, nor do they change in one. It is critical to analyse what variables they are connected to, the preceding conditions that need to be tackled, and how we can collaborate to chip away at entrenched norms and biases.

DEEP DIVE

In 2023, the Nobel Prize for Economics was awarded to an American economic historian, a labour economist, and a professor at Harvard University, Claudia Goldin. In what has come to be known as one of the most ground-breaking and substantial thesis on women and work, the Nobel went to Goldin for her U-shaped curve theory that has suggested that countries in the early stages of their economic development tend to have higher labour force participation by women due to household necessity, particularly when they are employed in the agricultural sector where labour is necessary and hard to afford.[5] As the country progresses to middle stages of economic development, this participation drops as family incomes rise, and social norms celebrate women staying at home as a mark of prosperity and status. The curve rises again when a country is in advanced stages of economic development, as women get higher education, find good opportunities in a growing services sector, and become part of dual-income households, all

[4]Confederation of India Industry (CII), 'India Skills Report 2023', 7 May 2023, https://tinyurl.com/4px9uznw. Accessed on 5 August 2024.
[5]Goldin, Claudia, 'Hours Flexibility and the Gender Gap in Pay', Center for American Progress, April 2015, https://tinyurl.com/5n6ujcwm. Accessed on 5 August 2024.

of which contribute to evolving social norms.

Goldin, after sifting through the archives and gathering over 200 years of data from the US, demonstrated how and why gender differences in earnings and employment rates have changed over time. In doing so, she has provided the first comprehensive account of women's earnings and labour market participation through the centuries, and has been able to collate and reveal the causes of change, as well as the main sources of the remaining gender gap[6]. What is even more exceptional is that the patterns discovered by Goldin may be used and exploited to understand trends in other countries including our own.

Given that India is in the middle stage of economic development, this research raises an interesting question about increases in women's participation in the labour force seen in the last few years. Could we be going through a similar U-curve phenomenon in India's FLFPR as the Indian economy grows?

There are two scenarios here. In the first, if we proceed with the general idea that our economy will also follow a similar curve as the United States's, then we have our work chalked out for us. At the most primary level, we need a way to travel up the U curve faster. However, there is a second scene wherein we cannot assume that this will happen automatically, as there is a real risk of falling into the middle-income trap as a country, a phenomenon where developing countries reach a certain level of income through low-cost advantages, but fail to move further ahead as that advantage disappears and lack of core technological advantages hold them back.[7]

---

[6]The Nobel Prize, 'The Royal Swedish Academy of Sciences has decided to award the Sveriges Riksbank Prize in Economic Sciences in Memory of Alfred Nobel 2023 to Claudia Goldin, Harvard University, Cambridge, MA, USA, for having advanced our understanding of women's labour market outcomes', 9 October 2023, https://tinyurl.com/msm562d2. Accessed on 5 August 2024.

[7]Zhou, S., & A. Hu, 'What Is the "Middle Income Trap"?', in *China: Surpassing the 'Middle Income Trap'*, *Contemporary China Studies*, Palgrave Macmillan, Singapore, 2021, https://tinyurl.com/j99jtb8k. Accessed on 27 August 2024.

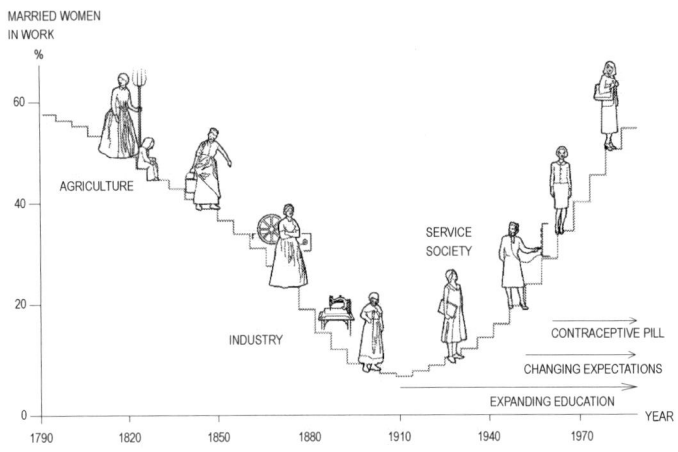

Women in Workforce

Source: The Nobel Prize Website[8]

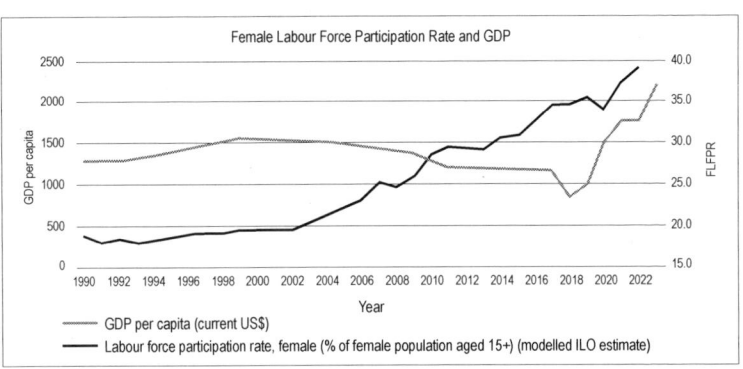

We can see promising signs in some demographic segments and sectors like IT and consumer services, where the percentage of women in workplaces is growing. The trillion-dollar question is how do we achieve progress at scale across the country, sectors

---

[8]Claudia Goldin – Prize presentation, NobelPrize.org, Nobel Prize Outreach AB 2024, 27 August 2024, https://tinyurl.com/4hrk4an8. Accessed on 27 August 2024.

and social classes. For this, we propose three key solutions that have the potential for large-scale impact and are doable—addressing demand-side barriers to women's employment in workplaces, enhancing compliance with existing policies, and lastly, but most crucially, taking into account the role of the care economy as an engine for growth

DEMAND BARRIER

Historically it has been observed across the world that once you create demand for jobs, supply-side issues get addressed faster.[9] In the Indian context, national-level survey data has consistently shown that Indian women are willing to work, provided the work is available at or near their homes.[10] The other important finding from other countries is that women transition in and out of the workforce many more times than men.[11] As such, if we are serious about retaining and bringing more women into the workforce, then we must redesign workspaces which have been curated primarily by men and with men as workforce in mind. We must systematically dismantle demand-side barriers like lack of flexibility, occupational segregation, unconscious biases in hiring and advancement, unwelcoming monocultures, and lack of paths for return to work after career breaks.

Given that the private sector plays a key role in creating quality

[9]Deshpande, Ashwini, & Jitendra Singh, 'Dropping Out, Being Pushed Out or Can't Get in? Decoding Declining Labour Force Participation of Indian Women', Social Science Research Network (SSRN), IZA Institute of Labour Economics, IZA Discussion Paper No. 14693, 17 August 2021, https://tinyurl.com/y48c9e7k. Accessed on 27 August 2024.
[10]Deshpande, Ashwini, & Naila Kabeer, 'Norms that matter: Exploring the distribution of women's work between income generation, expenditure-saving, and unpaid domestic responsibilities in India', WIDER Working Paper Series, wp-2021–130, World Institute for Development Economic Research (UNU-WIDER), 2021, https://tinyurl.com/jcm28pyn. Accessed on 27 August 2024.
[11]World Economic Forum, *Global Gender Gap Report 2023*, 20 June 2023, https://tinyurl.com/t8hh5rs6. Accessed on 27 August 2024.

jobs and is viewed as an engine of economic growth, addressing demand-side barriers in private sector organizations can have an outsized impact on improving women's participation in the workforce as a whole. The good news is that rich data is now available to track and measure the progress of gender diversity in Indian workplaces, especially in listed companies. The mandatory Business Responsibility & Sustainability Reporting (BRSR) with gender metrics for NSE-listed companies enables the capture and sharing of employment data from a gender lens. The 'Close the Gender Gap' data portal by The Udaiti Foundation enables granular analysis by industry and company size, revealing sectoral variations.[12] While IT shows the most substantial improvement in women's representation, sectors like automobiles and construction remain largely inaccessible to women.

What gets measured gets done. Now that we have the data, it is possible to dig deeper and build some actionable insights to address these demand-side barriers. Seventy-three per cent of hiring managers in 'The Women in India Inc.' survey report by The Udaiti Foundation reported that their organizations had set gender diversity goals, but only 21% reported having internal corporate strategies in place to implement these goals.

Based on the survey and subsequent analysis, we can break down demand-side barriers into four distinct categories, namely, hiring, retention, advancement, and return to work. Leading organizations across sectors are making noteworthy efforts to foster gender-inclusive workplaces. For instance, Godrej Industries[13] and Mahindra & Mahindra[14] have adopted holistic approaches covering the entire employee life cycle,

---

[12]The Udaiti Foundation, Close the Gender Gap, https://tinyurl.com/yt4ffr4p. Accessed on 27 August 2024.
[13]Godrej Industries Limited, *Annual Report 2023*, https://tinyurl.com/mr657jc7. Accessed on 27 August 2024.
[14]Mahindra & Mahindra Ltd, *Integrated Annual Report 2023-24*, https://tinyurl.com/2rsfs8rp. Accessed on 27 August 2024.

from recruitment to leadership development and facilitating smooth career re-entry. They have implemented targeted hiring efforts, extended maternity benefits, flexible work arrangements, and supportive employee networks. In the tech industry, HCL Technologies[15] has established comprehensive employee assistance programmes and flexible work policies that enable better work-life integration for all. Such company policies present to us an amalgamation of intent and practice. Upon further reflection and research, we can identify the main reasons for the success of the above-stated programmes. Three key critical success factors are common to all programmes that are showing results in their journey from intent to practice. These are the roles of explicit leadership commitment, measuring intermediate outcomes and celebrating progress, and public disclosure to stay honest to the commitment. These listed factors find their common point of origin in the overhauling of office structures and policy designs.

INTENTIONS MATTER

The importance of intentional design in creating gender-inclusive workplaces cannot be overstated. Successful companies critically examine every aspect of their employee life cycle, from attraction and recruitment to development and advancement, to identifying and addressing potential barriers. This requires a data-driven approach, leveraging insights from employee feedback, exit interviews, and industry benchmarks to pinpoint areas for improvement. For example, Delhivery's emphasis on gender-neutral job descriptions and diverse interview panels have fostered a significantly more inclusive recruitment process.[16]

---

[15]HCL Technologies Ltd, *Annual Report 2023-24*, https://tinyurl.com/2yh3v92d. Accessed on 27 August 2024.
[16]Delhivery, *Annual Report 2022–23*, https://tinyurl.com/5xptchb6. Accessed on 27 August 2024.

Several companies have implemented inclusive hiring processes for women in the workplace. Dr. Reddy's Laboratories engages in bench hiring, focused on identifying and nurturing talent within the organization, particularly at levels below the positions that need to be filled, with the aim of promoting qualified women to higher positions over time.[17] Sony Pictures Networks India has implemented Unconscious Bias training programmes to support the hiring and advancement of women, along with offering a 2X reward for diverse (women) referrals.[18] Hindustan Unilever Limited launched the global campaign Unstereotype to challenge gender stereotypes, accompanied by gender-neutral job postings and unconscious bias training for hiring managers.[19] Federal Bank introduced the FedRecruit Solution, an AI-enabled platform designed to eliminate any unconscious bias in hiring.[20]

On the other hand, another facet of policies that helps change are flexible work policies. These are critical to retaining women as traditional work schedules actively clash with care and family responsibilities. Options for compressed workweeks, part-time work, or flexible start-and-finish times enable women to balance these demands more effectively.[21] Normalizing access to flexible work arrangements for both men and women also combats the 'Mommy Track' stigma that women normally bear as

---

[17]Dr. Reddy's Laboratories Limited, 2022, *Integrated Annual Report 2022-23*, https://tinyurl.com/yucdtcye. Accessed on 27 August 2024.

[18]Sony, *Sustainability Report 2022*, https://tinyurl.com/59pyfm6w. Accessed on 27 August 2024.

[19]Hindustan Unilever Limited, *Annual Report 2022-23*, https://tinyurl.com/342jad82. Accessed on 27 August 2024.

[20]Saraswathy, M., 'How Federal Bank is Using Artificial Intelligence to Hire', *Moneycontrol*, 17 February 2020, https://tinyurl.com/bdd49669. Accessed on 27 August 2024.

[21]Chung, H., & C. Booker, 'Flexible Working and the Division of Housework and Childcare: Examining Divisions across Arrangement and Occupational Lines', *Work, Employment and Society*, 37 (1), 236–256, 4 August 2022, https://tinyurl.com/2ds85s3w. Accessed on 27 August 2024.

a burden.[22] The Covid-19 pandemic has accelerated the adoption of flexible work arrangements, with many Indian companies now offering greater flexibility in location, hours and workdays. IT giants like TCS[23] and Infosys[24] have been at the forefront of this shift, recognizing the benefits for both women and the broader workforce. Innovative policies like Zomato's period leave and HUL's Career by Choice programme for women returning from maternity breaks further underscore the potential of tailored initiatives to foster inclusion.

Several companies have implemented gender diversity initiatives to retain women employees and support them through different stages of their careers. Vodafone Idea has introduced the Maternity Signature Experience Program, which provides counselling support and accompanied travel until the child reaches two years of age, resulting in a 9% retention rate of women post maternity leave.[25] Novartis offers six months of parental leave, followed by flexible working options, six months of adoption leave, and reduced working hours for pregnant associates and nursing mothers.[26] HCL Technologies' 'Momtastic' initiative, launched by their Diversity, Equity & Inclusion (DEI) team, supports female employees transitioning to motherhood with carefully curated toolkits, insurance benefits, safe spaces for conversations with other moms, and buddy programmes to assist new mothers with a

[22]Sharma, R., & S. Dhir, 'An Exploratory Study of Challenges Faced by Working Mothers in India and Their Expectations from Organizations', *Global Business Review*, 23 (1), 192–204, 2022, https://tinyurl.com/yuy2p2fj. Accessed on 27 August 2024.

[23]Tata Consultancy Services, *Innovate; Adapt; Thrive: Integrated Annual Report 2022-23*, https://tinyurl.com/3nzjvy8k. Accessed on 27 August 2024.

[24]Infosys, *Navigating Change, Integrated Annual Report 2022-23*, https://tinyurl.com/2azb54js. Accessed on 27 August 2024.

[25]Vodafone Group Plc, *Annual Report 2023*, https://tinyurl.com/28xy95vh. Accessed on 27 August 2024.

[26]'Novartis Announces 26 week gender-neutral parental leave', *The Economic Times*, 1 July 2019, https://tinyurl.com/2a4yzkj5. Accessed on 27 August 2024.

smooth transition back to work.[27] Mastercard India's India Women Returnship Program aims to rehire women employees who have taken a career break, and the Mastercard India Alumni network reconnects with former colleagues, facilitating their return to the organization.[28] Abbott offers the Happy Feet programme, which provides pre- and post-maternity support, and the Second Career Engagement programme (ASCENT), which creates opportunities for women returning from career breaks.[29]

In addition to policies, human interventions also act as a major profit corner for women empowerment in the workplaces. Mentoring programme, sponsorship opportunities, and tailored leadership-development interventions are crucial to building a robust pipeline of women leaders and providing the necessary scaffolding as they balance career progression with family demands. Advocacy and sponsorship programmes go a long way in career acceleration through access to high-profile projects, leadership exposure, and opportunities for stretch assignments. Equally important is creating forums for networking opportunities, open dialogue and sharing of experiences, to build a sense of community and solidarity among women employees.

Several companies have launched gender diversity advancement programmes to support the career growth and leadership development of women within their organizations. Infosys offers the Women in Management (WIM) programme, an immersive, three-day residential workshop focused on building competencies in self-management, team dynamics, client relations, and business acumen. Additionally, their Women in Executive

---

[27]HCL Technologies Ltd, *Annual Report 2023-24*, https://tinyurl.com/2yh3v92d. Accessed on 27 August 2024.

[28]Hares, Sophie, 'As more women leave the workforce, this is a way back in', Mastercard Newsroom, 26 October 2020, https://tinyurl.com/yck7w2rc. Accessed on 27 August 2024.

[29]Abott, *Annual Report 2023*, https://tinyurl.com/f9534d8c. Accessed on 27 August 2024.

Leadership (WIEL) programme is designed to strengthen women in the leadership talent pipeline.[30] Moody's has introduced the TIDE programme, a nine-month career development initiative aimed at advancing careers of women. They also offer the Senior Women's Leadership Development Program, which brings together senior female employees for mentorship, coaching, training, and networking opportunities.[31] Genpact's Women's Leadership Program (WLP), developed in collaboration with Harvard Business Publishing, is tailored for women leaders at the Assistant Vice President level. Graduates of the programme are then placed on a fast-tracked career path.[32] Nestle runs the Nestle Women's Empowerment Program, which includes training and development programmes, mentorship, and networking opportunities. Their Nestle Women's Leadership Program focuses on developing leadership skills of high-potential women employees to help them advance to senior positions.[33] Abbott's Women Leaders of Abbott (WLA) platform is dedicated to attracting, retaining and advancing women within the organization. Additionally, their Wo-Mentoring programme is designed to accelerate the professional development of female colleagues.[34]

While the above examples are truly motivating and defeat the patriarchal rhetoric, to truly move the needle, we need a multi-stakeholder, data-driven approach. Collaboration between industry bodies, corporate leaders, and civil society is essential to

---

[30]Infosys, *Navigating Change, Integrated Annual Report 2022-23*, https://tinyurl.com/2azb54js. Accessed on 27 August 2024.

[31]Moody's, *Annual Report 2023*, https://tinyurl.com/ye8vu89h. Accessed on 27 August 2024.

[32]Genpact, *Sustainability Report 2022*, https://tinyurl.com/y27mz93v. Accessed on 27 August 2024.

[33]Nestle, *Creating Shared Value and Sustainability Record 2022: Advancing regenerative food system at scale*, https://tinyurl.com/mvuhpxyu. Accessed on 27 August 2024.

[34]Abott, *Annual Report 2023*, op. cit., https://tinyurl.com/f9534d8c. Accessed on 27 August 2024.

redesign workplaces with women's needs in mind. By dismantling demand-side barriers and creating enabling ecosystems, we can tap into the vast potential of India's female workforce and propel the nation towards its ambitious development goals. The impact of such efforts cannot be overstated—not only will they contribute to India's economic growth and development, but they will also create a more inclusive and equitable society.

While addressing demand-side barriers is crucial, it is equally important to ensure compliance with existing policies and regulations aimed at promoting gender equity and inclusive growth.

AN END AND A START

As per the State of Discrimination Report, 2022, by Prosperiti, India has over 53 laws which legalize gender-based discrimination at work.[35] In most states, women are not allowed to work as late at night as men, work in jobs that are deemed hazardous, work in jobs deemed morally inappropriate such as selling liquor, or even lift heavy objects. As a result of this discrimination, women do not get opportunities to learn high-growth skills with earning potential, limiting employment options. This is an opportunity to create a level-playing field by addressing laws that have outlived their utility.

The other area to address is policies which are progressive in intent but have unintended consequences when implemented. The Maternity Benefit (Amended) Act, 2017, a commendable step forward, enhances maternity leave to 26 weeks for two children and requires larger companies to provide crèches.[36] However,

---

[35]Anand, Bhuvnana, & Sarvipun Kaur, 2022, 'State of Discrimination Report: Sub-national comparison of legal barriers to women's right to choose work in India', Trayas Foundation, March 2022, https://tinyurl.com/3wczfpab. Accessed on 27 August 2024.
[36]The Gazette of India, Ministry of Law and Justice, 'The Maternity Benefit (Amendment) Act, 2017', 27 March 2017, https://tinyurl.com/3f8shsbn.

the financial burden needs to be borne by the organization. As such, the unintended consequence of this policy has been that subtle discrimination against women, especially married, now begins at the hiring stage in organizations.

A welcome move by the government has been the effort to increase transparency in reporting of gender metrics in the private sector. The Securities and Exchange Board of India's (SEBI) introduction of BRSR for the National Stock Exchange- (NSE-) listed companies is a great step in the direction of improving transparency and accountability in gender metrics. The Women on Boards directive has been a positive step towards gender diversity in Indian corporate leadership.[37] While progress has been made, further efforts are needed to achieve a more balanced representation and ensure women hold positions of greater influence within boards.

When it comes to entrepreneurship, India has implemented a number of programmes to support women entrepreneurs:

- Mahila Samridhi Yojana by SIDBI is a microfinance scheme which provides financial assistance up to ₹140,000 for women.[38]
- Mudra Yojana provides loans ranging from ₹50,000 to ₹10 lakh to women entrepreneurs for setting up or expanding micro or small enterprises.[39]
- Stand-Up India scheme facilitates bank loans up to ₹1 crore for one woman entrepreneur per bank branch.[40]

Accessed on 27 August 2024.

[37]Vohra, Neharika, "Women on Boards in India: Number, Composition, Experiences and Inclusion of Directors', Indian Institute of Management (IIM) & Federation of Indian Chambers of Commerce and Industry (FICCI), 2020, https://tinyurl.com/2ej58jwx. Accessed on 27 August 2024.

[38]Myscheme, Ministry of Social Justice and Empowerment, 'Mahila Samriddhi Yojana', https://tinyurl.com/3hx3tjmm. Accessed on 27 August 2024.

[39]Myscheme, Ministry of Finance, 'Pradhan Mantri Mudra Yojana', https://tinyurl.com/2tcme7fn . Accessed on 27 August 2024.

[40]Government of India; StandUp India; Mudra: A SIDBI Subsidary; Small

- Credit Guarantee Trust for Micro and Small Enterprises (CGTMSE) offers a discounted rate to women entrepreneurs.[41]

Two big challenges stand in the way of women availing these benefits. One is awareness—most women are not even aware of the benefits available to them due to information gap; second is ground implementation challenges. Many of these schemes are plagued by bottlenecks like collateral requirements, complex procedures, no credit history or digital footprints for women.

Collaborative efforts between the government, private sector, and civil society are crucial in addressing practical challenges of policy implementation, and improving adherence. By working together, these stakeholders can identify bottlenecks, share best practices, and develop innovative solutions tailored to the unique needs of different sectors and business sizes. Civil society organizations play a vital role in raising awareness, monitoring progress, and advocating for policy refinements based on on-the-ground realities. Such multi-stakeholder partnerships can create a more conducive ecosystem for gender equity, ensuring that progressive policies translate into tangible outcomes for women in the workforce.

US, AND THEM

While further policy changes, such as financial support and subsidies for MSMEs that maintain gender parity, could be beneficial, our focus should first be on refining the implementation of existing measures. Encouragingly, the government has shown openness to feedback and willingness to adapt, but we need more stakeholders to play a part in this.

Industries Development Bank of India (SIDBI); National Credit Guarantee Trustee Company Limited (NCGTS); Indian Banks' Association; https://tinyurl.com/4du6y6ep. Accessed on 27 August 2024.
[41]Credit Guarantee Fund Trust for Micro and Small Enterprises (CGTMSE), https://tinyurl.com/bdf48w7p. Accessed on 27 August 2024.

As citizens and members of the private sector, we have a role to play in this transformation. Rather than waiting passively for policy action, we can advocate for and initiate changes within our spheres of influence. Given the country's vast population and diversity, the approach of small, incremental changes with the potential for broader societal impact is a pragmatic strategy.

To navigate these challenges, interventions can be categorized into four areas:

- Well-designed but poorly implemented policies
- Well-designed policies with viable methods but lacking compliance
- Policies with design flaws leading to counterproductive effects
- Areas where policies are absent

The government has laid a progressive foundation with policies aimed at supporting women in the workforce; we now need collaborative effort on the part of industry bodies, corporate leaders, organizations and civil society to move the needle on the ground. There is a need to develop a true care economy in the country in the next few years.

CARE ECONOMY AS ENGINE OF GROWTH

A 2023 study done by a group of academics from the London School of Economics (LSE) and Princeton University measured the motherhood penalty in 134 countries, by comparing the careers of mothers and fathers with and without children.[42] They found that 24% of women leave the labour force in the first year, and 15% are still absent 10 years later. In developing countries, the motherhood penalty is subsumed by a marriage penalty, with

---

[42]Kleven, Henrik, et al., 'The Child Penalty Atlas', September 2023, https://tinyurl.com/xkhw5vn. Accessed on 27 August 2024.

women leaving jobs soon after marriage itself.

Although there are many factors affecting women's prospects in the workforce, if we could distil them down to one common factor, it would be the cost of motherhood. Families function as household economic units, and like any enterprise, they favour decisions that increase their net income. Unfortunately, these decisions tend to go against the interests of women, who become primary and unpaid caregivers, while men go to work and earn. When the same decision is repeated in households across the country, it has a butterfly effect on society, influencing everything from cultural norms to biases.

Entrenched biases impact women at all stages of their careers—hiring, advancement and return to work. Women who do return to work after a break, end up with lower cumulative earnings across their career span because of the break. Even women who only take paid maternity leave face slower advancement in their careers as they juggle domestic responsibilities along with their jobs. As a natural consequence, there are much fewer women in leadership positions, leading to more biases about women's abilities, and a lack of influential voices to counter biases in hiring and workplace policies. Most of the above challenges are due to indirect discrimination which is harder to impact.

These challenges impact every woman—from a corporate employee to a woman entrepreneur. Without independent capital and networks built through their careers, fewer women start their own businesses at a significant scale. According to the 2019 Google-Bain Report, women owned only 20% of all enterprises, with 95% of women entrepreneurs-led outfits in India being nano- and micro-establishments, typically out of their houses without employing anyone else. Even entrepreneurial spirit has been confined to four walls.[43]

---

[43]Google | Bain & Company, 'Powering the Economy with Her: Women Entrepreneurship in India', 2019, https://tinyurl.com/mrxh24d4. Accessed on 27 August 2024.

The cost of motherhood is essentially an economic problem and needs an economic solution. The problem is not that women are not working, but that the work they do is unpaid and invisible to the broader economy. Unpaid care work in India accounts for 31% of our GDP, as per the 2020 UN Women Report.[44] It is a topic that is covered extensively in the media and public discussions, but the solutions proposed are often idealistic, and impractical. The typical argument is that women should be paid for this household labour, but this does not give women any leverage, as they cannot simply find another employer and negotiate better pay and terms.

Governments, businesses and communities across the world are converging on the care economy as a strategic solution to address costs of motherhood, accelerate economic growth, improve demographic planning, and strengthen infrastructure delivery. Promoting the formal care economy, with crèches, daycare facilities, and elder-care facilities that employ caregivers and pay them a fair wage is central to unlocking women's equal participation in the workforce. Not only would this free up more working-age women to pursue dignified employment, it would employ many of them, and men. This kind of improved access to quality childcare, particularly centre-based care, is linked to increased women's labour force participation. A UNDP study evaluating Chile's care model found that approximately 60% of mothers benefitting from the programme were actively able to seek employment.[45] Further, a Sattva study from 2023 suggests the paid-care sector could employ 84 million individuals by 2030. It would have a direct bearing on our economic growth, with estimates by the ILO & NITI Aayog suggesting the sector has

[44]UN-Women, *THE WORLD FOR WOMEN AND GIRLS: ANNUAL REPORT 2019-2020*, https://tinyurl.com/mryfevrn. Accessed on 27 August 2024.
[45]Sattva: Delivering High Impact, 'Shaping the Care Economy in India: Lessons from Latin American Models', 21 November 2023, https://tinyurl.com/39w8fbcj. Accessed on 27 August 2024.

the potential to reach ₹24,401.4 billion by 2030.[46] To put that in perspective, the paid-care sector would then account for 3% of our targeted 10 trillion-dollar economy, comparable to sectors like textiles and automobiles.

Shifting to a paid-care paradigm would require many shifts in our thinking. The Indian family model has traditionally relied on joint families, with childcare support by grandparents or relatives who live close by, but as urbanization increases, families struggle to find new accommodations in cities. The rich can hire nannies or send children to daycare, but even then, it is not easy as mothers are rightly careful about who will take care of their children. Various platforms have cropped up to formalize and train workers for various household chores, but one is hard-pressed to find a widely used app to find good nannies. As a result, even educated women often stay at home. For the poor, even that is not an option, which is why one regularly sees toddlers at construction sites, playing with makeshift toys made out of building materials and tools. A challenge highlighted by many is that trained care workers are hired at low wages, making the expectation that caregivers will be motivated and engaged in the work, unfair. Other countries globally have had to address this challenge as well; Germany is an example of a 'general, statutory minimum wage policy' introduced in 2015.[47]

There are promising examples of success in parts of the country. Kudumbashree, a community-based poverty reduction initiative in Kerala, has built a network of Neighbourhood Groups (NHGs) consisting of women who run activities from micro-credit groups and entrepreneurial ventures to community farming, allowing them to share agricultural responsibilities and reduce

---

[46]Ibid.
[47]Jatia, Smita, 'It is time to recognise the value of unpaid care work in economic growth', *Forbes India*, 28 June 2024, https://tinyurl.com/38a6jnbx. Accessed on 27 August 2024.

the burden of unpaid care work.[48] The programme also runs BUDS Schools and Rehabilitation Centres, which provide care and education to children with special needs.

The Anganwadi Centres scheme under the Integrated Child Development Services (ICDS) is a well-known initiative that provides childcare and development services in Indian villages by employing women who are trained to give maternal care, impart nutrition education and teach pre-school activities.[49] There are opportunities to both strengthen and scale such initiatives.

LEARNING FROM GLOBAL BEST PRACTICES

Even with all this promising data and evidence-based initiatives, achieving gender parity and increasing economic growth can be a daunting task, especially in a country like India with deep-rooted patriarchal instincts.

Claudia Goldin's U-curve showed countries dipping in their female labour force participation rates and then improving, but how do we know we can follow the same curve to its conclusion in our own society?

Luckily, we have good examples to follow. South Korea and China, both historically patriarchal societies, have managed to do it before us, with South Korea showing the way decades ago and China, more recently.

Rapid industrialization in the 1960s and 1970s brought more women into the workforce in South Korea, leading to typical challenges with childcare. A major turning point was the Act for the Promotion of Early Childhood Education in 1982 and the subsequent Child Welfare Act in 1987, which recognized the

---

[48]Kudumbshree Organization, 'Organisation Strengthening', https://tinyurl.com/48x47sz3. Accessed on 27 August 2024.

[49]Department of Women and Child Development, Government of NCT of Delhi, 'Services under the Integrated Child Development Services', https://tinyurl.com/88bmsxsj. Accessed on 27 August 2024.

importance of government-supported childcare facilities and initiatives.[50] They were initially targeted at low-income families, but the government expanded the public childcare provision in the early 2000s to include all dual-earner and, later, single-earner families. Women's employment has been identified as a key factor, particularly in South Korea's economic development, transitioning the country from a developing country to a developed, knowledge-based economy.

More recently, China has taken significant steps to address childcare and support working women. For instance, the government provided tax concessions for the childcare industry in 2019, exempted business earnings from value-added tax and allowed deductions in taxable income.[51] This led to the development of affordable and quality childcare institutions, and community-based facilities. China has also been updating its maternity leave and maternity insurance systems, with pilot programmes in different regions to test different childcare leave schemes.[52]

LOOKING AHEAD: HARNESSING EMERGING OPPORTUNITIES

The future presents unique opportunities to further gender equity in the workforce, especially with evolving digital landscapes and shifting societal attitudes. Emphasizing flexible and remote work arrangements can be pivotal for women, allowing them to balance work with personal responsibilities effectively. The gig economy

---

[50]Rhee, Ock, 'Childcare Policy in Korea: Current Status and Major Issues', *International Journal of Child Care and Education Policy*, 1, 59–72 (2007), https://tinyurl.com/3474whd5. Accessed on 27 August 2024.

[51]Zhang, Zoey Ye, 'China's Tax Concessions for Elderly Care, Childcare, and Domestic Services Industries', China Briefing: From Dezan Shira and Associates, 24 June 2019, https://tinyurl.com/pwrknxpc. Accessed on 27 August 2024.

[52]Zhou, Dream, 'Maternity Leave in China: Understanding Policies and Employee Rights', MSA, 8 April 2024, https://tinyurl.com/2s49zbw9. Accessed on 27 August 2024.

and digital platforms are opening new avenues for women's economic participation, offering flexibility and entrepreneurial opportunities.

Advancements in AI and technology hold the promise of reshaping job roles and markets, potentially creating new employment opportunities for women. However, it is crucial to approach these advancements with a focus on gender sensitivity, ensuring that AI and technology-driven changes do not perpetuate existing biases. By actively building women's skills in STEM and digital literacy, we can prepare them to be at the forefront of these technological shifts.

The digital transformation in India offers a unique avenue for enhancing women's participation in the workforce. As India progresses towards becoming a digital economy, women stand to benefit significantly from this shift. For instance, the increasing penetration of smartphones and internet access in rural areas opens new ways for remote work and entrepreneurial ventures for women. Companies like Reliance Jio have played a pivotal role in this digital revolution, making internet access more affordable and widespread. This democratization of digital access can empower women to access educational resources, online training programmes, and e-commerce platforms, providing them with the tools to develop new skills, start their own businesses, and connect with broader markets.

Additionally, the rise of fintech and digital financial services in India has the potential to enhance women's economic independence. Companies like Paytm and PhonePe are revolutionizing the way financial transactions are conducted, making it easier for women, especially those in rural or underserved areas, to access financial services, receive payments for their work, and manage their finances. By capitalizing on these technological advancements, India can create a more inclusive economic environment where women have greater access to opportunities for growth and development.

The rise of the 'She Economy' also highlights the importance of women's roles as major economic influencers. This shift underscores the need for businesses to embrace gender-balanced leadership to resonate with a substantial segment of the consumer base.

As we move forward, it is essential to leverage these developments to build more inclusive workspaces and policies. This will not only aid in achieving gender parity but also contribute significantly to overall economic growth and societal progress.

WHY NOW IS THE RIGHT TIME

Historical data has traditionally helped inform most decisions. Our theoretical frameworks and analyses, whether examining the U-curve in gender economics across different countries or investigating how women rise to leadership roles, rely heavily on historical data. However, we are now experiencing a rapidly changing world that can be best described as VUCA—Volatile, Uncertain, Complex and Ambiguous. We are experiencing unprecedented change, driven by exponential advancements in digital technology at such a pace that historical data can no longer be the only navigator for future patterns of human behaviour.

While this fast-changing world is marked by turbulence and unpredictability, it also opens windows of opportunity to redefine workspaces that are more equitable, effective and efficient. Here are some examples:

- **Flexibility and hybrid work**: The Covid-19 pandemic drove a large-scale shift to remote work for organizations across the world, changing behaviours and the way teams and companies functioned. The advantages of remote work leading to more flexible work arrangements, access to a wider talent pool, reduced overhead costs for office space, and potentially increased productivity became evident. Policy shifts embracing remote work can be a game changer for women's participation at work, since they are often faced with a disproportionate share of childcare or eldercare responsibilities, and need higher flexibility.

- **Care economy**: As highly skilled jobs like programming are being taken away by AI, jobs in caregiving and social services, often dominated by women and undervalued and underpaid, are becoming more attractive as they are less replaceable by technology. It makes sense to systematically build skills for women in areas where human connection and empathy are essential, like palliative care, geriatric care, dementia care, and mental health support.
- **Burgeoning 'she economy':** This presents a significant shift in the global marketplace. Female consumers are reshaping economies by controlling spending worth $31.8 trillion annually.[53] This staggering number is driven by women actively influencing or driving 70%–80% of all consumer purchases. Every day, women spend more time than men making economic decisions for their families, encompassing everything from health and education to consumer goods and other services. Three segments poised to grow rapidly in the Indian e-commerce sector are beauty, fashion and grocery; and who is the decision-maker in these purchases? Mostly women. As organizations prime to tailor their marketing and product-development strategies to cater to this large segment of female consumers, they cannot afford gender-imbalanced leadership.

India as a country is very well positioned to grow rapidly over the next few decades, with a growing workforce, a large domestic market and a young population. The Indian government is actively driving initiatives to attract foreign investment, boost

---

[53]Nielsen IQ (NIQ), 'Shaping Success: A Deep Dive into Women's Impact on the CPG Landscape', 2024, https://tinyurl.com/tkpjvn9w. Accessed on 27 August 2024.

manufacturing and improve the business environment. Digital public infrastructure and its rapid adoption have been a game changer with new business opportunities like e-commerce, the gig economy and improved financial inclusion. According to the IMF, the Indian economy is projected to grow at 6.5% in CY24 and CY25.[54] This creates a significant demand for a skilled workforce, and a massive opportunity for women to enter the labour market, especially because the pool of skilled employable women is already large. The business case for having more women in the workforce has already been established and there is an active acceptance on the part of corporate leaders, politicians and bureaucrats that increasing FLFPR is a critical factor for realizing India's economic growth ambitions. There is an increasing pool of women role models in every sphere—from politics to armed forces to logistics and STEM. These factors are creating strong tailwinds to realize gender-equitable workspaces in India, and it is important that we leverage this momentum and attack the deep-rooted obstacles that stand in the way.

A rapidly changing world offers opportunities to change social norms along with everything else. We cannot start there, but if we change the preceding conditions and the economic calculations of households based on the earning power of its members, we will be on our way to having a society more receptive to change.

The cascading impact of women's economic agency goes far beyond increasing the national GDP. It creates ripple effects that enhance families and societies, contributing to a more inclusive and prosperous future for the nation as a whole. It is time for us to realize our dream of Atmanirbhar Bharat by dismantling barriers to women's participation in the economy and actively designing gender-inclusive workplaces.

---

[54]Press Information Bureau, Government of India, Ministry of Finance, 'India shines as IMF upgrades GDP forecast to 7% in FY24-25: Faster growth fosters more jobs, social security and wealth creation', 17 July 2024, https://tinyurl.com/4w946uc9. Accessed on 27 August 2024.

10

EMPOWERING WOMEN IN PRACTICE: MUSINGS BY CORPORATE AND SOCIAL LEADERS

Ganesh Natarajan, Dinanath Kholkar,
Anushri Alva, Mrinal Gharpure, Priya Patil,
Mridula Sankhyayan and Nikki Barua

In recent times, the near-equal percentages of women and men entering the services sector, technology and management programmes lends credence to the belief that the future, at least in these fields, will belong to both sexes. Our hypothesis is that once that happens in businesses, there will be a better chance of the numbers changing in other sectors, industries, and strata of society.

In this presentation, we profile companies and organizations that are making this happen as successful pilots, and later on a scaled basis, and draw some conclusions on how this can happen in a scaled and sustained manner. The stories are told by the builders of next practices who have made it happen!

ZENSAR'S ZENITH—A RETELLING BY GANESH NATARAJAN

The joy of empowering women lies in the fact that both men and women working for them feel more empowered, and enable the development of more productive and thriving organizations. Having become CEO of APTECH Computer Education at the very young age of 33 and getting the opportunity to build communities in four successful organizations that I have been privileged to lead in the last 30-plus years, I have no doubt in my mind that for a leadership role, if there are two equal candidates, pick a woman!

I will not dwell much on APTECH, where much of my experimentation and learnings on leadership happened. We expanded the company from 11 centres in India in 1991 to 1,200+ centres in 40 countries, with market leadership in over 20, including China. Many young women who started their careers with APTECH as students or young employees have blossomed into confident and capable leaders today. But my real work on enabling women to reach their full potential started in Zensar, which I took over as CEO in 2001, and grew the company from 30-odd million dollars to over three hundred million by 2016.

When I took charge as CEO, the team leaders were all men, with the exception of the financial controller and company secretary. Through a conscious effort and an empowered task force called Women for Excellence, led by a recently hired manager, Prameela Kalive, we worked on the agency and confidence of women, helped them through critical phases of their career, and ensured that the leadership team of a much larger organization by 2016 had 13 women, many in line for leadership roles. Prameela herself became Chief Operating Officer of the company, and a role model for women and men at Zensar, and in the larger RPG Group, our significant shareholder.

In the last ten years, our venture capital-funded enterprise, Global Talent Track, has been led by four women in succession, and today, is proud to have over 60% of its employees as women. The company has become a leader in skills and will soon be listed on stock exchanges. Going one better, we have been able to establish and run our social sector champion of sustainable livelihoods—Lighthouse Communities Foundation. The organization is headed by Ruchi Mathur, my co-founder and first CEO, and someone who has committed her life to the social sector. With the entire seven-member leadership team being women and six dynamic women on the Board of Directors, this organization has proven to be an exemplar of Nari Shakti.

What benefits have we derived from this strong support for women in these organizations? For one, the caring and sensitive leadership has delivered industry-beating retention across the board, and built a very open and collaborative culture. Second, the `never say die' attitude of our women have led to most business results being achieved. And finally, the participation of women at every level and in every activity in the organizations has enabled us to build a culture we are truly proud of—the five Fs: Fast, Focused, Flexible, Friendly and Fun. Looking back, I can confidently affirm that we could not have built these successful organizations in any other way!

TRANSITION TO BIG LEAGUES—A STORY BY DINANATH KHOLKAR

As I gather my thoughts, I realize how little I know about inequality with regard to women. Growing up in Mumbai, studying in some of the city's best schools and colleges, building a long career of 34 years with TCS, and living overseas in the US and Europe before settling down in the city of Pune, often, I did not get the feel of the ground reality in society at large.

During our school days, we had a good gender balance and equity. There were one-off cases we would hear about, but we were too young to understand these things. Having said that, when it came to certain communities and castes, one could clearly sense the gender inequality. As I went to the higher grades, and then to university, the number of female students started declining significantly, more so in engineering college. Specific streams in engineering were clearly out of bounds for girls. Fortunately, with the introduction of streams like electronics and computer science, and the IT-related curriculum, the number of female students has definitely increased.

Among the biggest concerns I had observed in my fellow female students were anxiety and family pressures. On completing their education, they hardly got an opportunity to further refine their thought process and harbour career aspirations. Interestingly, those who found their life partners during the engineering days fared better on the career front.

The initial few years in the IT sector are crucial to building a strong foundation. Focus and continuity are critical elements of that foundation. However, women would always be at a disadvantage because of their family commitments, and the breaks they may have to take in the initial years of marriage. The fast-paced IT industry renders technology obsolete in a few years; effectively, a long break from work means one has to start from scratch.

I always regretted losing some very good talent who would relocate post marriage and leave the workforce. In those days, there were communities who would discourage their women from continuing in a corporate job after marriage. Those who continued, ended up with a career break when they went the family way. It was a concern I always discussed with like-minded colleagues and our HR heads. Some of these concerns led me to create an empathetic and aware organization that would have the ears to the ground and call out any issue that needed the management's attention. Some cases called for a solution that could easily be achieved; for others, one had to go the extra mile to make it happen. But it was absolutely possible to support and enable our women colleagues.

As a leader, I felt it important to constantly reiterate the concerns in terms of business quantity and quality I had in the context of our business. Hence, the need was to create a culture that was caring and understanding of such situations. We did take certain steps locally within the account I was managing. However, I realized soon enough that such initiatives needed to be institutionalized and driven at a different level to make them effective, scalable, and sustainable.

In 2008–09, we were still in the midst of the world financial crisis when TCS launched DAWN—Diversity and Women's Network. It was received with a great deal of enthusiasm across the organization, and received all the support from the leadership team. I was updating my team during the townhall when one of my leaders asked me the reason for doing this especially for women, and if there would be something equivalent for men too. I played back the question in his personal context. I knew he had two daughters, so I told him to participate in this initiative and ensure that we create a TCS his daughters would aspire to join.

We ran this initiative by involving men in the core committee, especially those whose immediate female family members were working. This enabled us to get a more balanced perspective on the challenges faced by working women, and coach other men to appreciate situations our women colleagues often faced. When people understood the purpose and long-term benefits of DAWN, they whole-heartedly supported it and ensured they were making a conscious effort to make the initiative a success.

When I was managing the Business Process Servicing (BPS) operations, I noticed there were no women participants in the sales leadership development programme. I drew the attention of my HR head to the matter and encouraged him to understand the reason, and then put corrective measures in place to ensure the right participation from women leaders in this programme. One of the key reasons why there were no women nominated in the programme was the lack of visibility of such aspirants at the top leadership of my unit or some pre-conceived notion that women would not want to relocate to take up sales roles.

To address this, we conceptualized a new leadership

programme with only women leaders to give them the necessary visibility to the leadership team, thereby making them candidates to be nominated to the sales leadership programme. In the process, we oriented them for sales roles and also coached them to build their visibility at the leadership team level. For me, it was a business imperative to have women in frontline sales roles, as many of our client stakeholders were women, and some of our well-wishers were giving us improvement suggestions when they compared us to competition. It was important for us to take a step back, understand the root cause and design new ways.

In 2008, I attended one of the first Women in Leadership conferences, and as part of that, I was invited to a smaller group round-table conference. In the room of about 30 participants, we were only four men. It was that moment which made me realize the experience our women colleagues would be going through in many of our leadership meets. Since then, I have been associated with the Women in Leadership (WILL) Forum, and contributed as their executive committee member. I have also ensured the participation of many of our women leaders in WILL Forum events, have been a speaker at their conferences, and been involved in the follow-up mentoring process of some programmes.

I have worked closely with our head of Diversity, who led the diversity initiative right from its inception to its current avatar of Diversity, Equity & Inclusion (DEI).

The first version of the women leadership development programme called TCS Forward, and eventually renamed iExcel, has enabled us to scale up our diversity at the leadership level. I have been a faculty and a mentor for the iExcel programme, and have been fortunate to see many of those women leaders make an impact in the roles they have taken up.

One of the key elements of leadership has to be an inclusive approach. Any leader should consciously look for potential exclusions, which may happen because of the different cultural and social constructs of each region.

Since my days in engineering college, especially in my generation, we had less than 10% women in our class. Over the years, this percentage has steadily increased; now we see a very healthy balance of 50%, especially in some of the computer science, electronics and information technology classes

It is important for us as leaders to look for patterns and specific situations that warrant intervention or special exception to ensure there is equality in the team.

There are many instances I have come across either by observing them myself or because these were brought to my notice by my leaders. The reason my leaders drew my attention to these issues was because I always tried to address the concerns that emerged in the data.

Simple measures could address some of these issues. Once such example was, when a lady associate went on maternity leave, she would be taken off the customer account. As a result, she would lose touch with what was happening and the opportunities that were coming up. It was important to bring this to the notice of the customer, and ensure that they have a process to park the IDs of such associates for a defined period, and enable them to stay connected remotely.

We had many cases where women associates would resign because they had to relocate to another city with their husband. It was important to keep a tab on such requests and use our personal connections in other branches to see if we could retain such people by enabling their official transfer. This type of approach, if inculcated in the culture of each unit, would ensure there is awareness of the possibilities and necessary steps are taken before the damage is done.

Networking becomes a challenge for many women colleagues as they grow in the organization, because of the breaks they take and the relocations with their family, among other reasons. I have encouraged our women leaders to join professional bodies and volunteer to gain professionally from a skills perspective, and also build up their network beyond the work environment. I have been a volunteer at the Institute of Electrical and Electronics Engineers (IEEE), Pune Section, supported initiatives of Women In Engineering, and encouraged women to take on roles that would have otherwise been shunned by them.

We now have a woman as the Section Chair, and have a 50% diversity at the executive committee level.

There are certain rules I have learnt from my customers; one of them is to refuse being on panels or advisory boards which do not have support for diversity and inclusion.

There have been a couple of instances where I have formally registered my displeasure and ensured that the organizers and institutes appreciate my point of view and take corrective measures.

At TCS, when we came up with new publications, we ensured that we had equal participation of women contributors. We were fortunate that when we highlighted this approach, quite a few names were immediately referred to us by like-minded people.

Encouraged by the diverse talent we saw in women leaders, we decided to run a special webinar series for women leaders from business, social sector, academia; the research series was named 'Real Leaders, Real Stories'. We also came up with a publication showcasing these women leaders; this publication was launched by a well-known woman business leader, who is also driving a powerful initiative on higher education for girls.

While we are on the subject of diversity at workplace, in two of my businesses I had a different challenge in my Philippines Centre. Eighty per cent of our leaders were women, and the centre ran mostly according to the US time zone. During my visits to Manila, I would spend additional time with some of these women leaders to understand how they balanced their family commitments with their work commitments. It was amazing to hear how each of these women leaders had built their own support system, and how they managed time for their family, especially the time they spent with their children.

While at times I would be concerned about crossing the line and entering the personal space of these women leaders, I felt it was important for me as a business head to understand the social constructs of our people in this location.

We started an 'All Women Centre' (AWC) at Riyadh in the Kingdom of Saudi Arabia (KSA). This was at a time when women were not allowed to drive in the KSA, and there were considerable constraints on them working in offices. We set up this centre in partnership with one of our customers, and scaled it to house 1,000 associates. Initially, we had one of our Australian leaders deputed to manage the centre. Then we had a local woman leader to run the centre. Overall, we played a crucial role in this transformation journey as far as women employment in the KSA was concerned. Whenever I got an opportunity, I would share updates about the AWC with my customers, and they would be curious to connect and interact with them. This clearly demonstrated our commitment to social transformation and women empowerment.

My team was involved in creating and deploying AI-based automated sanitation inspection solutions for government schools of Andhra Pradesh for ensuring cleanliness of toilets and all other areas. Thus, we were able to bring down the dropout rate of girls in schools. This is a classic example of how digital technologies can impact lives of the poor.

There have been pockets of excellence in the form of unique programmes that have been run to support education of the girl child. One of them has been the Avasara Academy which has been set up on the outskirts of Pune. The focus of the academy has been to build leadership qualities in girls, and provide them state-of-the-art and progressive education.

Encouraging women to take up challenges and realize their full potential has given me tremendous satisfaction. My first assistant had started off her career at TCS as a receptionist, but has built her qualifications with a Master's degree and then by working for a very senior TCS executive.

PROFIT IN NON-PROFITS—THE JOURNEY OF
ADHYAYAN, BY ANUSHRI ALVA

Girls in India's government schools survive on a range of precarious privileges—privileges like cycles, financial aid, all-girl schools and a day to celebrate the girl child; privileges that are predicated on social structures that threaten the basic safety and freedom of girls. The girl child is simultaneously one of the most funded yet least invested-in person in the government school education system. For her personhood to become visible, two things are significant—first, the lived experience of the girl child needs to be seen as an important measure of the quality of education in school, not just her material presence in school; second, women leaders in government schools need adequate representation.

Let us examine questions at two ends of a long chain of hierarchy—the Department of Education and the girl child herself. 'Do you have material through which we can prepare children for the national academic survey and ensure their scores go up?' This is the burning question one is asked in almost every department of education as the deadline under the National Education Policy to ensure children have sound foundational literacy and numeracy skills by Grade 3, is fast approaching. This is a big conversation and begs an important seat at the table. On the other end of the hierarchy, one hears Deepa in Goa say, 'Walking home from school is really hard. Boys pass really vulgar comments. I feel ashamed and I feel even worse when I'm on my period. I want to be a dancer and a teacher, but I'm not sure if my parents will allow the former; it's not respectable.' In a border district of Arunachal Pradesh, Yaji shares, 'When I don't do housework, I'm defying my duty and when my brother doesn't, he is exercising his identity as a good man. I'm not allowed to climb trees, but I know how to and I want to. I want to be a deputy commissioner. I want to tell girls to try many things, like sports.' In South Tripura, Joshna of Grade 10 was left wondering, 'Who do I turn to when my own parents are trying to get me married secretly?' Across the 5,000-odd government schools in five states that we work with, only 4% have chosen to work on quality standards focused on some form of inclusion of the girl child in school to improve her lived experience. It is worth recognizing that in India, national quality frameworks like the Shaala Siddhi framework have specific standards that focus on improving the experience of the girl child, thus recognizing that these indicators are crucial when benchmarking schools as 'good' schools. However, while the possibility exists, the attention does not.

The second dimension of this problem lies in the fact that as one moves up the hierarchy of leadership in the government school system, the number of women in leadership positions reduces. In a state like Goa, 82% of hub leaders are women, and 67% of middle leaders like inspectors are women, whereas in states like Arunachal Pradesh and Tripura, there are hardly any women-led schools. However, even in a state like Goa, as one moves further up in the hierarchy towards more influential positions, the number of women drops drastically. 'There were fewer female college graduates in our state, so I'm hoping this number grows over the years', is one demographic explanation we heard in some states. While a system leader pointed to social and relational exclusion: 'Promotions are not merit-based. They depend on seniority and your network, and we are not friends with men who might decide this.' Perceptions of these relationships matter too, wherein a school head spoke about a female director in her state: 'She was incredibly good, but all the men thought she was arrogant because she tried to hold them accountable. She needed to be strict in a way men at her level don't need to be, as they can be friends and still be respected. That's not an option for her.' A complex leader stated, 'There are physical issues that disadvantage us because our terrain is tough and we don't drive, so men are given positions which require travel. Having said that, I also do not feel trusted as a female leader. I live in a deeply patriarchal culture. Men do not want to be told what to do by me.' Others point to societal structures that hold them back. A school inspector shared, 'When my peers wanted to become teachers, they were encouraged. It's a respectable profession with reasonable hours that would allow them to cook, clean and raise their children. But if they are to be considered for higher positions, they will not get the kind of support they need at home to take on more responsibilities at work.' Girls can be supported well only when women are represented adequately and have a voice at all levels within the system.

Girls thrive when their well-being is seen as an important part of the care taken by school they attend and when female leaders have a strong voice in the system. In South Tripura District, the Balika Manch programme is a good example of how the lived experience of girls was truly taken into consideration while taking action. Given the high rate of child marriage of girls, the district administration set up the Balika Manch programme wherein committees of teachers, female parents and girls are set up across schools to raise awareness about child marriage and provide resources. Joshna's story represents that of many girls in the district. One day when Joshna came home, she found out that her parents were trying to get her married secretly, and that her phone had been confiscated. Girls were seen either as an expensive burden or as cheap labour. Her older sister had already been married before she could complete school and Joshna knew the same fate awaited her. Being a Balika Manch student convener, Joshna was able to call for help. Social workers were able to arrive at her house and counsel her parents in the short term to stop the marriage, but also work with them and the community over a longer period to make them understand how child marriage impacted girls and why education mattered. Through concerted efforts of the district administration, local social workers, teachers, female parents and girls, strong communities have formed across schools and villages to drive this cause. This has also created the space for girls to feel supported while talking about their fears and aspirations.

We have seen female leaders play a role in making this an important issue when addressing the care taken in schools. They have worked to ensure girls have spaces to talk about menstruation. Where safety has been a concern, self-defence classes have been set up and resources have been made available. Unlocking potential has also meant pushing beyond the narrative of safety as the only way to engage with girls. Women leaders have encouraged girls to take on many activities like sports where they are traditionally underrepresented. They are taken on exposure visits with boys to ignite aspirations beyond the frames that have been set for them. 'How many parts does a car have?' a high school female student asked a manager at a car-manufacturing company during an exposure visit. He was surprised that a girl was as fascinated by cars as her male counterparts.

In schools where girls flourish, teachers recognize that girls need to feel entitled to ask questions in spaces scripted for boys. Schools that are trying to create a more equal environment opt for mixed seating over the conventional segregated seating of boys and girls, and also work on ensuring girls participate actively. Women leaders have also gone to the extent of tracking attendance and participation of vulnerable girls, and assigned teachers to talk to them one on one when they see at-risk behaviour. Female parents are also included in the school management committees of such schools. In Arunachal Pradesh, a student in a remote school that has really worked towards the inclusion of girls said it best: 'I feel us girls are locked in chains, but a good school can set us free.'

Do we have the audacity to dream of such a school system?

MAKING IT HAPPEN—THE GOYN WAY, BY MRINAL GHARPURE

'Continuous learning helps me move ahead with my business,' says Lakshmi [name changed]. Lakshmi is a 35-year-old single mother of two daughters living in Pimpri in Pune. Life's struggles and situations compelled her to earn a livelihood to support the family and the education of her daughters. Lakshmi was 12th-Grade pass with limited skills to be able to find employment in a formal job. It was her determination to provide a better life and good education for her children that helped her turn her passion for cooking into a business. Starting with snacks and tiffin services, she gradually expanded her menu to include Diwali specialities and gourmet cakes. The Junoon programme designed in Pune for Aspen Global Opportunity Youth Network (GOYN) helped her register a formal business and enhance her entrepreneurial spirit and skills. Today, Lakshmi not only provides financial support to her family, but also sets a powerful example for her daughters about the importance of hard work, perseverance, resilience, and pursuing one's passion.

'Age is just a number and I dream of going on.' These powerful words reinforce the notion that it is never too late to pursue one's dream and passion. At 51, Suman [name changed] too took the leap and seized an opportunity to turn her hobby into a business. Junoon provided her the platform and support needed to organize her ideas and advance her entrepreneurial journey. Suman has demonstrated perseverance through all the ups and downs of her business and emerged a winner. Today, her business has been incubated at a government institute and she exports her masalas to a couple of countries as well. As she aspires to further grow her business, Suman serves as a beacon of hope and inspiration for others who may have put their dreams on the back-burner, or are fearful of pursuing their passion.

For women in low-income/slum communities, entrepreneurship is often looked at merely as a necessity and not a choice. Faced with limited access to formal employment and constrained by socio-economic barriers, these women muster the courage to embark on their entrepreneurial ventures, fuelled by their own agency, determination, and courage. Operating within resource-constrained environments, women like Lakshmi and Suman exhibit remarkable resourcefulness and creativity. With minimal capital and infrastructure at their disposal, they leverage whatever skills they must to establish home-based businesses. Whether it is repurposing household items or maximizing the utility of all possible spaces, they demonstrate an ability to innovate and adapt. However small the business may be, it instils a sense of financial independence, enabling such women to contribute to the household, and in some cases, to become the chief wage earner at home. Such businesses also foster a sense of self-reliance among women.

Navigating structural barriers and systemic inequalities, women entrepreneurs often need to confront formidable challenges on their path to success. From limited/no access to financial services, limited capital, limited infrastructure, and lack of access to markets, they confront many obstacles that threaten to derail their ventures. Yet, armed with unwavering agency, resolve and resilience, they defy expectations and shatter stereotypes, challenging the narrative of marginalization and disadvantage.

Programmes like Junoon offer a variety of interventions, ranging from converting a business idea into reality, to providing business-skills training, connections to financing options, market linkages, to supporting with statutory licenses, and more. The programme also helps entrepreneurs build peer networks, which especially in low-income communities prove to help community development and become a source of inspiration for others who may fear taking the first step. The programme recognizes the volatility and dynamic situations in the lives of entrepreneurs that can lead to discontinuation or hurdles in smooth operations of the business, and helps with creating systems to anticipate and overcome such challenges. Mentors to such entrepreneurs play a huge role in this. Women entrepreneurs also need support to build agency to defy societal and structural barriers that may prevent them from moving forward in their livelihood journey. Most often women face resistance from family members, neighbours, and society in general. Moreover, perceptions about a woman's capabilities and competencies may hinder their access to networks and market opportunities. The programme is designed to help women deal with all these challenges and addresses individual needs too.

As women like Lakshmi and Suman prosper in their endeavours, they become role models for others, catalyzing a ripple effect of change. The stories of such women deserve to be celebrated and amplified. Their triumphs help us learn lessons in resilience, resourcefulness, and determination that resonate far beyond the constraints of life situations and inspire us to reimagine possibilities where every woman has the opportunity to thrive, regardless of her circumstances.

IN SEARCH OF HOPE—A MILLION JUGNUS LIGHT THE PATH, BY PRIYA PATIL

Million Jugnus has been created as a dream from Lighthouse Communities Foundation which works with slum youth in five cities across India, with the mission to make a million slum youth aspirational and engaged in sustainable livelihoods by 2030. In developing products that create agency in youth, we have also touched the lives of many children in municipal schools with Jeevan Shikshan.

The Jeevan Shikshan Social and Emotional Learning (SEL) programme offers children the opportunity to develop the language of emotions—at the heart of which is the fundamental human need to build relationships and trust. The programme curriculum enables children to build a bedrock of emotional language, leading to increased emotional stability. For girls, the curriculum changes how they engage with themselves, their peers and the adults in their lives. They take their first steps on the journey of moving away from their own vulnerabilities and socially-imposed constraints, to a space of strength.

Activities within the curriculum are standardized for children according to their age. However, each child's unique context and life influence the way she experiences the same set of activities. The context is established through a human or visual experience. This could be in the form of recalling a life experience, watching a film, listening to music or poetry, interpreting art, understanding metaphors, doing improvisations and bodywork (physical activities). Discovery begins with questioning what can be explored, within the established context. Understanding starts with the expression of insights about the self and the established context. And finally, sense-making uncovers what has been learnt and its value. This value is deeply personal and unique to each child and becomes a part of who she is.

On a daily basis, children are confronted with difficult choices that they have to make that others cannot make for them. As they experience the activities, they start developing the fluency to be able to talk to themselves, thus becoming reflective human beings. The curriculum helps a child tap into the person that exists within them. It does not require complex new learning and instead helps a child know themself better. Through these activities, children can go to uncertain and unknown places, understand how they feel, explore their responses and reactions, ultimately leading to better choices for themselves.

'I cannot walk into the future with my legs feeling heavy. I need a skip in my step. I need the lightness that will fuel my ability to move towards the future, with confidence, without fear. I was born for goodness. I was born for greatness.' These words of self-affirmation that are woven into the activities enable young girls to feel a sense of pride in themselves and overcome a culture that tells them they are less capable than others.

The evocative words of a 14-year-old girl, who discovers that it is not wrong to love oneself, truly brings out the power of the Jeevan Shikshan curriculum. Pratiksha experienced a visualization activity where she was invited to imagine her heart overflowing with love. As she shut her eyes and listened to the instructions, the face that appeared before her was her own. At first, she was confused. Why would I think of myself when I am invited to imagine love. When she was asked to delve deeper into her experience, she shared a powerful insight: 'When I was asked to imagine my heart overflowing with love, I thought of myself because I love myself. It is not wrong to love myself.'

In our own organizations—NGO Lighthouse Communities Foundation and social enterprise Million Jugnus, we have realized the need to get girls to believe in themselves from a very young age. Done systematically and at scale across the country, the results can be magical. India's female gender deserves equality and more!

PUMP UP THE CONFIDENCE, BY MRIDULA SANKHYAYAN

I would rather turn this much-debated question on its head and first reflect upon the following: What makes a woman succeed? I have observed five critical factors for success in women I have coached or worked with, or for women whose public career journeys I have seen. A woman who is driven by herself and not only by circumstances, who believes in her potential and not in preconceived notions about her gender, who has clarity of purpose and is not cowed down by people who dictate her life, who is intentional, who is determined about her dreams and goals and not intimidated by societal pressures, who follows her heart and not the herd, is often more successful than her peers. Thus, knowing what she is capable of, believing in her own self-worth, having clarity of purpose, intentionality to act upon it and the courage to sustain all of the above are key elements to becoming a woman of power—a veritable Nari Shakti.

Yet, millions of women are unable to nurture these qualities and hold themselves back from realizing their true potential. There are several factors that *Harvard Business Review* and many well-known business magazines and research institutes have written about. I am sharing those that have resonated with me in my experience of working with diverse women across ages, functions, nationalities, and socio-economic and cultural tapestries.

Three primary factors hold a woman back:

1. The woman herself
2. Her socio-economic support system
3. The absence of inspiration and relatable role models

Let us unpack each of these factors:

1. **The woman herself:** A common theme that comes up repeatedly is the lack of self-belief. I have seen very talented women suffer because of:
   a. **Lack of self-confidence:** Lack of self-confidence leads to absence of self-belief and other emotions such as anxiety, fear, sadness, which lead to low self-esteem.
   b. **Low self-esteem:** Constant comparisons at work, social media and at home can impact a woman's confidence level, making her feel she is less in comparison to others.
   c. **Work overload:** Unable to say no when a no is due, women take on work till there is such an overload that it starts to impact their work-life balance, and they end up engaging in negative self-talk.
   d. **Negative self-talk:** Not being able to do well either at work or at home, women feel overcome by guilt and

a sense of inadequacy, which can seriously impact their performance.

e. **Cycle of negativity:** Often, women feel they are not good enough, leading to a vicious cycle of negativity. To break free from this cycle, women must pause, reflect, and become self-aware!

f. **Imposter syndrome:** Many women experience the imposter syndrome, where they doubt their capabilities and fear being exposed as frauds, which can impact their confidence and career progression.

2. **Socio-economic support system:** Women face multiple challenges and hurdles from their environment that need to be addressed:

a. **Societal expectations**: Social norms and expectations about gender roles can restrict women's career choices and professional growth.

b. **Dual responsibilities:** Women often juggle dual responsibilities—of work and family—which limit their availability and energy for professional advancement. This can hinder their career growth and participation in the corporate sector.

c. **Career interruptions**: Women experience more career interruptions due to caregiving responsibilities. These interruptions significantly affect their career progression and earnings, creating barriers in reaching their full potential.

d. **Lack of supportive policies**: The absence of supportive labour laws and company policies hinder women's entry and retention in the workforce.

e. **Company size**: Research indicates that smaller firms, or 'micro-firms', may limit women's employment opportunities. Larger firms tend to have more formal structures and policies that support women's participation in the workforce.

3. **The absence of inspirational and relatable role models:**
    a. **Representation:** Women hold only 29% of senior management roles globally, highlighting the persistent underrepresentation of women in leadership positions.
    b. **Absence of role models**: The lack of female role models in leadership positions can discourage women from aspiring to high-level roles, and limit their career growth opportunities.

There is hope in all the success stories we see of women who have navigated these challenges successfully. Yet, we need to do a lot as individuals and as a society to awaken the Nari Shakti within. There is tremendous latent talent out there just waiting to be tapped into.

BREAKING BARRIERS—I DID IT MY WAY, BY NIKKI BARUA

It was a warm, sunny day in June 1997 when I set foot in America for the first time. As an immigrant, I had a heart full of hope and a suitcase full of dreams. Little did I know back then how many obstacles I would have to overcome to make those dreams come true—from adapting to a new society, to learning new norms and etiquette, to building entirely new skills—every challenge helped me grow into my future self.

But the hardest challenge was my struggle to fit in. I checked many boxes for diversity, but felt like I was on the outside of every inner circle. In my desperation to belong, I changed myself to fit into a box defined by others. The more I became like everyone else, the less of me there was to see.

My transformation began when I stopped trying to fit into someone else's world and started being myself—unapologetically. I discovered that authenticity is my ally and power. That is what helped me stand up for myself, navigate my career successfully, and achieve my ambitions. I did not just get a seat at the table; I built my own table.

The struggles in my journey made me realize I was not alone. Systemic barriers and lack of sponsors and mentors often hold women back from advancing in their careers. As a result, most women work twice as hard to get half as far. Consider your career journey and ask yourself what if you could get where you are today in half the time without double the effort. How might your life be different?

According to the World Economic Forum, it will take 257 years to close the opportunity and pay gap for women. It is unthinkable that we have so few women at the top, and it certainly is unacceptable for women to have to wait 257 years to achieve parity with men at all levels.

That is why our mission at Beyond Barriers is to help ambitious professionals go further, faster.

It is not the lack of ambition or ability that holds women back. It is not knowing what to do, how to do it, and from whom to seek help. With our AI-powered Career Fitness Platform, you can accelerate success by gaining clarity, mastering skills from leading experts, and boosting your confidence with a community of next-level peers.

It is time to make the world more inclusive—a world where women's voices and perspectives matter in defining products, services and policies; a world where women are no longer hoping for equal pay, career opportunities or simply a seat at the right table. It is time for women to change the game, play to win, and accelerate success!

Real-life stories from practitioners, men and women who have made women's empowerment their mission, should provide many pointers to the process of confidence building and opportunities that can be provided at scale—in the family, school or college setting, in rural as well as urban contexts, at an organizational or institutional level and indeed at the state and country levels.

Meeting entrepreneurs and practitioners as part of the process of developing and curating the content for this book, the authors and editors have found some of the examples incredibly empowering. We hope that bureaucrats, CEOs and social sector leaders will take a leaf from these experiences and replicate some of these blueprints to impact the lives of women positively, and create a more equitable world.

11

ONWARD AND UPWARD—WOMEN MUST SUCCEED!

Vandana Chavan, Uma Ganesh and Ganesh Natarajan

EDITORS' NOTE

We start this concluding chapter with a personal account by Advocate Vandana Chavan, ten-year Member of Parliament and an activist for social causes, particularly women and environment. We then summarize the key themes of this book and end with our comments on how we can all collaborate to take the Nari Shakti movement forward.

WOMEN'S POLITICAL PARTICIPATION IN INDIA— VANDANA CHAVAN

In February 1992, I, and many like me, totally inexperienced and new candidates, alien to active politics and not familiar with the working and governance of local bodies, hit the roads contesting and canvassing for the Pune Municipal Corporation local government elections, thanks to the reservation for women at local governments. Some of us literally got pushed into the fray even before we realized what we were in for. Looking back, all of us who got there feel immensely blessed to have had the most amazing opportunity of our lifetimes to have been able to connect to the grassroots and the people, and also to have been instrumental in making a difference in their lives, however small, on the huge canvas of aspirations, opportunity and development.

The 73rd and 74th Amendments to the Constitution of India marked a watershed for the women of India as these brought them into the decision-making process of local governments by laying the foundation for their participation at local levels. Through the 73rd Amendment—the Panchayati Raj Bill—the Constitution while recognizing the role of local governments in the three-tier system of governance, reserved one-third of all seats in Panchayats and urban local bodies for women. States like Karnataka and Maharashtra became front-runners in adopting the policy even before the Constitutional Amendment was passed and became law on 24 April 1993, attracting much interest, excitement and curiosity as to how the policy implementation would ultimately unfold.

As candidates of this first batch, the attention, expectations and speculations from the people and media were indeed daunting for us. Once elected, the women got on with their jobs in earnest, with great enthusiasm and energy; their wards now became their extended homes to administer and govern. In the first few days, cleanliness and garbage, sanitation, provision of toilet facilities, water availability, proper lighting of roads became natural priorities. These then extended to ensuring proper health and educational facilities and services, later extending further to issues such as provision of welfare measures—especially for women, children, seniors and the vulnerable—such as crèches for children of working women, working women's hostel, reserved seats for women in public transport, amusement centres for senior citizens and the like, and that too in a short span.

Despite the diversity of education, economic and social background that these women representatives came from, what gradually seemed to emerge not only in their wards but across the city was a 'women's agenda'. Even male corporators felt the invisible pressure to address women-centric issues taken up by their women colleagues. Daily quarrels at the common water tap in slums lessened, with women elected representatives prioritizing individual water taps for every household; open defecation came to an end with priority being given to the construction of community toilets in slums, and later wherever possible, individual toilets in houses; and provisions of properly cemented extremely narrow lanes and drainage system in settlements of the poor reduced disease and improved overall living conditions and quality of life.

In 1992, when reservation for women was first declared in Maharashtra, there weren't enough women candidates to contest elections; political parties had to hunt for women candidates and persuade them to contest elections. Five years later, in 1997, I became a member of the selection committee, and several confident women came forward wanting to contest elections, sometimes making it difficult for the committee to choose who would be a better candidate. Five years later, in 2002, it was a completely different scenario—women had become assertive; each one could persuasively convince how she was a better candidate than the other. From one election to the next, an evolution in the attitudes and vocabulary of women in politics was evident; the transition spoke volumes of their newfound confidence, leadership qualities and empowerment.

At the village level too, elected women *sarpanch*s (village heads) through the length and breadth of the country have made their mark by bringing positive change in their areas and by becoming role models to other women and young girls in their communities. Water conservation, provision of and access to clean drinking water, sanitation, irrigation systems, protection of environment, development of green belts and afforestation, installation of solar power, skill development, bridging the digital divide through mobile computer training institutes, construction of toilets and banks in villages, improvement of school infrastructure, ensuring zero dropout rate and balanced sex ratio, joyful learning and nutritious food for children, reviving traditional folk art, ensuring various government schemes reach beneficiaries, literacy campaigns, health camps, reproductive health awareness, immunization programmes, shelter to victims of domestic violence and destitute women, SHG formation—the list of initiatives taken by women sarpanchs, according to local needs, in different parts of India, is exhaustive, making it amply clear that women's leadership was setting the developmental agenda critical to village life, thereby transforming India at the grassroots.

With the reservation policy for women, the political landscape for women leaders, whether in villages or cities, started emerging from the shadows to reshape the future and redefine political leadership through their diverse and impactful contributions. During one of our earlier meetings, after we took charge of our new jobs, Sharad Pawar, then Chief Minister of Maharashtra, told the menfolk in a lighter vein, 'You will have to start working as your women counterparts are already outshining you all.' Senior officers told us that there was sanity in the corridors and meeting halls of the Municipal Corporation as now men had to mind their language and actions. More and more women from among the citizens now started approaching their women representatives as they felt more comfortable voicing their concerns and problems to them.

Despite enabling provisions of the law which give women the right to be in the decision-making process, there are inherent challenges in the system that need consideration to make their representation more effective. Firstly, women have to cope with ambitious and over-indulging male members in the family and yet remain patient to be able to tactfully handle the situation and make sure they have the final word. Secondly, the Municipal Corporation is a field where representatives have no formal training with respect to the work they have to do—management or governance, the laws they have to deal with, the policies, rules, precedents, urban development, etc.—and have to learn through experience after assuming office. As the belief goes, you either swim or sink. Thirdly, there is no security of tenure, as they have to fight elections every five years if they wish to remain in the job.

Elections are a different ball game where being meritorious may not be the only criteria to win. The electorate may not consider the big issues of the city you have handled or spoken for, but whether you attend all weddings, birthdays and deaths, which may not be possible for a woman who has other important roles as a mother, wife and homemaker. Caste considerations, too, determine the outcome of elections. Factors such as corruption, illegal gains, etc., play a decisive role during elections. Additionally, patriarchy, lack of cooperation from the administration, officials and sometimes even colleagues, still pose hurdles for women representatives. For women to be effective in politics, there will have to be a radical change of mindset, backed by sustained and sincere efforts for capacity building in order to enhance their participation.

Several studies indicated that inclusion of women in the decision-making process had brought about a sea change in grassroots development. Therefore, encouraged by the outcome of the political participation of women, as many as 19 states (Andhra Pradesh, Chhattisgarh, Gujarat, Himachal Pradesh, Jharkhand, Karnataka, Kerala, Maharashtra, Odisha, Rajasthan, Sikkim, Tripura, Uttarakhand, West Bengal, Madhya Pradesh, Assam, Bihar, Tamil Nadu and Telangana) enhanced the seats quota and offices of chairpersons for women from 33 to 50 per cent. Today, of the 3 million elected local government representatives, across 250,000 Panchayati Raj Institutions (PRI) and Urban Local Bodies (ULB), there are over 1.4 million women in the decision-making process in local governments. The latest data reveals that around 46.14% of seats in local bodies are held by women in India, much above the global average of 34.3%, thereby ranking 11 of 136 countries. Interestingly, there have been all-women panchayats (village councils) in states like Maharashtra, Odisha, Tamil Nadu, Karnataka, Madhya Pradesh, Himachal Pradesh, Gujarat, Haryana and Uttarakhand. All-women panchayats have been known to give courage and confidence to each other for initiating collective action and to establish strong bonds by standing up for each other and asserting their rights. Another important and welcome aspect of all-women panchayats is that the menfolk in these villages are ready to accept women in leadership positions.

Gender justice has been enshrined in the Constitution of India. However, since women have historically faced discrimination and marginalization in many areas like education, employment, health and politics, in spite of several efforts and affirmative actions by countries, many inequalities still remain. India has made pioneering efforts to bring women into the mainstream through local initiatives and also by responding promptly to declarations and covenants at the international level, to protect and promote women's rights and further ensure that women become equal partners in the development process through making policies and enacting egalitarian laws.

On 21 September 2023, the parliament of India passed the long-awaited, much-needed Women's Reservation Bill 2023, mandating that women would occupy 33% of the seats in the lower house of the parliament and state legislative assemblies. This provision would also cover seats reserved for Scheduled Castes (SC) and Scheduled Tribes (ST) in the Lok Sabha and Vidhan Sabhas of the states. The catch, however, is that the legislation is scheduled to come into force only after India publishes its next census, and after the completion of the delimitation procedure, thereby meaning that the implementation is not with immediate effect, and one has to wait for a few years for its implementation.

Reservation for women in local governments since 1992, through the 73rd and 74th Amendments to the Constitution, has served as a learning ground and a stepping stone for women to effectively graduate and participate in the state assemblies and the parliament of India, where presently they are in small numbers. Studies have revealed that female lawmakers exhibit higher levels of responsiveness, accountability, honesty and collaboration compared to their male counterparts. They also exhibit a propensity to prioritize matters pertaining to health, education, welfare, environment and social justice, all of which hold significant importance in the advancement of human progress. Thus, their increased presence is expected to bring important issues to the fore and improve legislative discourse. Studies have also revealed that exposure to the decision-making process at the grassroots, opportunity to show leadership skills, and training programmes have enabled many efficient and capable women to emerge as leaders in India's local political landscape.

The Bill was first introduced way back in 1996 and then again in 1998, 1999 and 2008. The first three Bills lapsed, with the dissolution of their respective Lok Sabhas. The 2008 Bill was introduced in and passed by Rajya Sabha, but it also lapsed with the dissolution of the 15th Lok Sabha. In 2010, a bill on women's reservation in the Lok Sabha and state legislatures was passed in the Rajya Sabha but it could not get the approval of the Lok Sabha. The Bill has now been passed, but can only come into effect after clearing the remaining hurdles. As of today, the time the process will take is unpredictable. So even after the Women's Reservation Bill has been passed, when will that translate into actual reservation for women in parliament and state assemblies is a question that still remains unanswered.

Though women have come a long way in the political arena, there are several measures that need to be taken to further enhance their contributions at the grassroots. First, concerted efforts must be made to address gender bias by changing deeply-held beliefs—by changing the way society sees women and also the way women see themselves. According to UNDP's 2023 Gender Social Norms Index (GSNI), it is not just men who think women cannot be effective politicians and business leaders, or that it is the duty of women solely to attend to the household, but even women think the same. There is a need to change attitudes with an effective affirmation policy for young girls and their parents. Second, it is important to recognize that a significant number of women contribute to addressing issues through informal structures that transform society, by remaining outside the realm of politics. Efforts will have to be made to support their initiatives, foster collaborations, help them amplify their work, and provide greater visibility to their efforts.

India's political landscape is being redefined by women. Their bold efforts are shaping policy and challenging the status quo. Their actions are already showing promise and potential. Their journey towards a community where men and women are equal has begun. Their resolve remains undaunted—and now nobody can stop them!

KEY MESSAGES OF *NARI SHAKTI*, THE BOOK

Throughout this book, we have looked at challenges faced by women at every stage of their existence and tried to understand the reasons for various gaps. We have also discussed at some length what could and should be done to address these. As we conclude, we will look at each stage in the lives and livelihoods journeys of women, and craft a how-to-make-it-happen set of prescriptions for enabling women to find their rightful place in society and in the world.

Education is the most important right for any human being and denial of this fundamental right must be seen as a crime. In a nation that has struggled with abortions and female infanticide for decades, it is not difficult to see why parents, particularly those in underprivileged sections of society, are comfortable not sending a girl child to school or pulling her out of it. An extra pair of hands for household or farm work, or just running errands for the primary caregiver is an obvious option when the girl herself is *paraya dhan*, and any investment in her mental development is seen as superfluous.

Safeena Husain suggests that we find every last girl in India and ensure that she is able to access the education that is rightfully hers. Many options exist for administrators and community leaders—inclusive enrolment programmes, mobilization of local champions to find local solutions to barriers that keep girls out of school, and community engagement to thwart all attempts at exclusion from education. A nation will be truly developed only when poverty, illiteracy and ignorance are defeated.

The impact in India would be transformational if through a combination of physical and open schools, every child has access to good-quality educational inputs. As envisaged in the National Education Policy (NEP), there is also an imperative for introducing technology into the pedagogy of education all over India. This will also offer continuing education pathways for women (and men). By designing it for the most vulnerable segments of society, the overall quality of education can be elevated in India.

In rural India, employment for women starts early at a very young age—in the house, on the farm, and occasionally, helping in production or sales. As we have already argued, it will need strong enforcement of the laws as well as active community engagement to ensure that children are not put to work, and most importantly, girls are not 'married off' before the age of 18. The right to work at the age of 18, and the ability to earn a livelihood and provide family support will also empower women with self-respect and self-worth, and must be encouraged by policy and societal approval.

Pooja Goyal has made several recommendations to ensure that women feel comfortable entering the workforce in the new VUCA world. She extols the virtues of hybrid work that offers flexibility for young women to balance careers with marriage and childbirth. Organizations like ICICI in the early years, and recent exemplars in the services sector, have implemented these levels of flexibility with excellent results. The advantages of remote work lead to more flexible work arrangements, access to a wider talent pool including women returning to the workforce, and potentially, increased productivity because women, spared the drudgery of travel, can contribute significantly more to work. Policy shifts embracing remote work can be a game changer for women's participation at work and need to be explored by small and large corporations across India.

A looming threat is technologies like Generative AI, where highly skilled jobs like programming are being automated. Pooja recommends that women should explore jobs in caregiving and social services, which have been undervalued and underpaid but will become more attractive as they are less replaceable by technology. It makes sense to systematically build skills for women in areas where human connection and empathy are essential, like palliative care, geriatric care, dementia care, and mental health support. There are other opportunities too, and the future of jobs is linked to the ability of women to train and opt for new professions.

The reality of employment in most organizations in India, barring exemplars like ICICI and Lighthouse Communities Foundation, has been that while early employment figures have shown steady upward movement in the percentage of women among first job entrants, the gender balance drops off as individual producers move to management and leadership roles. In fact, at the board level, the participation of women, even with the SEBI stipulation for larger companies, has been quite pathetic.

What this means for modern-day corporate and industry structures is the recognition of the fact that challenges to women in leadership roles are not external or contextual. We already have the context and the comfort of the woman in power. The actual problem is the realization by men and indeed women, that their own biases and self-limiting beliefs have to be discarded to expand their consciousness and create paths for success of women in the workplace, all the way from the desk in a corner to the corner office of the CEO and to the boardroom.

A number of recommendations for women to succeed have been made by many contributors to this book. A strong focus on mentorship programmes and reverse mentorship programmes spanning genders can open up new perspectives. It is important to ensure women employees are consulted on initiatives designed to provide them with equal opportunity. Men and women should both appreciate that men are not women's adversaries and both should be supportive and encouraging of not only women at home but also women at their workplace. This is true for colleagues as well as family members of both genders at home. It may be time for companies to develop and use monitoring platforms to track the impact and outcomes of gender equity programmes. The platforms should capture data of every granularity and level to tell senior management at a glance how the various initiatives are doing in terms of retaining women, upskilling them, and preparing them for roles they desire. These platforms should capture feedback and satisfaction levels to be used for constant improvement.

If participation of women in employment has been a challenge, ensuring women are motivated to set up businesses and take them to scale has been an even bigger one. The IndUS Entrepreneurs, a global entrepreneurship forum set up in the US, with branches across the world, has done yeoman work in nurturing young women and helping them in their journeys of idea validation, product or service area development, product-to-market fit, and scaling with the correct business model.

This book has argued that policies are available to be utilized and need to be enhanced to empower more women to participate and succeed. Our demographic dividend may be a fleeting opportunity for India, but the potential of empowered women can be sustained over decades and definitely contribute significantly to the realization of a Viksit Bharat. The business case for having more women in the workforce has already been established; there is an active acceptance on the part of corporate leaders, politicians and bureaucrats that increasing women's participation is a critical factor for successfully realizing India's economic growth ambitions. Strong tailwinds created by the move towards gender-equitable workspaces in India must now be supported by robust policies at all levels to leverage this momentum, remove deep-rooted beliefs and obstacles, and take half a billion women to success.

Other policy interventions too are needed for women to succeed nationwide. The growth of physical and digital infrastructures in the country and the slow but sure development of a National Optical Fibre Network will ensure decongestion of cities and access to markets and suppliers through the digital media. What should be particularly heartening for women in white-collar jobs or building entrepreneurial ventures is the ability to work flexi-hours and from anywhere. This takes the tension out of work-life balance and eliminates travel, which should be enshrined in a policy that makes it incumbent on employers to give gig workers the same opportunities as they would to those who show up at the workplace every day.

In blue-collar jobs and rural India too, women have a great opportunity to participate in and supervise automated operations. As Ejaz Ghani has suggested, female networks in labour markets and input-output markets need to be encouraged to promote more women entrepreneurs. Inadequate infrastructure affects women more than men, as women face greater constraints in geographic mobility imposed by safety concerns and/or social norms. Even to make women more productive in the home environment, policies facilitating easy and uninterrupted access to water and electricity would have a greater impact on women who bear a larger share of the time and responsibility for household maintenance and care activities.

ROAD AHEAD FOR NARI SHAKTI

Economic agency of women will have a cascading impact on prosperity which enhances the quality of life for families and societies, contributing to a more inclusive and prosperous future for a truly Viksit Bharat. The world has come through many evolutions and revolutions. The notion of industry itself has evolved from the Ford model of assembly line to an information economy, integrating cyber and physical experiences on factory floors through Industry 4.0, and more recently, by exploring streamlined interactions between human work and artificial intelligence (AI) in the workplace. For every Siri and Alexa assisting us and enabling us to live and work better, there will be a new creation of artificial general intelligence (AGI) that will not only enable and empower us, but also move to guiding many of our actions for the future. We need to move towards a society where the human–technology interface is seamless and we are able to move towards our desired goals as individuals and for society.

Adopting these principles will lead to everything we want to see in Viksit Bharat—a relentless push for economic growth, integration of cyber and physical capabilities, and focus on collaborative work and an inclusive society.

Dr Raghunath Anant Mashelkar and Dr Vijay Kelkar have mentioned the imperative of a peaceful co-existence of people in society in the pursuit of collective well-being, and emphasized that the significance of social harmony for a large and complex multi-religious, multi-ethnic and multi-cultural nation like India is paramount.

It is the collective belief of all the authors/contributors and editors of this book that as we commit ourselves to the challenge of nation-building at an unprecedented pace, we need a balanced focus on physical, digital and social development in

India. Women will have to make huge contributions towards a social construct that is built on the principles of cooperation, compassion, and respect for human dignity. Success of women will remain indispensable in realizing our shared aspirations for a better future.

To quote our founding father Mahatma Gandhi, 'To call woman the weaker sex is a libel; it is man's injustice to woman. [...] If by strength is meant moral power, then woman is immeasurably man's superior. [...] If nonviolence is the law of our being, the future is with women.'[1]

In *Nari Shakti*, we have cited numerous examples of individuals, social and profit-oriented organizations and businesses, and of political leaders who have seen the light, and are drawing more and more people into the fold of an aspirational vision and well-lit path to success. We believe that gender equality can be achieved and that will enable other forms of equity to be firmly installed in our minds, in our homes and in our workplaces. What better way to end than with the immortal words of Swami Vivekananda, 'Arise, awake and stop not till the goal is reached.'

---

[1] Gandhi, Mohandas Karamchand, 'To the Women of India', open letter published in *Young India*, 10 April 1930.

ACKNOWLEDGEMENTS

When Pune International Centre approached us with the idea of Nari Shakti, we were delighted at the opportunity. We thought it relevant to showcase the thoughts of diverse practitioners of Nari Shakti in a single book, given that over the decades, we had personally worked in many areas that were being explored under this overarching title. In our lives and careers, we have been fortunate to witness the stories of valiant women in urban and rural India who have refused to accept social norms, and embraced a way of life that best suited their own aspirations and circumstances. We thank all those who have inspired us with their endeavours.

With our desire to acknowledge some of these inspiring women, we would like to start with Parvathy, a woman born in Koottapana, a little village in Kerala, over 120 years ago—in 1903. Married at the age of 13, by the time she was 20, she'd had four children—a daughter and three sons. The unfortunate death of her husband at this juncture left her destitute, with four young offspring to fend for, with not much help from the immediate family. To add to her misery, she had to face accusations and taunts and was told to resign herself to her fate. Instead, for the survival and success of her family, Parvati chose to take up menial tasks in a nearby town and managed to find a job at the erstwhile Travancore Govt Printing Press and get her children through school and eventually employment. Sixty years later, her eldest son built a small business in New Delhi; the second son pursued a lifelong career at the State Bank of India; the third one became a career executive in All India Radio; and Parvathy's only daughter married young and moved to North India to bring up a fine family. Today, as is the case with many South Indian families, all of Parvathy's grandchildren, including author Uma

Ganesh, are well settled across the world, and the grandchildren and great-grandchildren are doing the family proud in many ways.

Move fifty years to the 1950s, and here is another inspiring life. Rajam spent her childhood in Mumbai, where her father had settled in 1929. The eldest of four girls and one boy, Rajam got married to the eldest son of a village schoolmaster, who had shifted to Kolkata after his graduation and was slowly moving his parents, seven sisters and three brothers from South to East India. In his early fifties, his elderly father was excited about his son marrying an intelligent woman who had completed her graduation. While Rajam was reconciled to being a good daughter-in-law, wife and mother, the elderly schoolmaster insisted on his daughter-in-law completing her post-graduation in Education so that she could become a schoolteacher. This gave Rajam the confidence to pursue other interests as well—singing classical music, reading and writing. Even after her two children were born, she retained her position as a well-read, worldly-wise woman who could hold her own in any conversation. When she passed on in her seventies, with all her husband's family and her own children, including author Ganesh Natarajan, well settled, she had accomplished, much like Parvathy, far more than many other women, and indeed, many men of her generation.

Manjiri's life is equally inspiring. Born and brought up in a simple Maharashtrian Pune household, she started a career in journalism at 18, got married and moved to Delhi. She joined a top computer magazine and was settling into a perfect life when divorce turned her life upside down. Manjiri moved back to Pune and joined the corporate sector. Rising quickly through the ranks, she moved into roles in marketing communication, business process outsourcing and human resources, and even co-authored a book with her CEO Ganesh Natarajan. Later, she moved to Mumbai with her daughter for a larger professional role. There she met her life partner Abhay Joshi and moved to the United Kingdom in 2008 and co-founded a charity—Maya

CARE Foundation—with him. After managerial roles in London and an MSc from Saïd Business School, University of Oxford, she served a three-year stint as CEO of author Uma Ganesh's company, Global Talent Track. She is now a consultant with her alma mater, Saïd Business School.

These are just three examples from different generations. Such exemplars abound in all sections of society, across businesses and entrepreneurships we have worked with and watched with admiration. There are many more who serve as role models in emerging India and the world. We salute their aspirations, their efforts and their achievements.

We would like extend our heartfelt gratitude to all the authors who willingly poured out their hearts, shared their ideas, and provided advice to all participants and enablers in the journey towards Nari Shakti.

For this book, we would like to acknowledge the leadership of Dr Raghunath Anant Mashelkar and Dr Vijay Kelkar at Pune International Centre, the authors who came forward willingly to share their thoughts and vision, and Richa Tewari, our development editor who added invaluable insights to the creation of the manuscript. We look forward to many such collaborative efforts in future.

END NOTES

CHAPTER 2

Ghani, Ejaz (2010), 'The service revolution in India', *VoxEU.org*, https://tinyurl.com/fhbtzmfh. Accessed on 22 October 2024.

Ghani, Ejaz (2013), 'Promoting Networking, Gender Parity & Shared Prosperity in India', Economic Policy and Debt, PREM, Seminar on Female entrepreneurship: Obstacles, innovative interventions, and impacts, https://tinyurl.com/2hu4tp7n. Accessed on 22 October 2024.

Ghani, E., A.G. Goswami, S. Kerr & W. Kerr (2016), 'Will Market Competition Trump Gender Discrimination in India?', World Bank Policy Research Working Papers, https://tinyurl.com/4skrntyw. Accessed on 22 October 2024.

Ghani, E., W.R. Kerr, & S. O'Connell (2012), 'What Explains Big Gender Disparities in India? Local Industrial Structures and Female Entrepreneurship', World Bank Policy Research Working Papers, https://tinyurl.com/634z5t9u. Accessed on 22 October 2024.

Ghani, Ejaz, William R. Kerr, and Stephen D. O'Connell (2014), 'Political Reservations and Women's Entrepreneurship in India', NBER Working Paper 19868, https://tinyurl.com/3dk39mpc. Accessed on 22 October 2024.

Ghani, E., W.R. Kerr, & S. O'Connell (2012), 'What Explains Big Gender Disparities in India? Local Industrial Structures and Female Entrepreneurship', World Bank Policy Research Working Papers, https://tinyurl.com/634z5t9u. Accessed on 22 October 2024.

Hausmann, Ricardo, Laura Tyson, & Saadia Zahidi (2011), *Global Gender Gap Report*, World Economic Forum, https://tinyurl.com/3y66fj25. Accessed on 22 October 2024.

Klapper, Leora, & Simon Parker (2011), 'Gender and Business Environment for New Firm Creation', World Bank Research Observer, https://tinyurl.com/2wu9bfwm. Accessed on 22 October 2024.

Marshall, Alfred, *Principles of Economics*, London, UK, MacMillan and Co., 1920, https://tinyurl.com/3atwzjhw. Accessed on 22 October 2024.

Mukim, Megha (2011), 'Industry and the Urge to Cluster: A Study of the Informal Sector in India', SERC Paper 0072, https://tinyurl.com/5crt7hpk. Accessed on 22 October 2024.

Najeeb, Fatima, Matias Morales, and Gladys Lopez-Acevedo (2020), 'Analyzing Female Employment Trends in South Asia', World Bank Policy Research Working Paper 9157, https://tinyurl.com/3bttwf9k. Accessed on 22 October 2024.

Pennings, Steven (2022), 'How much would GDP per capita increase if gender employment gaps were closed in developing countries?', World Bank Blogs, 4 March 2022, https://tinyurl.com/3jye4em7. Accessed on 22 October 2024.

World Bank Group (2012), 'World Development Report 2012: Gender Equality and Development', https://tinyurl.com/3879z3rm. Accessed on 22 October 2024.

World Bank Group (2022), 'Female labor force participation', 10 January 2022, https://tinyurl.com/4njsn3rc. Accessed on 22 October 2024.

CHAPTER 6

Dey, Anamika, Gurdeep Singh, & Anil K. Gupta, op. cit., https://tinyurl.com/yewbkf9b. Accessed on 27 August 2024.

CONTRIBUTORS

Dr Uma Ganesh is Principal Trustee of GTT Foundation and a Board member of 5F World, Emoha Health and Skills Alpha.

Dr Ganesh Natarajan is Chairman of 5F World, Lighthouse Communities and Honeywell Automation, and a board member of Hinduja Global Solutions, GTT, SBI Payments, 1 Crowd and Educate Girls.

Dr Ajit Ranade is Vice Chancellor of Gokhale Institute of Politics & Economics and former President & Chief Economist, Aditya Birla Group.

Dr Ejaz Ghani is former Lead Economist at The World Bank. He has also worked for ILO, UNCTAD, and UNICEF, and previously taught economics at Oxford and Delhi University.

Eika Chaturvedi Banerjee is Founder of Eikam Resonance and former CEO of Future Sharp Skills (a Future Group & NSDC venture).

Pooja Sharma Goyal is the Founding CEO of The Udaiti Foundation, and earlier led Avishkaar, a platform to support children learn next-gen tech skills like Robotics, AI, IoT and Coding and Intellitots.

Safeena Husain is Founder of Educate Girls, a social impact leader, and a recipient of the London School of Economics honorary doctorate and the NITI Aayog Women Transforming India Award.

Arundhati Bhattacharya is Chairperson and CEO for Salesforce in India and was earlier the first woman chairperson at the State Bank of India (SBI).

Sushma Rajagopalan is a Partner in Venture Capital firm Rittenhouse Ventures and Co-Founder, 2ndCareers.com.

Prashant Girbane is Director General at MCCIA.

Gunjan Bhojwani is a Youth Fellow at MCCIA.

Dr Anil K. Gupta is Professor, IIM Ahmedabad.

Dr Raghunath Mashelkar is President, **Dr Vijay Kelkar** is Vice President, and **Abhay Vaidya** is Director of Pune International Centre.

Vandana Chavan is former Mayor of Pune Municipal Corporation, a former Member of Parliament for ten years, and founder of two social organizations, ALERT and SMILE.

SEGMENT CONTRIBUTORS

Dinanath Kholkar is an Independent Consultant and was formerly with TCS.

Anushri Alva is CEO, Adhyayan Quality Education Foundation.

Mrinal Gharpure is CFO, Lighthouse Communities, and former Director, Aspen Global Opportunity Youth Network, Pune.

Priya Patil is CEO, Million Jugnus Pvt. Ltd.

Mridula Sankhyayan is Founder of Vatt Vriksh, and a trainer and coach.

Nikki Barua is CEO and Co-Founder of Beyond Barriers.

Anamika R. Dey is Professor, IIM Ahmedabad.

Volunteers of Honeybee Network

Made in the USA
Monee, IL
15 May 2026

75a1bac9-28ab-4df1-9b90-ed64df413c5cR01